MW01173136

LAST YEAR ON THE JOB

LAST YEAR ON THE JOB

A Battalion Chief's Final Year on the Chicago Fire Department

KEVIN STAWIARSKI

Copyright © 2023 by Kevin Stawiarski

All rights reserved. NO part of this book may be used or reproduced by any means, graphic, electronic, or mechanical, including photocopying, recording, taping or by any information storage retrieval system without the written permission of the author except in the case of brief quotations embodied in critical articles and reviews.

The events, places, and conversations in this book have been recreated from memory. When necessary, the names and identifying characteristics of individuals and places have been changed to maintain anonymity. Views expressed are the authors own and are not intended to offend or malign any organization, group, or individual.

Book cover and interior formatted for print and ebook by Phillip Gessert (gessertbooks.com)
Cover photo by Lens Cap Tim Photography (lenscaptim@gmail.com)

TABLE OF CONTENTS

PREFACE

"WHAT'S THE BIGGEST fire you've been to?" After serving twenty-nine years on the Chicago Fire Department and still today, this is the question I have been asked most frequently by friends, relatives, and people I've met who were curious about my line of work. A common and understandable misconception by the general public is that "big fires" are always the most interesting. Over the years, what became obvious to me was that people who asked this question weren't necessarily looking for a story about a large fire, but more so an insight into what it's like fighting a fire, or what an emergency scene looks like through the eyes of a firefighter.

So, with that in mind my stock answer to the "biggest fire" question had become, and still is, "The big, spectacular fires are the ones that make the news, but are usually not the most interesting." To those who ask me to elaborate, I explain that many times large fires seen in the media involving unoccupied structures, such as warehouses and factories with flames shooting high into the sky look very dramatic, and they are, however, from a firefighter's perspective, they can be uneventful and not very challenging. Basically, these are what we in the business call "water carnivals" where the structure is surrounded and crews throw water from a safe distance until the fire is out.

I then follow-up by relating a story or two about a more

compelling fire or other type of incident I've worked. This usually satisfies their curiosity and explains what I meant when I said the biggest fires are not usually the most interesting. Many times, my "stories" will further pique their interest and I will be asked to tell another. Some have even gone as far as suggesting I write a book...ME? A book? I don't think so. There are way more firefighters with way more interesting experiences than me.

When I first entered the Chicago Fire Department in July of 1986, I was fortunate enough to work with many older and very experienced firefighters. Most of them had come on the job in the 1960's or 70's and had seen a lot of action. When these guys would talk about fires, car accidents or other incidents they'd been to, I, as a young firefighter, would keep my ears open and my mouth shut. I can recall sitting at the firehouse kitchen table and learning just as much about techniques, tools, innovative ideas and how to work as safely as possible as I did during formal drills. These "coffee talks" would also usually include a lecture aimed at me on how I should learn every aspect of "the job" and pass that knowledge along to the next generation of firefighters, who would some day be looking to me as the "old-timer." In addition to passing along their insightful experiences, many of these seasoned firemen also suggested that I keep a personal journal of all the interesting things that I was sure to see in the next thirty years...all of them also noting that this is something they regretfully had not done themselves. At the time, not fully realizing the nostalgic value of such documentation, I, like most others on the job, did not heed their advice. Throughout my career I, too, used only my memory to store my personal experiences. This was however, until I had exactly one year left on the job.

My retirement date had been set for November 26, 2015. So, on November 28, 2014, with exactly one year left on the Chicago Fire Department and holding the rank of citywide relief battalion chief, I decided to keep a personal journal of my remaining workdays. Throughout my last year some of the shifts and runs were routine while others were way out of the ordinary. If something interesting happened on a particular day, it was noted. If nothing happened, that too was documented. At home, after each shift day I would roughly transfer my notes from paper to computer. Then, during the winter of 2016, once in full retirement, I sat down at my computer and began reading my personal journal. A spelling correction here and a grammar correction there and I began to feel that this was starting to look more like something that could be a good answer to that question, "What's the biggest fire you've been to?" I never intended to publish my personal accounts. I only took this on as a hobby to keep busy through my first winter of retirement. My thought was that when it was completed, I would have a keepsake to share with my family and a few friends. Well...here we are...it's a book.

INTRODUCTION
PART I

CHICAGO, ECKHART PARK (CIRCA 1970)—Bottom of the third, one out, man on second. There's the windup and the pitch. The batter swings and hits a sharp grounder to third. Just before the old beat-up hard ball reaches the third baseman it hits a piece of broken glass and takes a tricky hop to the left. Well aware of the field's condition the shortstop is prepared. He fields the ball and before the runner makes it to first, throws it to the pitcher's hands for the out. The runner on second is now on third. (Ten young boys, ages 9 to 12, on summer break playing their second pick-up baseball game of the day on a very hot July afternoon—five per team, right field is out.) As the next batter steps up to the flattened cardboard beer box that represents home plate, the pitcher checks to make sure his fielders are ready. Everyone's set. There's the windup and the..."SMOKE!!" shouts the centerfielder. Immediately all ten kids stop and turn to look in the direction that the centerfielder is pointing. There, in the sky just beyond the tall steeples of Saint Boniface church, is a large column of billowing, black smoke. (Fires were not uncommon in this area of Chicago in the 70's and all the ball players on the field knew the drill.)

Each kid grabs a bat, ball or glove and runs as fast as they can across the street to hide their gear in the pitcher's front hallway before running to watch the fire. This one seemed to be on the 1400 block of Walton Street, the next block over from the park. With the baseball gear secured, the group takes off running west down Chestnut Street towards the smoke. Just as they pass Saint Boniface school the first siren can be heard in the distance. "We're gonna get there before the firemen this time!" shouts one of the kids as they cross Noble Street. The sirens grow louder, and the smell of smoke gets heavier as the kids turn onto Walton. "There it is!" yells one of them. About midway down the block a two-story frame building can be seen with fire blowing out of its second-floor windows. As the boys get closer, flames from the wooden back porches can be seen over the rooftop spewing large embers into the smoke-filled sky. Still panting from their sprint to the scene the group of kids take a position directly across the street from the vacant fire building. Taking in all the chaos, they watch as residents of the two neighboring buildings hurriedly carry out pets and personal possessions in anticipation of the fire spreading to their apartments.

Then, only seconds after the boys arrive, the first fire engine, a pumper, rolls up on the scene. Stopping just past the building on fire, two of the three firemen riding on the back step hook large, heavy looking hoses over each of their shoulders and jump off the engine onto the street. "GO!" shouts one of them as the pumper pulls away carrying the third fireman in the direction of the nearest fire hydrant. Simultaneously a fourth fireman, the company officer, runs down one of the gangways to get a look at the rear of the building. When he returns to the front, he begins helping the other two lay out the hose on the street and sidewalk. Suddenly, the people who were beginning to gather across the street with the kids feel a rush of heat. Looking up they see that another window, that was previously intact, had just broken and flames were now shooting from it. Absorbing everything happening, and with eyes watering from the smoke, one of the boys points down the street back in the direction from where the pumper came. There, standing ominously behind the whiffs of smoke, was the hook and ladder truck. Its lights could barely be seen through the smoke but the sound of its motor, much like an old farm tractor, was deafening. The hook and ladder and its crew were eagerly waiting a few houses back for the signal from the pumper that their hose was out of the way. The smoke on the street was now so thick that some of the kids and onlookers began to disperse. The few that remained wiped their eyes and coughed waiting to watch this monster of a truck pull up to the front of the building. It didn't take long. Within seconds the engine crew had its hose laid out and out of the way.

Standing in the street the officer of the pumper waves and yells for the hook and ladder to pull forward. With a loud roar and giving off almost as much black smoke as the fire, the hook and ladder truck drives forward and takes a position directly in front of the fire building. The truck itself is about forty feet in length and has a long wooden ladder mounted to it. At the rear of the ladder, on top, is a seat with a steering wheel. From this position a fireman steers the rear wheels making it easier to get down small streets.

As quickly as the truck stops, two men jump off and begin helping the firemen from the pumper stretch out the hose in the gangway between the fire building and the apartment building next door. The fireman who sat atop the ladder stands from his perch and forcefully steps on a long steel pedal just to his left. Quickly, and almost violently, one end of the large wooden ladder attached to the truck springs into the air scaring many of the people watching the scene. Not the kids. They've seen this before. After releasing this spring-loaded ladder, the fireman who pushed the pedal scurries to the other end of the truck and begins laboriously turning two large cranks, one that makes the ladder turn from left to right and another that makes it extend. A second fireman, the driver of the truck, also works feverishly as he manually lowers the large stabilizing jacks on the rear of the truck. With the jacks down the driver looks up and begins directing the fireman at the cranks, "LEFT, LEFT, LFET!" he yells. "NOW, DOWN, DOWN! GOOD RIGHT THERE, STOP!!" Now with the ladder in place at the roof, both the driver and the man at the cranks slide axes into their belts and, already looking totally exhausted, climb through the smoke to the roof.

While all of this is going on, the officer of the pumper stands in the middle of the street and waves his arms back toward his driver and third fireman who are waiting at the hydrant. "SEND THE WATER!!" he yells. Then, just as quickly as that ladder jumped into the air seconds before, the hoses laying in the street begin flapping and flailing as they fill with water. One hose is led out to the men at the gangway and one to the firemen waiting in a crouching position at the front door that leads to the second floor of the fire building. Over the sound of the hook and ladder's motor and breaking glass, the officer then yells, "BLEED 'EM!" This was the cue for the two firemen to open their nozzles away from the fire in order to expel all the air inside the hose. As each of the firemen opens their nozzles, air begins sputtering out with extreme force sounding like a broken steam pipe. This, too, catches the attention of the onlookers. Once all the air is expelled and a solid flow of water is coming from the nozzles, the men at the gangway begin shooting water between the buildings in order to protect the house next door. The other two, the officer and one fireman with nozzle in hand, are at the base of the stairway looking up. With a pat on the back from the officer the nozzleman begins ascending the stairs towards the fire. The officer follows and both disappear into the thick smoke. The third fireman, now back from the hydrant, positions himself at the doorway and helps push the heavy hose up the stairs.

Looking up, the kids can now see the two hook and ladder firemen straddling the peaked roof and vigorously swinging their axes through the ebb and flow of the still billowing smoke. While all of this is going on another pumper truck arrives. Its crew drags hoses to the rear of the building while another fireman in a white helmet quickly and methodically surveys the scene.

Then, only about five minutes after the arrival of the first fire engine, the flames are gone, and the smoke begins to turn white.

"Look!" says one of the kids as he points to a second-floor window, where only minutes ago the roaring fire caused onlookers to retreat from the intense heat. He is pointing at two firemen with their heads hanging out of the window. Their faces are covered with soot and mucus is running from their noses. They spit and cough as they gasp for a breath of fresh air. Both men are soaking wet, and their watery, bloodshot eyes can be seen from the street. It was the fireman and officer who seconds ago went up the interior staircase to the second floor to extinguish the fire. "Man, I wouldn't want to do THAT," says one of the kids..."I would," I replied.

To this day I can vividly remember the day described above. As a kid growing up in Chicago in the 1960s and '70s I saw a lot of fires. Back then it was common for neighbors to gather to "watch a fire." There were many. Even though I, like many kids, wanted to be a fireman, this day was different. It was one of the few times we beat the fire trucks to the scene and got to witness what they saw and what they did immediately upon their arrival. I recall being intensely fascinated by how calmly and systematically those guys handled that chaotic scene. You could say that day was life changing for me. That day, at the age of ten, I KNEW this was what I wanted to do.

INTRODUCTION PART II

FAST FORWARD

At the age of twenty-one and employed as a truck driver, I made the decision to follow my boyhood dream of being a fireman. Because Chicago was not offering an entrance exam at the time, I decided to start taking entrance exams for suburban fire departments in the Chicagoland area. All in all, I tried out for about ten different suburban municipalities. The turnout for these tests was very large. Literally thousands of applicants tested for less than fifty or so jobs. Although I scored fairly well on most of these written and physical exams, I wasn't called for any of the positions. That really didn't bother me much because I knew deep down that what I really wanted was to be a Chicago firefighter. Had I been called for one of the suburban jobs I would have gladly accepted and given it my all...always knowing, however, that if "the big city" called I'd jump on it in a heartbeat. I was always grateful for the opportunity to participate in any fire department entrance exam. The experience was invaluable.

What also turned out to be invaluable was a friendship I made in early 1983 with a fireman at a local firehouse. I had just taken up photography as a hobby and was carrying my camera wherever I went. One evening, on my way home from work, I came across a fire a few blocks from my house. It didn't look like much, just a lot of smoke but I thought to myself, "This could make for some interesting photography!" So, I quickly parked my car, grabbed my camera, and began shooting away. What caught my eye as much as the fire, were the numbers on the trucks. Engine 30, Engine 14 and Truck 19 were the same fire companies I witnessed as a young boy years ago at that unforgettable fire noted above.

After developing the photos, I decided to stop at the firehouse where Truck 19 was quartered and offer the guys in the pictures these "souvenirs." With extra prints in hand, I stopped in at the firehouse on Chicago Avenue. I walked up and introduced myself to a younger fireman sitting in a chair out front and gave him the pictures. After looking them over we had a brief conversation that turned mostly about me not being a photographer but really someone who wanted to be a fireman. "You know, there's hot rumors about an entrance exam soon," the fireman said. "Really?" I asked. "When can I apply?" He went on to tell me that all I could do at this time was to go down to City Hall and fill out a self-addressed post card that the city would mail to me when the test was announced. He also told me that I was welcome to stop by and visit him at the firehouse on any of his shift days. Before leaving I asked, "What was your name again?" "I'm Roy," he replied. Over the next few months, I took Roy up on his offer to visit and even got to ride along on a few runs.

On one of my visits to the firehouse in the spring of 1985, Roy told me he heard that the entrance exam was going to be given sometime within the year. He added that he knew of a bunch of guys my age who were already training for the physical part of the test and, if I wanted, he'd take me to where they were working out and introduce me to them. I told him I was VERY interested in anything that would prep me for the entrance exam. We then made arrangements for me to meet the group.

Rumors were that the entrance exam would probably be the same as the last one given in 1975. All applicants would take a fairly simple reading comprehension test on the same day. Then, if your written score was 70% or higher, you would be scheduled for the physical agility test at a later date. Applicants would ultimately be ranked on a list by their combined written and physical scores. The physical agility part was what we trained for. That was the "separator." It was what got you your place on "the list." The agility test consisted of five parts—each event was timed.

- Stair Climb (up a fire escape three stories, wearing an air tank, touching every stair)
- Hose Coupling (connect 3 hoses to a standpipe)
- Bar Hang (how long you could hang on a bar with arms bent)
- Dummy Drag (drag a 150-pound dummy about 75' up, around and down a ramped platform)
- Obstacle Course (a very physically taxing three laps around a large course)

That following Saturday morning around ten o'clock I got in my car and followed Roy to a large vacant lot on the Near Westside. As I pulled up, I saw about ten guys stretching and warming up for a workout. Some looked to be my age and some younger. Roy and I walked over, and I was introduced to the group. "Hey guys, this is Kevin," he said, "he's in the same boat as you." The entire group was very welcoming and took me in like I had known them for years. At that moment I had a weird feeling, kind of like that "age ten" experience noted at the start of this introduction. I KNEW that meeting these guys would be the start of my path on to the Chicago Fire Department. I couldn't have been more correct!

After some stretching and light exercise we all walked across the property over to a garage. Attached to the garage was a bar for practicing "the hang" and a makeshift hose coupling device. Inside the garage were all the pieces to form an obstacle course! The overhead door opened, and everyone pitched in as we assembled the obstacle course complete with a long tunnel to shimmy through, a ladder to scoot across, a wood frame window prop to crawl through and heavy sandbags to run with. The last item in the garage was a weight vest. One of the guys grabbed the vest and said, "Let's go." I had no idea where we were going but I followed as we walked north through an alley. (This is probably a good time to note that in 1985, some parts of this area were a bit rundown. As a matter of fact, we were only a block or two from what was known back then as Chicago's "skid row.") As we walked down the alley, I heard a female voice call out, "Hey cutie!" Looking up I saw a woman in a second-floor window that was covered with bars. "Hey Loretta. What's up? When you gettin' out?" one of the guys called back. "I dunno and I don't care. It ain't too bad here." Loretta was incarcerated. She was calling out from the window of a halfway house and knew the guys from their previous walks down the alley. We all smiled, waved, and continued walking north. About a half a block from Loretta's house we arrived at a large abandoned five-story building with the fire escape still attached. One of the guys ran up to the second level with a stopwatch while the rest of us lined up at the bottom. One at a time we put on the weighted vest and at the command "GO" ran up the stairs trying to beat our best times. After everyone completed three turns, we went back to the lot to continue the workout. This is how I spent most of the summer of 1985. We met at the lot and trained three to four times a week.

Over time I got to be very good friends with all the guys in the group, most of who lived on the far northwest or southwest sides of the city. We all wanted the same thing and wanted it badly. One day during one of our workouts I happened to casually mention to one of the guys that I would be perfectly fine with just making the list and that even if I had to wait a few years to be hired I'd be happy. His reply was a game changer. With a stone face he looked at me and said, "You better change your attitude. We're all in this to be in the first class off the new list. If that's not what you're working for, find another group." It only took about two seconds for me to answer. "You're right, first class it is. We'll work hard and we'll get it!"

In June of 1985, about 32,000 people took what some called a sixth-grade level reading comprehension test as the first part of the entrance exam. The tests were corrected, and the scores were sent out in late July...with one glitch. After the city of Chicago committed in writing that anyone who scored over a 70% on the written portion of the exam would be allowed to take the physical, they decided to change the rules. Because of the high number of passing scores on the written exam, they now said that instead of allowing all of the passing applicants to take the physical agility portion, they would only be testing about half and that the half to be tested were going to be drawn using a "lottery" system. This would mean that some, all, or even none of our group would be allowed to continue in the testing process to become Chicago firefighters. As the scores were sent out guys in our group began getting their letters. Some, like mine, read "Congratulations," and others read, "We are sorry to inform you..."

Needless to say, this rule change in the middle of the game saddened and angered a lot of people. It was a big thing. All the major, local television news channels and newspapers covered the story for weeks. Lawsuits were threatened and some aldermen held public meetings. About a month before the physical exams were to begin, two young firefighter applicants hired lawyers and took the lead. Things came to a boil at a City Council meeting where these two young men were allowed to plead their case. Guided by their strong desire to become Chicago firefighters (and their attorneys), they both gave compelling speeches in front of the entire Chicago City Council and Mayor Harold Washington. Clips of their speeches were shown on television and transcripts were printed in *The Chicago Sun Times* and *The Chicago Tribune.* Ultimately, their presentations persuaded the City Council to reverse their decision and allow every applicant with a passing score of 70% or higher to continue on to the physical agility portion of the firefighter exam as originally promised.

In August of 1985, the city began administering the physical agility portion of the entrance exam. All applicants with a written score of 70% or higher were notified by mail of their test date and time. A few of the guys in my workout group were called early on. After taking the exam they reported back to the rest of us on what it was like. Most of our group wasn't scheduled to be tested until late September, October and, like me, in November. By September, because of the shorter days and colder weather, we moved our workouts from the vacant lot on Monroe to an indoor location on the northside.

November finally came and with it my turn to take the physical exam. The pressure I felt the night before the exam was immense to say the least. As much as I tried to put it out of my mind, I knew that one slip, a bad turn or a fall could knock me back thousands of places on the list meaning that it could take years to be hired or maybe not even called at all.

On the morning of my test, I reported to The Quinn Fire Academy at the specified time. About one hundred of us were corralled into a small room where we signed waivers, watched a short video and were given a brief overview of the rules. We were then broken into groups of ten and led through a door that opened into the Chicago Fire Department drill hall. I remember feeling very nervous at this point and itching to get started. I figured the sooner I got my blood flowing the sooner I would calm down. Our group administrator led us to our first event, the stair climb. While in training for this day I was pretty good at all five events but the stair climb just happened to be my strongest. This was a great way to start, I thought. Then, by pure chance, my name was called first. Two proctors monitored this event, one at the bottom of the fire escape and one three stories up at the top holding a stop-watch. The proctor at the bottom helped me strap an air tank on my back and read me the rules. "If you miss a stair you have to return and start again...the clock doesn't stop," he said. I nodded, put my head down and gripped the railings tightly. "READY...SET...GO!" Like a dragster on the green light, I took off. Using mostly my arms to pull myself up I toed each stair like a tap dancer. The weight on my back was less than the weight vest we trained with, so I felt almost no resistance as I ascended. I could hear the other nine applicants and the proctor down below cheering as I reached the finish line at the third landing. "7.2 seconds," said the proctor at the top of the stairs, "I'm gonna have to check but I think you beat the record so far." As I descended the fire escape, I could hear the proctor at the bottom of the stairs telling the rest of the group, "I've been doing this since August. I think this guy's got the record." What a way to start!

I did okay on the next three events, the hose coupling, the bar-hang and the dummy drag. The last event was the obstacle course. (Because of their difficulty, the bar hang and obstacle course were probably the biggest separator events. One second on either could mean one hundred places up or down the list.) I was doing well so far and figured if I performed this last event as well as I did in my training sessions, I'd be all right.

For the last time of the day my name was called and I stepped up to the starting line. Once again, the proctor read a list of rules as I psyched up with my eyes looking straight down at the floor. "Kevin, are you ready?" the proctor asked. I took a deep breath and nodded my head. "READY...SET..." with the word "GO" off I went like I was shot out of a canon. I jumped onto the ladder that was lying horizontally set on two saw horses and quickly shimmied across using only hands and feet—jumping off the ladder I dove into the tunnel still moving swiftly on hands and feet—out of the tunnel I stood up and ran about ten feet to a window prop made of two by fours and crawled through—once through the window I picked up the two heavy sandbags and ran with one in each hand about thirty feet—dropping the sandbags I then ran serpentine through a series of cones that ended back at the ladder. Everything was a blur as I continued on to complete two more laps of the course at full speed. My heart was pounding through my chest, and I was breathing heavily as I dropped the sandbags for the last time and headed through the cones to the finish line. Running past the proctor I heard him yell, "ONE TEN...nice job." I remember catching my breath and thinking, "I'm eight seconds shy of the record!" A few weeks earlier one of my training partners was told he had the fastest time in this event with a score of one minute and two seconds.

On my way out of the hall I was handed a copy of my scores. I took a quick glance at them and walked out to my car. I can still remember that gloomy November day sitting in the parking lot staring down at my score sheet. "This is it," I thought, "it's over. I've done all I could. Now all I can do is wait and hope."

The physical testing for the remaining applicants continued through December. The combined final scores and the hiring list would not be out for months. All the guys in my workout group remained close friends and kept in touch through the winter and spring.

Around May of 1986, rumors began to float around that the scores would be out soon and that the first class of firefighter candidates from the new list could be called as early as July. Trying not to get my hopes up too much, I patiently checked my mailbox every day. It didn't take long. The rumors were correct. A few weeks into May I received a formal letter with my list placement number. Out of the original 32,000 people who took the exam, my number on the list was 95! With the letters now out, the phone lines were burning up. Calls from guys in my workout group were coming in fast ... #42, #3, #107, #210...all great numbers!

The next rumor going around was that the first 150 people on the list would be called very soon! The objective now was to stay healthy and to not do anything stupid to get hurt (like the ski trip our workout group took in February, but that's another story). We could be called to start the academy at any time.

It was sometime in early June that I received a letter telling me to report to a specified local hospital for a medical evaluation. There, I, and about 200 of the top scoring applicants underwent a mandatory physical/medical exam. After the exam, representatives from the Chicago Department of Personnel who were on hand told us to expect something in the mail very soon.

Then, in mid-June, it came...the letter telling me to report to the Quinn Fire Academy at 0800 hours, July 16, 1986. It was official. I was going to be a Chicago firefighter!

Those in my core workout group who didn't make the first call were hired in the next few classes only three or six months later. Everyone was happy for themselves and for each other!

INTRODUCTION
PART III

FAST FORWARD (SO FAST I STILL CAN'T BELIEVE IT!)

November 2015

THE LAST TWENTY-NINE years flew by. I am so grateful for the experiences I had, the people I worked with, and that I was able to help others in their times of need. I'm also extremely grateful to be leaving the job without any serious injuries or illnesses. With the ambition and drive instilled in me by my original workout partners, so many great mentors and by surrounding myself with good hard-working firemen, I rose through the ranks from fire candidate to firefighter to lieutenant to captain and finally to battalion chief. The next title I'll hold will be at the end of this month..."Retired Firefighter Kevin Stawiarski."

NOTES TO THE READER

BEFORE GETTING TO the body of this writing, there are a few things that are very important to me that I need to address:

- Most firefighters are very humble about what they do. When one of us gets cornered into a news interview it's not uncommon to hear, "It's just our job" or "It's what we do." Within this writing the word "I" is used quite often. It's very important to me that I clarify and respectfully ask the reader of this work not to interpret it as a "brag book." Using the word "I" just happens to be inherent when presenting a perspective through one's own eyes.
- This writing is not a "greatest hits" of experiences. It is a personal journal of the daily activities of my last year on the job. The primary focus of this work is not to relate "fire stories," but rather to give the reader a perspective of what one year can be like for a battalion chief on a big city fire department.
- Throughout this book I used quotation marks to indicate conversations and or radio transmissions. I felt this was necessary to make things more realistic for the reader. Please know that, even though I used my personal notes to recall each of the incidents in

this book, a great deal of this writing was done by memory. Therefore, not all, but much of the "quoted" material has been paraphrased by me.

- I feel it's also important to mention stress levels as they relate to those in the fire service. It's not always being at the actual incident that gets a firefighter's heart pumping and fight-or-flight responses to kick in. Stress levels and anxiety can rise significantly while on the way to a run just listening to the radio reports of the first arriving companies. For example, "We have a fire" or "It's going through the roof" or "I have a four-car rollover accident with multiple victims pinned in." Sometimes it's the comments section of a run sheet that reads, "people trapped" or "offender still on the scene." Sometimes it's just the loud tones of the computer dispatch system. And yes, sometimes it's that you just woke from a sound sleep four minutes ago and now find yourself crawling down a dark smoky hallway with zero visibility pulling hose and listening for the crackle of fire and or signs of life.
- Lastly, I would like to mention that there are a few times in this writing where I might have not worked entirely "by the book." Yes, I may have gone outside the lines a couple of times, but it's imperative to me to note that these instances were not me "hot-dogging it," but rather doing what I thought, at the time, was the best way for me to get the job done, and most importantly, watch out for the well-being of the members working under my command.

Below is an overview of Chicago Fire Department apparatus, ranks, responses etc. Many of these terms are used often throughout this book. I strongly suggest a quick scan through this information prior to starting into the body of this writing.

CHICAGO FIRE DEPARTMENT APPARATUS

Engine

- Also known as a pumper
- 1 Officer, 1 Engineer/Driver, 2 or 3 Firefighters
- Carries hose and puts the water on the fire
- An Advanced Life Support (ALS) engine is manned with one of the Firefighters as a Paramedic and one as an Emergency Medical Technician (EMT). An ALS engine can administer the same medical care as an ambulance but cannot transport a patient.
- ALS certified rigs are housed sporadically throughout the city

Truck

- Also known as a hook and ladder
- 1 Officer and 3 or 4 Firefighters
- Carries ladders, forcible entry and vehicle extrication tools
- Primary responsibilities include search and rescue and ventilation
- An Advanced Life Support (ALS) truck is manned with one of the Firefighters as a Paramedic and one as an Emergency Medical Technician (EMT). An ALS

engine can administer the same medical care as an ambulance but cannot transport a patient.
- ALS certified rigs are housed sporadically throughout the city

Tower Ladder

- An apparatus similar to a Truck with the major difference being that a Tower Ladder has a platform ("basket") attached at the end of its main ladder from where firefighters can apply water to a fire, make rescues, ventilate, etc.
- Primary responsibilities are the same as a Truck Company
- At the time of this writing there were eight Tower Ladders located throughout the city

Snorkel

- An articulating boom apparatus with a platform ("basket") attached at the end of the boom from where firefighters can apply water to a fire, make rescues, ventilate, etc.
- In Chicago each Squad Company runs with two rigs, one of which is a 55' snorkel
- At the time of this writing there was one "auxiliary snorkel." The auxiliary snorkel was an extra apparatus. It was manned only when requested by an on-scene incident commander to respond to very large fires.

Squad

- Special Operations Unit
- There are four squads in the city (Downtown, North, South and O'Hare Airport)
- Has very large response district
- 1 Officer and 5 specially trained Firefighters
- Duties include fires, water rescue, hazmat, extrications, trench and high angle rescue etc.
- Carries many specialized tools as well as standard tools found on trucks
- Runs with two rigs: a snorkel and a large box type vehicle

Buggy

- A Chief's car—usually an SUV

Hazardous Incident Team (HIT or Hazmat Team)

- There are two Hazmat teams in the city. 5-1-1 and 5-1-2
- 5-1-1 covers most of the city—5-1-2 is quartered at O'Hare Airport

5-1-5

- Also known as the Special Operations Battalion Chief
- A Battalion Chief that responds to all "Special Operations" runs citywide
- 5-1-5 also responds to all fires in high-rise buildings and all extra alarms

ALS Company

- Advanced Life Support company
- An ALS company can be either an engine or a truck
- An ALS company is manned with at least one FF/EMT and one FF/PM
- About half of the fire companies in Chicago are certified as ALS

BLS Company

- Basic Life Support company
- Every engine and truck are certified at minimum as BLS. If it's not BLS it is ALS
- A BLS company is manned with at least two EMT-Bs

PARTIAL LIST OF CHICAGO FIRE DEPARTMENT RANKS IN TOP-DOWN ORDER AND PERTINENT TO THIS WRITING

- Fire Commissioner
- Deputy Fire Commissioner
- Assistant Deputy Fire Commissioner
- District Chief
- Deputy District Chief
- Battalion Chief
- Captain
- Lieutenant
- Engineer
- Firefighter—Firefighter Paramedic—Firefighter EMT
- Candidate Firefighter

CHICAGO FIRE DEPARTMENT JOB TITLES

Fire Commissioner

- highest rank on the Chicago Fire Department
- rides in a black buggy with a personal driver

Deputy Fire Commissioner

- also known as a DFC
- one rank above an ADFC
- works 8-hour shifts but can also be on call anytime
- drives alone in a black buggy

Assistant Deputy Fire Commissioner

- also known as an ADFC
- one rank above a DC
- works 8-hour shifts but can also be on call anytime
- drives alone in a black buggy

District Chief

- also known as a DC
- one rank above DDC
- works 8-hour shifts but can also be on call anytime
- drives alone in a black buggy

Deputy District Chief

- also known as a DDC with call numbers such as 2-2-1, 2-2-2 etc.

- one rank above Battalion Chief
- has administrative command over all 20 houses in his/her district
- rides in a red "buggy" and has a driver to assist at incidents and with daily administrative duties

BATTALION CHIEF

- also known as a BC
- first level Incident Commander
- drives alone in a red "buggy"
- administratively responsible for the four firehouses in his/her battalion
- manages most fires and other incidents
- if an alarm is escalated, the Battalion Chief remains on scene as a supervisor but is relieved of overall command by a higher-ranking Chief (usually a Deputy District Chief).

CAPTAIN

- second level fire Company Officer
- works on an engine, truck or squad
- responsible for the crew and apparatus he/she is assigned to for a 24-hour shift
- also responsible for his/her assigned apparatus for all three shifts
- engine Captains are also responsible for the care and upkeep of their quarters

Lieutenant

- first level fire Company Officer
- works on an engine, truck or squad
- responsible for the crew and apparatus he/she is assigned to for a 24-hour shift

Engineer

- drives an engine and operates the pumps
- this is a tested and promoted rank

Paramedic

- also known as a Single Role Paramedic (does not work as a Firefighter)
- works on an ambulance only
- highest medical training

Firefighter/Paramedic

- also known as a FF/PM
- same as Firefighter but with third (highest) level medical training

Firefighter/Emergency Medical Technician

- also known as a FF/EMT
- same as a Firefighter but with second level medical training

Firefighter

- works on an engine, truck or squad
- medically trained as a basic First Responder

Candidate Firefighter

- works on an engine, truck or squad
- medically trained as a basic First Responder
- still in probationary period

Reliever

- an Engineer, Lieutenant, Captain or Chief without an assigned company
- relievers fill in for regularly assigned members who are on Daley day, furlough, medical leave, etc.

BASIC CHICAGO FIRE DEPARTMENT RESPONSES

Automatic Alarm

- a response summoned by a monitoring service rather than a phone call—example: a monitored smoke alarm activates, the system sends a detailed notification (floor, room number etc.) to a manned 24/7 alarm monitoring service who then dials 911 to alert the fire department
- response: 1 engine and 1 truck—add 1 Battalion Chief if the automatic alarm is in a high-rise building
- Automatic Alarms are usually false due to cooking, dust in the detector or a malfunction

Automatic Alarm High-Rise

- see above

Box Alarm

- dispatched by either the Main or Englewood Fire Alarm Office upon receipt of an alarm from a fire alarm box usually located in a lobby of a school, nursing home, hospital, theater or other place of public assembly
- can be activated by a manual pull or connected to an automatic alarm system
- usually false due to malicious pulls or malfunctions
- responses: vary depending on the type of assembly and time of day—example: a Box Alarm at an elementary school at one o'clock in the morning would not draw as large of a response as an elementary school alarm at one o'clock in the afternoon when classes are likely to be in session

Cold Box

- similar to a Box Alarm response but mostly specific to hospitals and nursing homes
- a Cold Box alarm is usually false due to a malicious pull, a dusty or malfunctioning smoke detector, cigarette smoke or burnt food in a lounge room microwave
- response: 4 engines, 2 trucks, 1 Battalion Chief

Still or Still Alarm

- standard first level response when someone picks up a phone and reports smoke and or a fire
- response: 2 engines, 2 trucks, 1 Battalion Chief—sometimes a squad

Working Fire Response

- a slight upgrade to an initial Still Alarm response when fire or smoke is reported by an on-scene company or chief officer
- depending on the location, either the Main or Englewood Fire Alarm Office can also start a "Working Fire Response" at their discretion if they are receiving many calls or if they can confirm an actual fire using street cameras
- response: 1 RIT, 1 command van (for communications), 1 squad

Still & Box Alarm

- an escalation in response to a Still Alarm.
- initiated by a Chief or first arriving fire companies if they determine more help is needed
- usually requested by radio as "Emergency—Gimme a Box"
- depending on the location, a Still & Box could also be dispatched by either the Main or Englewood Fire Alarm Office prior to the arrival of the first fire companies—this is done when the dispatchers are

receiving many calls reporting a fire at the same address or there are reports of people trapped

- response: several additional engines and trucks

Still In a High-Rise

- standard first level response when someone picks up a phone and reports smoke and or a fire in a high-rise building
- response: massive

Still & Box In a High-Rise

- initial escalation in response above a Still In a High-Rise when there is a confirmed fire in a high-rise building
- this response is very involved—it brings many more engines, trucks, Chiefs and specialized apparatus

EMS Plans

- an EMS Plan I is a standardized medical response when more than 3 ambulances are needed
- an EMS Plan I initially sends a total of 5 ambulances to the scene (two more can be requested before an EMS Plan II is necessary)
- can be followed by an EMS Plan II and an EMS Plan III if more ambulances are needed

Extra Alarm

- an escalation in response resources above a Still & Box alarm
- identified as 2-11, 3-11, 4-11 and 5-11
- anything after a 5-11 is called a "Special"
- note: 4-11s and above are very rare
- responses: vary—usually anything above a 3-11 summons mostly engines

Rapid Intervention Team (RIT)

- dispatched to every Working Fire
- the RIT does not fight the fire
- the RIT stands by in case a Mayday is called for firefighters in trouble—its only job is to rescue firefighters if something goes wrong
- the RIT consists of 1 Battalion Chief, 1 truck, 1 ambulance and 1 Paramedic Chief

Water Flow Alarm

- similar to an Automatic Alarm with the exception that the initial alarm is caused by a flow of water from a sprinkler system rather than the activation of a smoke alarm
- usually false due to a broken pipe, a water surge in the city supply or the accidental operation of a sprinkler head
- response: 1 engine, 1 truck

OTHER TERMS

Time Notations

- Fire Departments use military time. With the non-fire department reader in mind, I've opted to use a.m. and p.m. in this writing.

Building Side Designations

- a specific system to designate work sectors of a building or other incident
- the front or address side of a building is Side A—Sides B, C and D are added clockwise from Side A

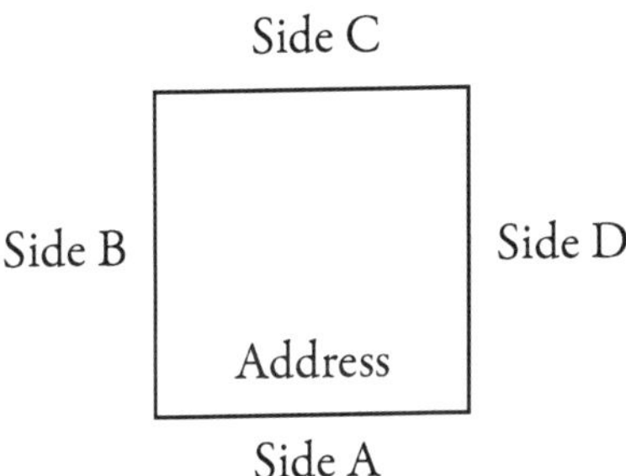

CPD

- Chicago Police Department

Daley Day

- a day off in addition to the normal 48-hour period between shifts—this extra day off (named after Mayor Richard J. Daley) was added to the Chicago Fire

Department schedule to get the normal work week down to 46 hours

DECK GUN

- A large water nozzle permanently piped in and mounted to the top of an engine
- A deck gun can deliver a significantly higher volume of water than a handheld hose line

ENGLEWOOD

- Englewood Fire Alarm Office
- southside dispatch
- referred to as "Englewood"

FIREGROUND (radio frequency)

- a low power radio channel separate from the dispatch channel used by units operating at a scene to communicate with each other
- the Fireground radio channel is only good for about a 1-mile radius
- the term "fireground" is also used to describe the area of operations at a fire

HAND PUMP

- a five-gallon manual pump water extinguisher carried on all engines and trucks

Hold or Held (short for held while en route)

- when a unit is dispatched and en route but is subsequently told to disregard before arriving on scene, this is called being "held" or "held up"
- companies are usually "held" when another unit arrives first and either doesn't find anything or will handle the situation themselves

Hot Spots

- when the bulk of a fire is extinguished small areas of hidden fire or hot smoldering debris can remain, these are called "hot spots"
- typically, hot spots can be found inside walls, behind window trim, up and around ceiling joists or roof rafters and in piles of debris
- at larger fires where a roof has collapsed, hot spots are often hidden under hundreds of pounds of tarpaper and can be difficult or impossible to get at safely—in these cases firefighters will stand by and wait for a rekindle to flare up, then apply water from a distance.
- the majority of times, however, firefighters will pick and pull with hand tools to expose hot spots and then give them a good wash—searching for hot spots can be extremely physically taxing on a firefighter

IDOT

- Illinois Department of Transportation (highway tow trucks)

Incident Commander

- The highest-ranking fire officer on the scene of any incident

ISP

- Illinois State Police

Main

- Main Fire Alarm Office
- northside dispatch
- referred to as "Main"

Meat on the Stove (MOS)

- Meat on the Stove or Pot of Meat (interchangeable terms)
- a term that applies to burnt food causing an alarm—example: someone leaves home with a pot of chili simmering on the stove, the liquid in the pot evaporates causing the food and pot itself to emit smoke—this could cause a smoke alarm to activate or neighbors to call in a smell of something burning
- also very common, is burnt popcorn in a microwave—this is also sometimes referred to as a "pot of meat"—a radio report would sound something like "Hold all responding companies. We have a pot of meat. We'll handle it."

OFI

- Office of Fire Investigation
- Chicago Fire Department investigators that respond to selected incidents to determine the cause of fire

Overhaul

- the search for and extinguishment of hidden fires that could potentially rekindle
- this phase of operation can be very dangerous due to structural damage and toxic fumes

Pot of Meat (POM)—see Meat on the Stove

Red X Building

- a vacant building identified by the Building Department as having significant structural damage
- Red X buildings are identified by several large red colored "X" placards affixed to the structure's exterior
- Chicago Fire Department protocol in Red X buildings initially calls for an exterior attack so as to protect firefighters
- an interior attack on a Red X Building can only be initiated when certain criteria are met—example: a minimum of two Chiefs must be on the scene and complete a systematic survey to assure firefighter safety before anyone can enter

REKINDLE

- the re-ignition of hot spots
- rekindles are rare and mostly occur after very large fires where hot spots are difficult or impossible to get to

RIB

- Radio In a Box
- a radio mounted in a briefcase that can be plugged into an electrical outlet to get more power for communicating within steel and concrete high-rise buildings or subways

RUN

- a response to a dispatch
- includes all types of dispatches
- example: "Truck 3 had 15 runs yesterday, three fires, four stuck elevators and eight ambulance assists."

"Choose a job you love, and you will never have to work a day in your life."

No one knows for certain who authored this old adage but I, for one, consider myself very lucky to be one of those who can wholeheartedly attest to its accuracy.

NOVEMBER 2014

11/28/14
ASSIGNMENT—5-1-5 (SPECIAL OPERATIONS—ENGINE 5'S QUARTERS, DESPLAINES & JACKSON)
PRIMARY RESPONSE AREA—CITY WIDE
WEATHER—TEMPERATURES IN THE LOW 20S, VERY WINDY

Black Friday, the day after Thanksgiving, one year and one day until retirement. My assignment for the day was 5-1-5, Special Operations. 5-1-5 runs out of Engine 5's quarters just west of the downtown area and responds to all incidents within the city limits where technical rescue may be required. (i.e., water rescue, entrapment in machinery, high angle rescues, collapses, etc.) 5-1-5 also responds to confirmed fires in high-rise buildings and all extra alarms.

"CAR IN THE WATER"

Sometime late morning I was dispatched to a "Car in the Water" at Lake Shore Drive near Division. As I was responding, the first companies arrived on the scene and reported via radio that they were being waved down by several people near the reported location. Battalion 1 arrived less than a minute later and reported that he had a pickup truck in the lake but that everyone was safe, and no one was in the water. He then held all responding companies but had the ambulance continue in to the scene. I was only a few blocks away so I continued my response out of curiosity. When I arrived Battalion 1 filled me in on what occurred.

Apparently, a park district worker in a pickup truck was driving along the lakeshore bike path when he spotted two women on foot sliding around on the ice near the frozen shoreline. When he stopped to offer them help his truck began sliding down towards the water. Luckily, he was able to jump out of his vehicle just before it plunged into the icy lake. While the truck was sinking the women were able to crawl up the snow and ice to a safe area where the first arriving companies found them. The driver wasn't physically injured but was pretty shaken up and transported by ambulance to the hospital. The women declined medical attention. Battalion 1 released all companies and notified the fire alarm office that this was now a vehicle recovery incident and that he was turning the scene over to the police.

The month of November is a big month for retirements. On a member's last workday, the crew at the firehouse where the retiring member is assigned will host an informal "last day" open house luncheon. Family, friends and department members stop by to wish the retiring member well. Today was Battalion 18, Chief Tom McCarthy's, last day. Around 1:00 p.m. I took a ride to Engine 95's house near Madison and Pulaski to wish Tom well.

On my way from the front door back to Engine 95's kitchen I could already hear the chatter and laughter of the gathering. Tom was a popular guy, and the kitchen was full of well-wishers.

Through the crowd I could see Tom standing at the far side of the kitchen surrounded by friends and family. As I made my way across the room towards the guest of honor, I was greeted by several old friends that asked about my own retirement. "One year and one day," was my reply. When I finally got to Tom, I gave him a quick handshake and wished him well in his retirement. Just as I turned away and before I could have something to eat, a call came across the radio, "Main to Battalion 1—you have a Car in the Water at Lake Shore Drive and Balbo."

"Battalion 1 message received."

"Main to 5-1-5."

I answered, "5-1-5's got it ... Car in the Water ... Lake Shore Drive and Balbo."

With that I made a quick exit through the crowd towards the parking lot. Opening the door to the outside I was hit in the face with a cold blast of fine snow. The weather had suddenly turned very blustery.

"CAR IN THE WATER"

As I made my way east on the Eisenhower Expressway, I heard the first radio report from the scene. Companies were reporting that several eyewitnesses with corroborating accounts were saying that a car came barreling down a hill backwards from Lake Shore Drive at a high rate of speed and "flew into the water" sinking about 20' off the shoreline. (The most important piece of information we can get on a water incident is a good "last seen point." In this case all witnesses were pointing to the exact same spot telling rescuers where the vehicle entered the water. As a general rule the depth of the water at the last seen point will provide rescuers with a good start in locating a victim or vehicle. Example: If a vehicle or person sinks in twenty feet of water the rescuers will go to the last seen point and dive straight down to the bottom. Using this general rule, the vehicle or victim should be found within a twenty-foot radius.)

Surprisingly the wind and snow didn't delay my response too much and my arrival on scene was rather quick. Exiting my buggy, I could hear companies on shore communicating the last seen point with 6-8-8, the Chicago Fire Department Fast Boat. The Fast Boat is docked less than a mile north of where the incident occurred and was on the scene within minutes and ready to deploy divers. Once at the shore I got a quick briefing from Battalion 1 and took over communications with the Fast Boat.

"5-1-5 to 6-8-8."

"6-8-8 go ahead."

"Pull up about 20 yards and drop your divers. The last seen point is about 25 feet due east of where I'm standing."

"6-8-8 ... message received."

Two specially trained SCUBA divers immediately plunged into the icy water. Via radio I communicated the last seen point to the captain of 6-8-8 who I could see standing at the bow of the boat. Carefully watching over his divers, he relayed my information to them through a communication line connected directly from a radio on the boat to their face masks. In less than a minute one of the divers reported that they found the car and that there was one victim inside. Keeping the radio silent we waited for the diver's next report. It came in less than a minute. Over the sound of the diver's laborious breathing one of them reported, "We got 'em out ... we're comin' up." The first diver's head appeared out of the water almost exactly where the witnesses reported the vehicle went in. The second diver, who was holding the victim, surfaced next and was guided by his partner towards the shore.

Waiting at the wall were firefighters dangling a nylon strap ready to remove the victim from the water. Also standing by was an ambulance crew with a stretcher and more firefighters to assist if needed. Once the divers had the victim at the shore wall, using the dangling rescue strap, the divers tied what is called a handcuff knot on the victim. The firefighters on shore then hoisted him out of the water and placed him onto the waiting stretcher. Quickly, the victim was wheeled to the ambulance where three paramedics jumped in the back and shut the door. After only a minute or so the back door of the ambulance swung open and one of the paramedics reported, "We're going to Northwestern!" Off they went with lights and siren escorted by a Chicago Police car. Our initial estimations were that it was approximately fifteen to twenty minutes from the time the vehicle entered the water until the victim was brought to shore and in an ambulance.

With the victim now on the way to the hospital we began trying to piece together what happened. From witness accounts, a man driving northbound on Lake Shore Drive got out of his car at the red light for an unknown reason. (Possibly car trouble or an iced windshield???) While he was out of his vehicle it began to slowly move forward. Witnesses reported that the man jumped back into the driver's seat and tried to put his vehicle in Park, but that he must have missed gears and put it in Reverse instead. When the car began moving backwards, he apparently panicked and hit the gas pedal instead of the brake causing the vehicle to take off in Reverse at a high rate of speed through a snow fence, down a hill, across the concrete walking path and into Lake Michigan. The police found one of the driver's shoes on Lake Shore Drive where the car jumped the curb, a possible indication that he may have tried to exit the vehicle while it was moving.

With the victim out of the water the scene was officially turned over to the Chicago Police Department. Their divers along with an Illinois Department of Transportation (IDOT) tow truck would now be removing the vehicle from the water and while the vehicle recovery operation was in progress, the CFD dive team truck, 6-8-7, would stand by as a backup for the Chicago Police divers. I, too, remained on scene until about 5:30 p.m. when the car was lifted out of the water. While still on the scene I received word that the driver of the vehicle did not survive. By the time I left the lakefront the sun had gone down and the temperature dropped into the low teens.

Being that it was Black Friday, the day after Thanksgiving, I knew that some of my family would be gathering at my in-law's house for holiday leftovers. Their home was very close to my quarters located downtown, so before heading back to my firehouse I stopped by for a few minutes to say "hi," grab a quick bite to eat and thaw out a bit. Just as I sat down at the kitchen table my radio crackled and I heard Battalion 1 report on the scene with a "fire on the fourth floor of a high-rise building." Per protocol, he also immediately requested a Box and EMS Plan I. As Special Operations chief one of my responsibilities was to respond to all confirmed high-rise fires. With that I stood up from the table and grabbed some bread for the ride. The radio cracked again, "5-1-5 take in the high-rise fire 300 W. Illinois." I radioed back, "5-1-5's got it—fire in a high-rise 300 W. Illinois." I thanked my family for the "almost" meal and headed for downtown.

"FIRE IN A HIGH-RISE"

My initial responsibilities as Special Operations at a high-rise fire was to first let the Incident Commander know that I was on the scene and then ascend to a location two floors below the reported fire floor where Forward Fire Command was set up. There, I would report to the Forward Fire Commander (another battalion chief) and set up my Radio In a Box (RIB).

The fire address was only about a mile and a half from my in-law's home so I arrived on scene quickly. With my RIB in hand, I entered the lobby and reported to Battalion 1.

"Hey Aaron ... I'm here. I'm heading upstairs ... you need anything?"

"Not now ... the fire's on 4. Chet's up on 2 ... go see him."

"Got it."

In full gear, and carrying my RIB, I entered the stairwell and headed up to the second floor where I met the Forward Fire Commander, Battalion Chief Chet Lynch.

"What's up Chet? "

"Hey Kev. It's crazy as usual. I haven't even got a report on conditions on the floors above the fire yet."

"I got it." I said as I handed him my RIB and headed up the stairway to get a look at the 5TH, 6TH and 7TH floors.

Making my way up the fire attack stairway I could see a charged hoseline connected to the standpipe on the 3RD floor. It was led out up the stairs, through the hallway door and down the hall on the 4TH floor. Radio traffic was chaotic, but I was able to hear Engine 42 report that they had water on the fire and were making progress.

In the 4TH floor stairway were a couple of firefighters crouching and looking down the hall. Before going up the stairs above the fire I tapped one of them on the shoulder and, for accountability, told them that I was going up three floors to check conditions. They nodded and I continued past the fire floor to the 5TH, 6TH, and 7TH where I made a quick assessment of the smoke and heat conditions.

"5-1-5 to Forward Fire Command."

"Forward Fire Command."

"Smoke on the 5TH, 6TH and 7TH and stairwell is moderate to light. I'm gonna stop on 4 on the way down."

"Message Received."

Back at the 4TH floor I let the two firefighters know that I was no longer above them. I then decided to take a look at the fire. The smoke in the 4TH floor hallway was still a little thick so following the hoseline I made my way to the involved apartment. When I got there the fire was out and companies were in the process of washing down and checking for hot spots. Sizing up the scene, it was obvious to me that coordination and aggressive tactics by the first arriving companies kept this fire from spreading beyond the apartment where it started. "Good job 42," I said through the smoke. I then went back to the 2ND floor, retrieved my RIB, and returned to the lobby where I stood by until released.

When all companies were picked up from the fire, I followed Squad 1 back to their quarters for a night visit and brief critique of the fire.

"GUNSHOT VICTIM"

Around 8:30 p.m., while chatting with the crew at Squad 1's house, Engine 42 and Ambulance 42 were dispatched to a "gunshot victim" inside Nordstrom's at 55 E. Grand Ave. From the kitchen table I, and the remaining members in the house, watched as the engine and ambulance pulled out. A call for a gunshot victim downtown on Black Friday immediately drew everyone's attention. Downtown fire companies and ambulances are always on alert for possible incidents of terror including mass shootings. With this in mind Battalion 1, who also happened to be at Engine 42's house when the call came in, jumped in his buggy, and told the fire alarm office via radio that he was taking in the shooting run with Engine 42. I radioed in the same message and jogged out to my buggy. The run wasn't too far from the firehouse but while we were all still in route, a notification from the alarm office came over the radio, "Companies responding to the gunshot victim at Nordstrom's...we're now getting a report of a second person shot. We're starting in another ambulance."

Turning onto Grand Ave., we could see a ton of blue lights up ahead indicating that the police were already on scene. As Battalion 1 and I walked up to the front door, we were met by a police sergeant that told us the shooting was bona fide. He added that the scene was secure and that it initially appears to be a domestic related murder/suicide. The ambulance, engine, Battalion 1 and I all went up to the second floor where we were guided to the cosmetics department. There we found the two gunshot victims, a male and a female. After a quick assessment the ambulance crew determined that the male was DOA but that the female was still showing signs of life. We watched intently as the paramedics worked on the female victim. "Okay...we gotta get her to the ambo NOW!" one of them said. Engine 42's crew assisted getting the woman onto the stretcher and helped wheel her out to the ambulance. A medic jumped in the driver's seat and off they went.

I returned to my quarters around 10:00 p.m. and completed all my paperwork for the day's events before lying down. In contrast to the busy day, my night was quiet. I had no runs and got in a full five hours of down time. The following morning around 5:00 a.m., I packed up my stuff and headed downstairs to the kitchen for coffee and to wait for my relief to come in. The television news was on and reporting that the shooting we had last night was in fact domestic related. The male apparently shot the woman then turned the gun on himself. He died at the scene and the female died at the hospital later that night.

About 5:30 a.m. I was relieved by an old friend of mine, Battalion Chief Sid Cullen. Over the years Sid and I not only worked together as firemen but also did construction together on our days off. Over coffee I filled him in on the events of the previous day.

DECEMBER 2014

12/01/14
ASSIGNMENT—BATTALION 14 (ENGINE 109'S QUARTERS, 22ND & KEDZIE)
PRIMARY RESPONSE AREA—WESTSIDE, LITTLE VILLAGE
WEATHER—TEMPERATURES IN THE MID 20S, WINDY

Battalion 14 is quartered at Engine 38's house at 16TH and Pulaski. It was one of my favorite battalions to work but it had been over a year since I had been there. I arrived at the firehouse at my usual time of 5:15 a.m. and peering through the glass front door I could see the firefighter on watch sweeping the area near the officers' desks. Rather than ring the doorbell and wake everyone up I tapped lightly on the glass to get his attention. Looking up he recognized me as the relief battalion chief showing up for work. The giveaway was me standing there loaded down with all my gear and uniform pieces for the day. He gave me a wave as he propped his broom against the wall and walked toward the door. He and I had worked together in the past and knew each other, but not by name. Unlocking and holding the door open he greeted me with a surprised look, "Hey Chief. What are you doing HERE?" As soon as he said that, I realized I was at the WRONG firehouse! I had forgotten that within the last year Battalion 14 had been reassigned from Engine 38's quarters to

Engine 109 at 22ND and Kedzie, about a mile or so away. We both laughed and chatted for a few minutes before I went on my way.

The first twenty-three hours of my shift were pretty uneventful. Throughout the day, evening and night I had several runs, nothing out of the ordinary.

"STILL ALARM"

At about 5:00 a.m. while getting ready to be relieved by the oncoming chief, I was dispatched along with Engine 109 and Truck 32 to a fire at 3200 W. 31ST St.

We arrived at the address and found no sign of smoke or fire. There wasn't even a building.

"Battalion 14 to Main...do you have a better address? This is a vacant lot."

"Main to Battalion 14...we had a female caller state that she was inside a Public Storage building and said that she saw smoke coming from one of the units."

"Main, there's no storage building at this address. We'll look around and I'll get back to you in a minute."

Upon hearing this radio exchange between me and the fire alarm office, Engine 99 who was also dispatched to this run and standing by, called me on the Fireground radio channel. "Chief, there's a storage building about a block or so east of here. You want us to check it out?" "Yeah, all companies here with me on 31ST follow 99." I then notified the alarm office that per Engine 99's information we were all relocating and that I'd get them a better address in a minute.

Upon arrival at our new location, we found a storage facility locked up with no alarm sounding and no sign of fire.

"Battalion 14 to Main...we're at the new location with

nothing showing. Can you contact the caller and have her let us in?"

"Will do."

"Main to Battalion 14...the call came from a cell phone number. We called her back and it went to voicemail three times. No further information."

Okay...decision time. Do we force entry or call it a false alarm and leave? My first thought was that this was a malicious call. We get quite a few phony runs of this nature. Someone falsely reporting a building on fire or seeing or smelling smoke is not uncommon.

Two scenarios came to mind:

- If we force entry and break the door the owner could say, "If you saw no sign that there was a fire why did you break my door?!"
- If we leave without checking inside there might be a woman inside who needs help.

As one last check I ordered Truck 32 to put their main ladder to the roof to see if there was any sign of fire from up there. I also had the remaining companies on scene do a complete walk around the perimeter. When all reports came back negative, I decided to call it a false alarm and return all companies. However, just as I reached for my radio microphone, I happened to notice one lone vehicle in the small parking area directly in front of the building. Change of plans, we're gonna force entry. My thought was that the vehicle could very well belong to the woman caller who was inside and possibly in need of help. We HAD to check this out. The police were now on the scene.

I instructed the members of Truck 32 to force entry to a

steel door on the D side of the building and to try to keep damage to the door at a minimum. I then went back to the parking lot in front of the building where the police were running the license plate of the car.

A minute later I returned to the D Side and found Truck 32 using their gas powered K12 saw with a metal cutting blade on the door. Sparks were flying everywhere! From my position it appeared that they were making a triangle cut at the lock right through the door. "Oh man...they're ruining the door," I thought. I could yell but they probably wouldn't hear me and besides, the damage was already done. After about ten seconds the saw stopped, and I saw the door swing open without any damage. What Truck 32's crew did was surgically insert the saw blade between the door and the jamb to cut the throws on both locks. There was no damage to the door itself, and now the only repair needed was to replace the lock. Great job! With the door now open I radioed to the fire alarm office that we made entry and were going inside to check it out.

We only got in about ten feet when the alarm office radioed back,

"Main to Battalion 14...we finally reached the caller. She said she was mistaken. There is no fire."

"Battalion 14 to Main...we already forced entry. The police are here with us. We're gonna look around."

After walking around the entire inside of the structure and finding no sign of fire or of the caller I picked up all companies and put myself "in service." We all left the scene. The police had it from here.

When I got about three blocks away from the scene, I realized that I forgot to get the corrected address I needed for my paperwork, so I turned my buggy around and went back.

When I returned the police were still there outside next to their vehicles, probably waiting for the owner to show up. Just around the corner from where they were standing was an overhead garage door with small windows about chest high. Through one of the windows, I just happened to catch a glimpse of a man cupping his hands over his brows and looking out from the inside. I stepped out of my buggy, walked over to the police, and told them what I saw. Together we went over to the door that we forced earlier and entered the building. Once back inside the man greeted us while wiping sleep from his eyes. He appeared clean but with a scraggly beard and a worn look.

"What's going on?" one of the police officers asked.

"Awww man. Me and my lady had a fight and she's tryin' to get me in trouble," replied the man.

After a few minutes of questioning by the police it was determined that the couple had been illegally living in one of the storage units. After some sort of dispute, the woman left and called 911 reporting a fire. Her intent was to get the man arrested for living in the unit.

Upon returning to the firehouse, I went directly to the kitchen where many of the off-going and on-coming shift members were gathered. Over coffee I complimented the members of Truck 32 for their nice work on that steel door and told everyone about what happened after they left. The main take-away I wanted to impress from this quick coffee talk was to never assume that a storage facility is unoccupied...even overnight.

Done for the day.

12/04/14
Assignment—Battalion 2 (Engine 8's Quarters, 22ND & Wentworth)
Primary Response Area—Chinatown, South Loop, Bridgeport, Near South Lakefront
Weather—Temperatures in the high 20s

"STILL AND BOX"

I was riding in my buggy about 3:30 p.m. when Battalion 4, John Stevens, reported over the radio that he was on the scene of a garage fire on the 1700 hundred block of west 21ST Place. His initial report was that he had a 15'x 20' brick garage totally involved. John is usually pretty calm on the radio, but in this report I could tell from the tone of his voice that he might have something more than just a usual garage fire. Knowing that I was due to respond if he escalated the alarm from a Still to a Still and Box, and hearing what I felt was an anxious communication from a normally calm guy, I began making my way south and west from Roosevelt and Michigan towards the fire address. Sure enough, just as I got to 22ND and Michigan the call came over the radio from Battalion 4,

"Battalion 4 to Main, Emergency. Gimme a Box."

The fire alarm office quickly acknowledged his request and announced over the radio, "A Still and Box Alarm on the 1700 block of west 21ST Place on the orders of Battalion 4 ... Battalion 2 you're the Box Chief."

"Battalion 2 Box Chief," I confirmed. My job as Box Chief was to take command at the rear of the fire building.

(Side Note: At a post fire critique the next workday, Chief Stevens explained that when he first arrived on scene, he found a garage with its overhead door wide open and fire coming out like a blowtorch. The flames, he said were already engulfing overhead electrical wires and threatening wooden back porches across the alley. After he did a quick once around the entire scene, he discovered that a wall inside the burning garage was breeched into an adjoining brick garage making the original structure twice as large. He also found that the fire was communicating quickly to an enclosed back porch on the occupied frame structure in the front of the property.)

Driving west on 22ND Street, I could see clouds of dark smoke billowing in the sky ahead. As I got closer, I began hearing the radio chatter on Fireground. Battalion 4 was directing units on where to set up and I could hear engine officers yelling to their engineers, "Send the water!" As I drove up to the scene, I was able to get a look down the alley where I would be taking command. I was at the far end but could see that if I drove down the alley towards the fire there was a good place to park my buggy and be out of the way. With that I pulled in and parked about five houses down from the fire making sure I wasn't under any compromised span of electrical wires. While donning my turnout gear at the back of my buggy I did a quick visual survey of the scene, then reported via radio to 2-2-1, the Incident Commander, Deputy District Chief Mike Wrobelinski that I was assuming command on Side D.

By the time I got down to the garage Engine 18 already had knocked down the main body of fire with their two 2 ½" lines led out from their engine parked on Wood Street. As I walked up, the captain of Engine 18, Nick Benson, briefed me that there were live electrical wires down in the alley just to the west of us and that there were also firefighters operating on the roof of the garage. I took a quick look at the downed wires and saw a policeman standing nearby warning incoming firefighters about them. With the wire situation under control and most of the fire out, I had Engine 18 shut down both of their 2 ½" lines so I could get a better look at what we had inside the garage. Peering in through the residual smoke and steam I could see a couple of smoldering cars and a burned-up workbench area. I also saw that the roof rafters were pretty charred and there were still small areas of fire. "Okay, we're good," I thought, all we needed to do now was give this thing a good wash down. I turned to the captain of Engine 18 and said, "Go ahead and throw a hundred feet of 1 ¾" line on one of your 2 1/2s." The smaller hose line would give them better maneuverability to reach the remaining hot spots and good penetration to wash down the roof rafters. I also stepped back outside and ordered all firefighters off of the garage roof because of the many heavily charred rafters.

While waiting for the firefighters to return with the smaller hose, the captain of Engine 18 and I again surveyed the interior of the garage from the overhead doorway. Using flashlights and a thermal imagining camera we saw a steel I-beam running perpendicular to the roof rafters but supported by very charred 6"x 6" wood columns. The rafters themselves were also burned up pretty good. We also identified an area just inside the garage where the roof was still supported by steel columns. From there we could safely operate the 1 ¾" line once it was ready to go. When Engine 18's crew returned they connected the smaller line, and we entered the safe part of the garage to wash down. After a few minutes I stepped outside leaving the captain and his crew to do their work.

Once back out in the alley I happened to look to the east and saw a company dragging a line from the far end of the alley in my direction. My first thought was, "Why are they dragging a line 600 feet down the alley rather than coming through a gangway the next block over?" Plus...we really didn't need another line at this point. I radioed the approaching company and told them to stop where they were and stand by. Before giving them a "disregard", I wanted to check with the boss, 2-2-1, just in case he gave them an order I wasn't aware of. The return message I got from 2-2-1 was that he did send Engine 105 to the rear but if I didn't need another line, I could pick them up. With that I radioed to Engine 105, "Battalion 2 to 105. You can pick up your line. We're good down here."

Now focusing back on the garages, I saw that Engine 18 was almost done washing down. Looking up, I also saw that there were about five firefighters still on the roof of the garage after I had already told them to get off. I immediately yelled up and ordered all companies off the roof again. This time they complied...or so I thought. About 3 minutes later I heard a saw start up. Someone up there was getting ready to continue cutting into the roof of the garage. Over the coping I could see a helmet shield from the Tower Ladder. I immediately got on the radio,

"Battalion 2 to the Tower, is there a chief up there with you?"

"Negative."

"I want everyone off that roof right now. Meet me in the alley and bring everyone up there with you."

When they all came down, I gathered them in the alley just outside the garage overhead door. Two at a time I took them into the safe area of the garage and showed them from below where they were standing on the roof. I explained that they, five firefighters each weighing over 200 pounds, all in wet gear, with tools, were standing on an area of the roof where the joists were almost completely burned through. I told them that I appreciate their aggressiveness but to remember, "risk vs. reward." What were we going to gain by opening that roof any further? The fire was out. I also reminded them that when given an order they are to comply and ask questions later. Everyone understood, apologized, and thanked me for the quick drill.

Later that night, about 9:00 p.m., I got a phone call from 2-2-1, Chief Mike Wrobelinski. Rhetorically he asked, "Hey...why would an engine company drag hose from 600' away rather than come through a gangway on the next block?" He said that he specifically told Engine 105 to lead out from 21ST Street through a gangway where he already had a truck company clear a path for them. He added that there was also a hydrant at that location close to the gangway that would have made that lead-out much easier. I knew where he was going with this and trying to take some heat off of Engine 105, I mentioned that radio communications on the scene were pretty hectic at the time and perhaps they didn't hear the part about bringing the line through the gangway. "Yeah...maybe," was his doubtful reply. Hey...I tried.

12/10/14
ASSIGNMENT—BATTALION 13 (ENGINE 95'S QUARTERS, PULASKI & MADISON)
PRIMARY RESPONSE AREA—WESTSIDE
WEATHER—TEMPERATURES IN THE LOW 30S

Uneventful day.

12/13/14
ASSIGNMENT—BATTALION 13 (ENGINE 95'S QUARTERS, PULASKI & MADISON)
PRIMARY RESPONSE AREA—WESTSIDE
WEATHER—TEMPERATURES IN THE HIGH 30S

"STILL ALARM"

At about 2:00 p.m. while holding an informal drill at Engine 113's quarters, both 113 and I were dispatched to a Still Alarm on West Monroe Street. Also dispatched were Engine 95, Truck 26 and Tower Ladder 14. With my buggy parked out front and already pointing in the direction of the run, I took off. I knew 113 would get a good push-out and be close behind me because:

- All the members were at the kitchen table for the drill and close to the rig.
- The address of the run was just about midway between Engine 113 and Engine 95's quarters. Because of this, both engines would try to be first on the scene.

This is probably a good time to briefly explain the pride mentality of a firefighter. Basically, it's a "no one takes MY work" attitude that dates way back to the early days of organized firefighting. One aspect of this is arriving first at incidents within your assigned response area. Slide the pole, jog to the rig, get dressed and out the door as quickly as possible. Drive safely, arrive first and do your job. This pride mentality also pertains to the use of tools and equipment. From day one on the job, it is instilled in young firefighters that you never give your tools or your pipe (hose line nozzle) to any other company. If, for instance, another firefighter was to ask to borrow your axe for a second, your answer would be, "Whaddya need? I'll do it."

Heading eastbound on Harrison about three blocks into my response I saw 113 in my rear-view mirror closing in. With lights and siren, I approached the busy intersection of Harrison and Cicero. I had the red light and had to stop before proceeding through. Even though I had my lights on and the siren wailing, none of the cross traffic was stopping. It wasn't until Engine 113 was inches from my bumper blaring their air horn that enough of the traffic stopped to let us through. We made the left turn and headed south another four blocks. At Monroe we made a right turn and pulled up to the address about halfway down the block.

I reported on the scene, "Battalion 13 to Main. I'm on the scene with Engine 113. We have a vacant 2-story brick with light smoke on the first floor. 113's eastbound. I'll get back to you with more in a minute."

It's important that the first engine on the scene reports their direction of travel over the radio so the other responding companies hear it and know how to set up. Bread and butter protocol is that the first engine to arrive pulls down the street and stops just past the fire building. This is done for several reasons:

- So that their back end, where all the hose is carried, is beyond the building making it easier to lead out their hoselines.
- So that they have the option to drive forward unimpeded to secure a hydrant.
- So that the truck can position directly in front of the address to use their main ladder to access the roof.

This also makes it a lot easier and more efficient to access and raise ground ladders for rescue.

After a quick look around the outside of the building, I ran up the front porch stairs to the entrance door that was wide open. The building had a common layout with a small foyer and two doors, one to the left leading to the upstairs apartment, and one to the right leading to the first-floor apartment. Conditions weren't too bad. While Engine 113 was leading out their hoseline, I decided to quickly scout out the location of the fire. About 15' inside the apartment I found a rubbish pile burning in a closet under the staircase leading to the second floor. The flames were just starting to impinge the underside of the stairs. I returned to the front porch where I was met by two members of Truck 26, each carrying a hand pump. Through the smoke I grabbed one of them and said, "It's in the closet under the stairs. It's starting to take off. We're probably gonna need a line. See what you can do with your hand pumps for now." From the elevated front porch, I could also see Engine 113 was down in the front yard straightening out their line. "Good," I thought, "we'd have water in a few seconds."

(Side Note: A common occurrence in vacant buildings like this one is that they are often taken over by squatters and/or drug users. They'll use the building for a few weeks or months then for some reason, usually an argument or fight between themselves, they try to burn it down. Typically, a small pile of trash is lit somewhere within the building. Many times, however, before the rubbish fire communicates to the structure, neighbors see the smoke and call 911. Many of these small fires are typically extinguished using only a 5-gallon water hand pump carried on all CFD rigs. However, there are times when these attempts at arson are very successful. I recall one time where some drug users had a beef with their dealers. Late at night while the users were sleeping on the upper floors, the dealers lit up all of the stairwells and back porches. Because of this we consider ALL buildings to be occupied.)

I knew that eventually we were going to have to make the second floor to perform a search and to look for fire extension. Intent on checking the stability of the staircase, I took a quick breath and re-entered the foyer. When I opened the door leading to the second floor, I could see bright orange between the cracks in the staircase indicating that the fire in the closet under the stairs was intensifying. If we wanted to use this stairway, we'd need to get water on this thing quickly. I stepped back out onto the front porch and heard members of Engine 113 saying that they were having a problem getting water. (This could mean a number of things: a kink in the hose, an unintentionally closed valve, trouble with the pumper, etc.) Now knowing that our big water might be delayed a few seconds I wanted to see how the two firefighters were doing inside with the hand pumps. Grabbing a breath of fresh air, I re-entered the first floor and headed for where the fire was. The smoke was getting heavier so a few feet inside the apartment I had to get on my knees. Through the smoke I yelled, "Truck 26 how you doin' in there?" I couldn't see them but heard their reply, "Our pumps are empty...we're gonna need a line in here fast!"

Things were rapidly changing for the worse. The fire was growing too fast to get with hand pumps and the first engine was having problems getting water. Most importantly the smoke generated by the quickly progressing fire was now thicker and beginning to move in a way that indicated a possible flashover. It was time to go. "Truck ... back out right now!" I yelled but got no reply. In need of a fresh breath of air I shimmied back out to the front porch. Quickly, I radioed to my second engine, "Engine 95 lead out to the front door right now!" The heat and smoke at the front door were getting hotter and darker. "Shit!" In my haste, and because I initially treated this as a routine rubbish fire, I had not put on my turnout gear. I was still dressed in only my work uniform: dress pants and button-down dress shirt, no hat or helmet. I screwed up. Still not getting a reply from Truck 26, I took a deep breath and re-entered the apartment pounding on the floor with my hand and yelling, "TRUCK ...TRUCK!" The small rubbish fire we found on arrival was quickly making its way up the walls and out of the closet into the living room. The heat on top of my head and face was intense. I had to get out now. Looking back through the smoke I could see flashlights near the front door. That was the way out and that's where I headed on all fours. A few feet from the front door I was grabbed and pulled forward by the firefighters on the front porch. It was the two guys from Truck 26! Somehow, they must have slipped past me in the smoke. Before I had even a second to let out a sigh of relief, the gasses and smoke at the ceiling level of the first floor lit up and flames began to roll over our heads out onto the front porch. "Back down...Back down," I yelled, and with that, we all began our retreat staying low and trying not to take a breath. A few short seconds later I heard the welcome sound of water gushing out of a nozzle. Engine 113 now had water and was knocking down the fire over our heads. We all got out of their way as they pushed past us advancing into the apartment continuously extinguishing fire as they moved in.

Once I was down the front steps and out on the sidewalk,

I quickly gathered my thoughts. Okay, we were in good shape again. 113's got water on the fire, 95 has a second hoseline waiting on the front porch ready to make the second floor, and we have ladders on three sides of the building. With that, I took a deep breath and calmly gave my progress report to the fire alarm office, "Battalion 13 to Main, we have a small fire on the first floor...we have water on it and searches are underway."

My next concern was that there could be more than one fire. Because of how rapidly the fire in the closet progressed, it was very possible that whoever started it may have used some type of accelerant. If this were the case, there was also a good possibility of a second or even third fire somewhere in the structure. Reports from crews in the basement were negative but we still needed to get to the second floor. Surprisingly, the staircase over the closet was in decent shape. Engine 95 and Truck 26 carefully made their way up. When they got to the second floor, they reported finding two more small fires, a smoldering mattress in one of the bedrooms and another in the middle of the kitchen floor. They also confirmed that both Primary and Secondary searches were complete and negative.

After about ten minutes Engine 113 was done on the first floor. Engine 95 reported that they had the fires out on the second and Truck 26 reported that all searches were complete and negative. Tower Ladder 14 had all utilities shut off and reported the basement as "all clear." Fire out. No victims. Nobody hurt. All good. I gave the "Everyone can pick up" order and companies began exiting the building picking up hose, ladders and tools.

Because of the three separate fires set within the structure, I requested our Office of Fire Investigation (OFI) to respond to the scene. As I sat in my buggy across the street awaiting their arrival, a snow/sleet mixture began to fall.

Just as all companies on the scene were almost done picking up and ready to leave, I received another radio transmission from the fire alarm office,

"Main to Battalion 13 do you have anyone available for a Pin-In at Cicero and Jackson?"

"Battalion 13 to Main. You can have 95 and Truck 26. I'll take it in too."

"Message received...95 and the truck and Battalion 13 to the Pin-In Accident at Cicero and Jackson."

Cicero and Jackson was only two blocks away. Quickly 95 and Truck 26 took off with lights and siren. As I started to pull away from the curb, I could see the OFI investigators arriving in my rear-view mirror. I waited and gave them a very quick briefing on the situation then told them that I would return after the pin-in run.

"PIN-IN ACCIDENT"

As I pulled up on the scene, I saw a very large crowd and about seven or eight police cars at the intersection of Jackson and Cicero. Engine 95 was already in the process of dropping a hoseline and I could hear Truck 26's Hurst Tool's generator starting up. (The Hurst Tool, more commonly known as The Jaws of Life, consists of a gas generator that supplies hydraulic power to an assortment of extrication tools. The most commonly used tool is the spreader, often referred to as "the jaws." Any time the Hurst Tool is used, a hoseline is led out and charged as a precaution.) Apparently, an SUV hit and ran over a teen-aged girl who was standing at the bus stop, and she was still pinned underneath.

As I approached the driver's side of the vehicle, I could see that Tony Vitale, a good friend of mine and a very experienced firefighter, would be manning the jaws. Tony spent most his long career on Truck 26, consistently one of the busiest trucks in the city. Lifting a vehicle off the ground was something he and his company drilled on often. With this particular situation our concerns were:

- That the SUV came to rest in in the entrance of what used to be a gas station. Because of the pitch of the driveway the crew would have to take extra precautions to stabilize the vehicle while lifting it off the victim.
- The weather was causing ice to form on the ground where we would be working. Because of these conditions this job would be a little less than routine.

Our plan was to first double-chock the SUV's wheels. Then, while slowly using the Hurst Tool to lift the vehicle, we would simultaneously place heavy wooden blocks as cribbing under the frame as it was raised off of the victim. With everything in place, Tony began to move the vehicle upward. Another firefighter, lying on his belly in front of the vehicle, gave the commands "up" and "stop" while Tony manned the tool. Things were going well but then suddenly the jaws slipped on the ice and with a loud bang, the SUV dropped triggering a collective "Oh No!" from onlookers. Fortunately, the wood cribbing worked as it was supposed to. Because of this precaution the vehicle only dropped about two inches and rested on the wood. "Damn it!" Tony said as he repositioned the jaws. "It's good Tony," I said, "We're all good. Keep going. You got this," I told him. As the vehicle once again began to rise, FFPM

Larsen, who was lying on his belly assessing the situation from the opposite side, reported that the unconscious victim was "folded in half" with her knees up near her chin. This meant we'd need to raise the vehicle higher than usual to get her out. Hearing this report Tony let out an apprehensive groan and paused to think. Before I had a chance to say it, he called out, "Gimme a 20-ton jack!" We had the same idea. The jack was a screw type and could be raised in minute increments along with the jaws. The jack combined with the wood cribbing would provide the best protection for both the victim and firefighters. With everything in place Tony again began lifting the SUV. It only took another three inches of lift to allow the girls legs to drop putting her into a prone position on her back. A backboard was cautiously slipped under her, and she was carefully removed from under the vehicle. Once cleared from the SUV, the crew of Engine 95 began administering medical treatment. A few minutes later our ambulance arrived and transported the patient to the hospital in critical condition.

As Engine 95 and Truck 26 were picking up their equipment I notified the fire alarm office via radio, "Battalion 13 to Main, all companies here are picking up and in service. Keep me on the air back to Monroe to finish up with OFI from the earlier fire."

Then, while walking back to my buggy, I heard the unmistakable sound of a gang fight. From behind my vehicle, I watched as several police officers from our accident scene ran in the direction of a gas station across the street where about 20 people were screaming, fighting, swinging objects, and throwing bottles at each other. The fight was unrelated to our incident. I waited until things were under control and the police reported that no one needed medical attention before heading back to Monroe Street.

12/16/14
ASSIGNMENT—BATTALION 13 (ENGINE 95'S QUARTERS, PULASKI & MADISON)
PRIMARY RESPONSE AREA—WESTSIDE
WEATHER—TEMPERATURES IN THE LOW 40S

One run—Check the box—False

12/19/14
ASSIGNMENT—BATTALION 13 (ENGINE 95'S QUARTERS, PULASKI & MADISON)
PRIMARY RESPONSE AREA—WESTSIDE
WEATHER—TEMPERATURES IN THE HIGH 20S
OTHER—BUSY DAY IN THE 13TH

"RIT"

At around 9:30 a.m. while doing my morning rounds, I was sent as RIT Chief to a fire on South Keeler Avenue. The fire was on the second floor of a 2-story occupied building and was under control by the time I arrived. I stood by for about 15 minutes and was released by Battalion 14.

A RIT (Rapid Intervention Team) is dispatched to every Working Fire. It is made up of one truck, one battalion chief, one ambulance and one EMS (Emergency Medical Service) chief. The purpose of a RIT is to facilitate rescue of other firefighters should they become lost or trapped. A RIT is not part of the actual firefighting operation. Their assignment is to stand by and be at the ready. In a situation where RIT is activated, the RIT truck members and the RIT battalion chief immediately search for and remove any missing, trapped, injured or unaccounted for firefighter(s).

"STILL ALARM"

At approximately 10:45 a.m. I was dispatched via radio to a Still Alarm at 5257 West Harmon. While en route I heard Engine 113 arrive on the scene and report a fire in a 3-story occupied apartment building. I arrived within a few minutes and gave the following report to the fire alarm office, "Battalion 13's on the scene. We got a 3-story occupied apartment building about 100' by 50'. Fire on the second floor. 113's got a line in the front door. All companies are working. I'll get back to you with more in a minute." I then called Engine 113 on Fireground for a progress report. They responded that they were in a vacant apartment on the second floor, they had the fire knocked and were in the process of washing down. Trucks 29 and 26 followed with, "All searches complete and negative." Based on that information I radioed the fire alarm office, "Hold the Working Fire Response." By "holding" the Working Fire Response this cancelled all further in-coming companies.

Outside, I began interviewing residents of the building and was told that a family had recently been evicted from the apartment where the fire was. After the eviction, police were called several times to this address when a relative of the evicted tenant and his friends returned and broke into the apartment to party. I was also told that when another tenant of the building confronted the trespassers, one of them allegedly said something like, "This mutha #%^# gonna burn down." I thanked them for the information and went inside to get a look at the apartment. On the way up the stairs, I passed a firefighter cradling a soot-covered cat in one hand and an axe and pike pole in the other. The semi-conscious cat appeared to have taken what is known in the fire service as "a beating." It was obviously suffering from smoke inhalation. "I'm gonna try some O2 with the pet mask on this thing," said the firefighter calmly. "Good luck with that," I replied. That cat didn't look good at all.

When I got up to the apartment the officer of Engine 113 told me that his crew extinguished two separate fires, one in each of the bedrooms. Because of the two separate fires and information I got from interviewing the other tenants, I requested OFI and CPD.

The fire investigators arrived about 30 minutes after my request. I took them upstairs and showed them where the two fires were and also relayed what the tenants told me about the possible threat to burn down the building. Leaving them to do their work, I went back downstairs and outside where I saw several firemen on the parkway grass hovering over and administering oxygen to the beat-up cat. "Ha! We got it!" said one of them. The cat had regained just enough consciousness to freak out and take off running down the alley.

"STILL ALARM"

At about 1:45 p.m. I was sent via radio to a Still Alarm. Engine 117 arrived first and reported light smoke from a 1-story brick manufacturing building 100' by 100'. Upon investigation we found that a printing press overheated and ignited an air filter on top of the machine. The small flames it produced lit up some cardboard boxes stacked nearby and activated the sprinkler system. The sprinkler did its job.

Engine 117 led out a hoseline to wash down and overhaul. We shut down and drained the sprinkler system.

"STILL ALARM"

At 3:15 p.m. a full Still Alarm response was sent to an address on West Adams Street when a tenant of that building called 911 from another location. The caller stated she thought she may have left a pot on her stove with the burner on and was afraid it would start a fire. Truck 26 was able to get into the apartment through a rear porch window without causing any damage. They entered the apartment and did find a pot on the stove with the burner on. They shut off the burner, took the pot to the sink and ran some cool water over it. No fire. All was good.

"STILL ALARM"

At about 5:30 p.m. companies were dispatched to a call for a fire on the 3900 block of West Wilcox. When we arrived a woman met us out front and explained that her baby's father, who she had an order of protection against, kept calling in false fire and police runs to her apartment. The police pulled up right behind us. "Battalion 13 to Main. There's no fire. Hold all companies. I'm returning 95 and the truck. CPD is on scene and will handle this ... it's a domestic."

"STILL ALARM"

Just as I backed into quarters from my previous run I was sent to another Still Alarm. On my arrival I reported, "Battalion 13 to Main, I'm on the scene on Franklin Boulevard. Nothing showing on a large 3-story occupied courtyard building. 44

and the Truck are checking it out." Hearing that I was on the scene, the officer of Engine 44 radioed to me on Fireground, "44 to Battalion 13, we got some curtains and a little bit of a window frame. It started with a candle. It's all on the surface. We got it with a hand pump. You can hold everyone up."

"Okay 44, did you force entry?"

"Yeah, to the original apartment and the one on the floor above to check for heat in the wall. We got no reading on the camera. There's no extension. We're good."

"Message received. I'm pickin' up. The police are here and will handle the forced entry."

No extension. Fire out. All was good.

"STILL ALARM"

At 6:45 p.m. I was dispatched to a Still Alarm in a store on South Pulaski. The first arriving companies found an arcing electrical box in the ceiling. Using thermal imaging cameras, they checked for heat in the ceiling and found none. All circuit breakers were shut off and I advised the owner of the business who was on the scene that she needed to get an electrician to look at the fixture before turning the breakers back on.

"STILL ALARM"

Engine 95, Truck 26 and I were all in quarters around 1:30 a.m. when a run came in for a Still Alarm at 5257 West Harmon. As I was wiping the sleep from my eyes and trotting to my buggy, it hit me that this was the same address where we had that second-floor apartment fire earlier on our shift. My first thought was that the evicted tenant returned and started a fire at night while the other tenants were sleeping so that it would go undetected longer.

On the apparatus floor, as everyone in the firehouse was getting on their rigs, I yelled to them, "This is the same place we had that fire this morning!" With just that little reminder everyone was now thinking on the same page. This was a very large, occupied building in the wee hours of the morning. The likelihood was that this time, everyone was home sleeping rather than at work or school. The address was only a couple of blocks from Engine 96 and Truck 29's quarters so we all knew that they would arrive before us. While responding we all listened anxiously to our radios to hear their initial on scene report. We were only a few blocks out of our quarters when Engine 96 reported, "96 on the scene. We have a fire." They didn't say how much fire or where it was located, they only said, "we have a fire."

As I pulled up on the scene about 30 seconds after 96's initial radio report, I didn't see any fire but did smell smoke and saw Engine 96 leading out a hoseline down an alley to the rear. I drove my buggy down the alley to get a look at where they were heading and could now see flames at the roof level of the back porch. This was actually somewhat of a relief. A fire at roof level in an occupied building that size and at that time of night is WAY different than a fire set on the first floor. Smoke and fire go up.

Before I had a chance to call them, Engine 96 and Truck 29 reported that the fire appeared to be only at the roof level of the back porches and that they had it under control. I radioed in my report to the fire alarm office and held the Working Fire Response. Because of the suspicious fire we had earlier at the same address, I once again requested an OFI response. While 96 and Truck 29 were working on the back porch, I had Truck 26 check the vacant apartment where the earlier fire was. "Negative Chief, no fire here," they reported. After about 30 minutes companies began to pick up. While waiting for the fire investigators to arrive several of us discussed how odd it was that we would have two unrelated fires in the same building on the same shift. Anyone who would have started this second fire on purpose surely would have lit it up on a lower floor so that it could burn up, not at the roof level.

OFI Investigator, Josh Daniels, a friend of mine, arrived and already knew about the earlier fire. He was the one who did the investigation. With a flashlight and a few small tools in hand, Josh climbed Truck 29's main ladder to the roof. After about 20 minutes he came down. "Accidental," he proclaimed. "What?" I asked. He went on to explain that this morning after we left the scene, the owner hired roofers to patch the ventilation hole that Truck 29 cut in the roof at the earlier fire. To make the repair the roofers used a rubber patch that is commonly applied using a torch. Apparently, they accidently lit something in the roofing that smoldered all day until it finally ignited at 1:30 in the morning. Good call by Josh. Fire out. No one hurt. All good.

> 12/21/14—12/22/14
> Assignment—Battalion 13 (Engine 95's Quarters, Pulaski & Madison)
> Primary Response Area—Westside
> Weather—Temperatures in the low 30s

Due to the large number of retirements in the month of November, the Department was short on battalion chiefs. Because of this, I was offered to work overtime on both my off shift and my Daley Day. This means that I worked a 48-hour shift. I did both shifts in Battalion 13. Surprisingly, unlike my previous shift in the 13TH Battalion, both days were pretty uneventful.

> 12/25/14 (CHRISTMAS DAY)
> ASSIGNMENT—BATTALION 3 (ENGINE 14'S QUARTERS, MILWAUKEE AND CHICAGO)
> PRIMARY RESPONSE AREA—NEAR WESTSIDE, WEST LOOP
> WEATHER—TEMPERATURES IN THE MID 30S

Traditionally, on Christmas Day, my wife and I host a relaxing informal "open house" at our home. This annual gathering usually draws about twenty to thirty family members, friends and neighbors. We always provide a large pot of gumbo and warm hospitality. Over the years, due to my work schedule, there were many times I wasn't able to attend our social gathering. This Christmas Day, my last Christmas Day on the job, I was assigned to Battalion 3. Battalion 3 is quartered with Engine 14 and Truck 19 at 1129 W. Chicago Ave., about three blocks from where I live. About 3:00 p.m. I put myself "available on the radio" and was able to spend a few hours of Christmas with my family and friends. At about 7:00 p.m. as things were winding down, I took off for my night visits to Engine's 30 and 22. It was a great day for my last Christmas on the job!

12/28/14
ASSIGNMENT—BATTALION 10 (ENGINE 124'S QUARTERS, KEDZIE & MONTROSE)
PRIMARY RESPONSE AREA—LINCOLN SQUARE, NORTH CENTER, ALBANY PARK
WEATHER—TEMPERATURES IN THE LOW 30S

This was my first time working as Battalion 10. Other than getting a chance to chat with some old friends, the shift was uneventful.

12/31/14
ASSIGNMENT—BATTALION 14 (ENGINE 109'S QUARTERS, 22ND & KEDZIE)
PRIMARY RESPONSE AREA—WESTSIDE, LITTLE VILLAGE
WEATHER—VERY COLD—TEMPERATURES IN THE SINGLE DIGITS
OTHER—NEW YEARS EVE

"STILL ALARM"

Around 9:00 p.m. I was dispatched from quarters to a Still Alarm at an approximate address of Ogden and Pulaski. About a minute prior to my arrival, Engine 38 and Truck 48 reported that they we were on the scene with nothing showing. They then asked the fire alarm office if there was any more information or a better address for this run. "Smoke in the area," was the reply from the dispatcher. As I pulled up, I rolled down my window. Quickly judging from the familiar smell in the air, I thought to myself, "We have an auto fire somewhere in the area." Before I had a chance to report this to the alarm office, Engine 38 called me on the radio to say they could see a large column of smoke coming from the junkyard behind the strip mall. I acknowledged their message, notified the fire alarm office, and followed the engine and truck to the new location a block away.

Looking in from the locked junkyard gate we could see that there were about five or six cars burning. There was way too much fire for one or even two engines to extinguish with the 500 gallons of water they each carry on board. Oh well. This meant dropping a large amount of big hose in freezing and windy weather. Because there were no exposures to protect, other than junk cars, I returned the second responding companies and kept 38 and Truck 48 on the scene. I figured the less firefighters exposed to the frigid temperatures the better. Engine 38 hooked a hydrant on Pulaski then drove 150' into the yard. From there they led out 200' of 2 ½" line and worked it on the burning cars. When the fire was extinguished, we all helped roll up 38's hose and returned to quarters. No big deal. Just really, really cold!

I got to bed around 11:00 p.m., and at midnight was awoken by the sound of New Year's celebratory gunfire just outside my window. It didn't last long though, probably because of the extreme cold. I didn't have any more runs that night, but the engine and truck got slammed. I heard them going out all night, like every forty-five minutes or so on medical runs. I felt bad for them but thought I'd have a little fun with it in the morning.

At 5:00 a.m. I got out of bed, packed up my stuff and went to the kitchen to wait for my relief to arrive. When I turned the corner into the kitchen/lounge area all the members of Engine 109 and Truck 32 were there. They gave up on trying to get any bed sleep. Some of them had their arms folded on the kitchen table resting their heads, some were sprawled out on the sofas and a couple of guys were cleaning the kitchen and making coffee. “Gooooood Morning!” I said cheerfully. “Did you guys have any runs last night? I was out like a light and didn't hear a thing.” No one said a word but I’m not sure if it was a cookie or muffin that whizzed past my head.

JANUARY 2015

01/03/15
ASSIGNMENT—BATTALION 14 (ENGINE 109'S QUARTERS, 22ND & KEDZIE)
PRIMARY RESPONSE AREA—WESTSIDE, LITTLE VILLAGE
WEATHER—TEMPERATURES IN THE HIGH 20S

"LEVEL I HAZMAT"

At the start of our shift around 7:00 a.m., Engine 109 and Ambulance 34 were dispatched from quarters to a medical run at an address near 21ST and Rockwell. The nature of the call was a "Carbon Monoxide Inhalation Victim."

Upon arrival Engine 109 and the ambulance met a woman standing on the sidewalk in front of a 2-story brick 4-unit building. She identified herself as the landlord. The building had two apartments in the front and two in the rear. In broken English the woman told the crews that she smelled something "funny" in the hallway earlier and now someone was ill. Armed with a Carbon Monoxide detector, 109's crew followed the woman down the gangway to a side door in the center of the building. (This is a common layout for buildings in this area of the city. The center door in the gangway provides access to all four units and the basement.)

Just inside the doorway sitting on the stairs, was a male in his 40's who appeared to be in a daze. He was identified by the landlord as the tenant of the second-floor front apartment. One step into the hallway and Engine 109's CO meter began to show higher than normal readings. Normal readings are below 9 parts per million. The meter, upon entry, was at 25 ppm. Capt. Alex Galvan of Engine 109 immediately had one of his firefighters escort the man and landlord to the sidewalk out front where the paramedics were standing by. He and another firefighter then proceeded to the second floor. When they opened the unlocked door to the front apartment their CO meter began beeping and the reading spiked to 700 parts per million! (35 ppm is the threshold that requires the use of Self Contained Breathing Apparatus—SCBA.) Alex immediately withdrew his crew, evacuated all residents, and called for a Level I Hazmat Response. Back at the firehouse, hearing Alex's radio report, I immediately jumped in my buggy and told the alarm office via radio that I was taking in the Level I.

Upon my arrival I reported on the scene, set a staging area, and requested the gas company. I then proceeded down the gangway where I was met by Capt. Galvan.

"Chief, we were getting 700 ppm in the second-floor front apartment. We're all masked up and we shut down the gas to the entire building. We also started opening windows to ventilate. It's going down pretty fast. We're already at about 500."

"Okay, good. Wasn't there supposed to be someone sick here?"

"Yeah. Ambulance 34 has a guy out front from that apartment who says he was feeling sick."

"All right, it's pretty windy. I don't think we'll need fans. Just keep the windows open for now and let me know when you find the cause."

"Got it."

At this point I turned my attention to the patient who was

now inside the ambulance. As I approached the ambo, one of the paramedics opened the door and informed me that the patient did not want to be transported to the hospital. I was told that the patient's vitals were all good but that both paramedics still strongly advised him to get checked out at the ER. The patient declined and signed a release form.

After a few minutes Capt. Galvan reported back to me,

"109 to Battalion 14. We have all the windows opened up here. It's dropping fast. We're down to around 200. We also found the cause ..."

"Go ahead 109, what's the cause?"

"There's a large space heater up here with the vent pipe completely disconnected from the chimney. It's laying on the sofa."

"Message received."

With the source of the CO leak determined I radioed the alarm office, "Battalion 14 to Main. Secure the Level I Hazmat on my orders and return all companies. I'll keep 109, Truck 32 and Ambulance 34 here with me. We should be done in a few minutes."

Once the levels dropped below 35 ppm, I went up to take a look. Entering the apartment, I saw the vent pipe lying across the arms of a sofa just as Capt. Galvan described. With no vent pipe between the space heater and the chimney, all the carbon monoxide produced flowed freely into the apartment. I also found that there were no working CO or smoke alarms anywhere in the building.

I then went back outside to tell the police what we found and to advise the landlord of her responsibilities regarding smoke and CO alarms. Because of a language barrier with the landlord, a Spanish-speaking police officer translated everything I said. While listening to the police officer translate my message to the landlord, I was called over the radio by Capt. Galvan,

"Engine 109 to Battalion 14...the entire building is down to 000 ppm."

"Good job, Al. Go ahead and close all but a couple of windows up there. The gas company should be here soon. They'll handle getting the heat back on."

"109, got it."

The police officer interviewing the landlord informed me that the second-floor occupant, who at this time was still in the ambulance, was in fact a "squatter" and wasn't supposed to be in the apartment in the first place. I was told that the people who rented the apartment were in the process of being evicted and they were letting random people stay there without the landlord's approval. Just then, the ambulance door opened up. "He signed a release. He's not going to the hospital...we tried." said one of the paramedics as the man stepped out of the ambulance. The man then walked over to where we were standing and sincerely apologized for everything. He told the landlord and the police that he would leave and not come back but only needed to go back into the apartment to get his shoes. During this whole thing he was only wearing a thin pair of socks. "It's cold. Where ya gonna go?" asked the police officer. "I have some friends a couple of blocks away. I can go there," the man replied. The cop nodded and said, "Go get your stuff together. I'll drive you over there."

When the gas company crew arrived, I filled them in on what we had, then returned to quarters about 7:45 a.m. Engine 109 stayed on scene a few minutes longer to secure their equipment. When they got back to quarters, Capt. Galvan informed me that right after I left the scene, the police and landlord accompanied the man back into the apartment to retrieve his belongings. As soon as they got up to the apartment, the man collapsed. 109 and the ambulance, who were both still on the scene, carried the patient in a stair chair to the ambulance and he was transported to the hospital.

Whenever we encounter something out of the ordinary or something that could arise as an issue later, we fill out what is known as an Incident Case Report. This was now one of those runs. I completed an ICR explaining that, while in the ambulance, the patient's vitals and O2 levels were normal and that the paramedics did all they could to try to convince him to go to the hospital. Later, when Ambulance 34 returned to quarters, they informed that after further examination at the hospital it was believed the man's sudden collapse was possibly not due to CO but from previous medical issues.

> 01/06/15
> ASSIGNMENT—BATTALION 13 (ENGINE 95'S QUARTERS, PULASKI & MADISON)
> PRIMARY RESPONSE AREA—WESTSIDE
> WEATHER—TEMPERATURES IN THE SINGLE DIGITS, SNOW

The regularly assigned chief of the 13TH battalion retired back in November creating a vacancy that would be filled in a few months on the next transfer order. In the interim, relieving battalion chiefs would be filling in or "sitting on the spot." During my last work shift Manpower Central informed me that I would be sitting in the 13TH Battalion for two consecutive furlough periods, which is ten workdays. This stint in the 13TH began today.

Battalion 13 has one of the highest run to fire ratios in the city, meaning that although the 13TH doesn't do as many runs as some of the other battalions, the odds of catching a fire are pretty high. Because of its work potential Battalion 13 is one of the most sought-after spots in the city. Transfers within the department are determined by seniority. It usually takes thirty plus years to land an open spot in the 13TH Battalion. Whenever there is an opening in the 13TH because of a Daley Day, Furlough, Medical Lay-Up, Transfer or retirement, relief battalion chiefs like me, are happy to fill in.

This day, however, was pretty slow. I only had a few runs but nothing out of the ordinary.

> 01/09/15
> ASSIGNMENT—BATTALION 13 (ENGINE 95'S QUARTERS, PULASKI & MADISON)
> PRIMARY RESPONSE AREA—WESTSIDE
> WEATHER—TEMPERATURES IN THE SINGLE DIGITS

After my usual morning ritual of relieving my partner: getting a briefing on anything that happened on the prior shift, drinking twelve cups of coffee, and paying the cook for the day's meals, I retreated to my room to start my paperwork for the day. Right around 7:30 a.m. I heard seven gunshots just outside my window. The windows in my room were up high and the walls were cinderblock, so I wasn't too worried about strays. However, I still felt it would be safer to put a few more walls between me and what was happening outside, so I walked back into the kitchen.

"Did you guys hear those gunshots?" I asked.

"Yeah," someone replied calmly, "they're probably coming from that abandoned building just behind the firehouse parking lot."

"I thought they tore that place down?" I replied.

"Nah...it's still there."

After a few minutes of waiting, we didn't hear any more shots, so I went back to my room to finish my morning paperwork. About twenty minutes later as I was pulling out of the house to begin my morning rounds, there was still a large police presence in the area.

"STILL ALARM"

My first run of the day was for an "Electrical Fire" where the resident said he heard a scratching noise in his living room wall near an electrical outlet. After using our thermal imaging cameras to examine the walls in the living room, the room above and the basement, we determined there was no fire and what the resident heard was probably a rat in the wall. I held all companies. We advised the resident to ask his landlord to hire an exterminator.

"STILL ALARM"

My second run of the day was around 2:00 p.m. for a fire that turned out to be an overheated electrical outlet. The first engine on the scene handled it and held me up before I got there.

The rest of the day was pretty slow. As the sun went down so did the outside temperature. By 10 p.m. the wind-chills, as reported on the local news, were down to around -30 degrees. I was really hoping for a quiet night.

Around 11:30, just before hitting the bed, I went to the kitchen for a piece of apple pie and a glass of milk. As I was washing my plate and glass, four bells rang throughout the house signaling that the engine was getting a run. Usually there is a computer tone and voice dispatch heard throughout the house first, and then the bells would be manually rung by whoever is on floor watch. Immediately after the bells, the man on watch announced over the house PA, "Engine, we got a walk-in ... there's a car on the apron with a gunshot victim in it." With that announcement we all went to the front to see what was going on. As soon as we walked from the hallway out to the apparatus floor, we were blinded by blue flashing lights. About four police cars were parked on our front apron along with the gunshot victim's car. A few of the guys from Truck 26 and I watched through the window as the crew from Engine 95 went outside to tend to the victim who suffered one gunshot wound that shattered his left leg. When Ambulance 10, who is actually assigned to this firehouse, arrived at the scene, the patient was immediately transported to the hospital. (Side Note: Ambulance 10 is one of the busiest ambulances in the country and usually doesn't spend much time in their quarters.)

With the police and ambulance gone and our apron back to normal, I returned to my room to do a little reading before hitting the sack. I was only in bed about ten minutes when I heard another ten gunshots, this time a little more distant. Still mostly awake, I turned on the police scanner in my room and almost immediately heard a police officer report that he heard several shots fired in the area of Madison and Kostner, about four blocks from our firehouse. Seconds after that transmission the same police car reported they were now in a foot chase after the alleged shooter and heading north on Kostner from Madison. This was toward the firehouse. Thankfully, the next radio transmission from the police in pursuit said that the offender was in custody. A subsequent report from another officer said they had two people shot at Monroe and Kostner. Within seconds the computer dispatch tone went off in the firehouse and Engine 95 was on their way to their second shooting victim of the hour. Listening to my radio I heard 95 report they had one gunshot victim with a wound to the lower abdomen, and that another victim left the scene in a car. It was later broadcast over the police radio that the second victim showed up at another local hospital. Engine 95 returned home, and things calmed down, at least for a little while. Between midnight and 5:00 a.m. Engine 95 had 3 runs and Truck 26 had 8. I had none.

> MAN DEAD, 3 HURT IN SEPARATE SHOOTINGS—CHICAGO TRIBUNE 1/10/15
>
> *A man was shot to death and three other men were wounded in separate shootings on the West Side Friday evening, police said.*
>
> *In the latest shooting, a 35-year-old man died and a 31-year-old man was wounded after a shooting around 10:40 p.m. in the West Garfield Park neighborhood, said Chicago Police News Affairs Officer Ron Gaines.*
>
> *The two were standing outside in the 0-100 block of South Kostner Avenue when they heard gunshots and were wounded, Gaines said.*
>
> *The 35-year-old was shot in the stomach and was taken to John H. Stroger Jr. Hospital of Cook County where he was later pronounced dead, said Chicago Police News Affairs Officer Hector Alfaro.*
>
> *The Cook County medical examiner's office could not confirm the fatality immediately.*

The 31-year-old was shot in his left calf and right ankle and was able to make it to Rush University Medical Center. His condition stabilized there, Alfaro said.

At the scene, police officers blocked off a block of Kostner Avenue from Monroe to Madison streets with yellow tape. A neighborhood grocery store, a barber shop and a boarded-up building were on one side of the street, and a three-story building and a parking lot filled with U-Haul trucks lined the other side.

Behind the crime scene tape, a Styrofoam takeout box and a red plastic cup sat on the sidewalk. A couple of feet over, a red cap was lying on the ground. Two other pieces of clothing also lay nearby.

Less than a mile away, a 21-year-old man was wounded in another shooting around 10:17 p.m., Gaines said.

The man was sitting in the driver's seat of a parked car in the 4000 block of West End Avenue when he heard gunshots and realized he was shot in the leg, Gaines said.

He was transported to Mount Sinai Hospital where his condition stabilized, Gaines said.

01/12/15
Assignment—Battalion 13 (Engine 95's Quarters, Pulaski & Madison)
Primary Response Area—Westside
Weather—Temperatures in the teens with blowing snow to arrive in the afternoon

I reported for work at 5:15 a.m. A chief's shift officially starts at 6:30 but as a courtesy we always relieve our partners early. The earlier we get there, the earlier the off-going chief can go home. Firefighters and company officers officially start their shift at 7:00 a.m. and also make their relief earlier.

After an exceptionally busy and cold morning of running around completing administrative duties, I returned to my quarters just in time for lunch. A hot bowl of soup and a sandwich and I was ready for some "me" time. Retiring to my room around 1:30 p.m., I plopped down in my recliner with a crossword puzzle hoping to doze off for a few minutes. I never really slept well at the firehouse so squeezing in a little catnap in a recliner after lunch was always appreciated if time allowed. You never know when you'd be up all night.

"STILL ALARM"

At about 3:15 p.m., while in a sleepy trance-like state, I was jolted by the sound of the computer dispatch tones and robotic voice, "Engine 95—Battalion 13—Fire—26 S. Pulaski Road." The entire time I was in the recliner I had not been fully asleep and was aware of all earlier radio transmissions broadcast over my handi-talkie radio. Because of this, I knew that Truck 26 had been dispatched to an ambulance run about five minutes earlier and was not in quarters. Still in a bit of a daze, I quickly rose out of the chair, grabbed my radio, struggled to throw on an extra sweatshirt and rubbed my eyes while bouncing off the hallway walls heading for my buggy.

When I got to the apparatus floor Engine 95 was already idling with its lights on. The crew was getting dressed and climbing into the rig. As the overhead door slowly rose, we could see that the blowing snow predicted earlier by the weather forecast had begun to fall, causing almost whiteout conditions. 95 pulled out of the house first. My response was delayed a bit as I had to close the overhead doors. 95 was about a block and a half ahead of me as I turned on to Pulaski from West End. The blowing snow was so bad I could barely see their lights. Poor visibility and heavy traffic at the corner of Madison and Pulaski also drastically slowed our response. Looking ahead through my windshield wipers and ahead of Engine 95, I could see a haze in the air but couldn't tell if it was smoke or just blowing snow.

I was only about a block behind Engine 95 when they reported on the scene, "Engine 95 to Main. We're on Pulaski. We have a fire in a Red X Building." (A Red X Building is a structure identified by the Chicago Building Department as having significant structural damage.) I pulled up seconds later and parked my buggy at the curb across the street near a small crowd that was gathering on the sidewalk. From there I gave my initial report to the fire alarm office, "Battalion 13's on Pulaski office. We do have a fire in a 2-story brick 150' by 150'... Red X...I'll get back to you in a minute with more." I got out of my buggy without donning my fire gear and ran across the street to do a fast size-up.

As I crossed Pulaski through the blowing snow this is what I saw. Heavy smoke was coming from a vacant 2-story Red X brick building about 150'x 150'. The building, when it was in use, had stores on the first floor and apartments on the second. Some of the first-floor store windows were intact and some were boarded up. All the doors appeared to be open. On the second floor, heavy black smoke was pushing through cracks around the plywood covering the windows. Although there was no visible flame, the pressure and color of the smoke indicated that there was a large amount of fire inside. Just to the north of the building was a small alley where I could see a group of civilians pointing and directing me towards the rear of the structure. Even before getting a look at the back of the building, with what I saw and, most importantly, the possibility of frozen hydrants, I escalated the alarm.

"Battalion 13 to Main. Emergency. Gimme a Box. Set the Staging Area at Engine 95's quarters."

"Message received. A Still & Box Alarm at 26 S. Pulaski on the orders of Battalion 13. Companies responding to the Still & Box, the staging area is at Engine 95's quarters."

Still needing to get a look at the back of the building, I shuffled as quickly as I could down the alley through the calf-high snow while continuing my radio report: "Office, I've got a 2-story ordinary 150 by 150 with heavy smoke on two. 95's leading out to Side A. I'll get back to you in a minute." When I got to the rear of the building, I found that all the doors and burglar gates on the first floor had been removed, leaving the first floor wide open. There were no outside back porches, just a couple of wooden stairways that looked like they should have collapsed years ago. Looking up I saw that a couple of the second-floor windows were not boarded up. Through these windows I could see a large amount of fire rolling at the ceiling level. This is what the people on the street were pointing to. Continuing my size-up I approached one of the first-floor rear doors and took a look inside. Smoke conditions were minimal making it easy to do a visual scan for any vagrants or homeless people who may have been inside. I didn't see anyone but off to my right I could see a stairway leading to the second floor. If this had not been a Red X building, this stairway would have been the way up to extinguish the fire. However, because of the Red X and obvious safety reasons, we were going defensive from the start. Surround and Drown.

With my size-up up now complete, I needed to get back to the front of the building to start setting things up for incoming companies. From where I was standing at the rear door, I could see a straight path to the front door that was wide open. If I made a quick dash, I could get back out to the street without trudging through the snow around the alley. I also wanted to take a quick look at that stairway just in case anyone may have been on the second floor when the fire started and didn't make it down. I took a deep breath and quickly made my way over the rubbish-covered floor to the foot of the stairway. Looking up and around I didn't see anyone but what I did see was a ton of fire at the top of the stairs. One turn, a few steps and I was back on the street out front.

Before giving my next radio update I wanted to take one more look and gather my thoughts. I saw Engine 95 on Side A with a charged line ready to apply water. However, because the entire front second floor was boarded up, they would have to wait until we could get some of that plywood removed. Also in the distance, I could hear the sirens of my responding box companies and squad. My next radio report to the fire alarm office was, "Battalion 13 to Main, we have heavy fire on the second floor and need to get this opened up before we can hit it. Have Squad 2 back down from the north and Tower 14 from the south. I'm gonna need both baskets. Also, have Engine 38 come in from the south to supply Tower 14 and have one of my Box engines get a hydrant near Madison and Pulaski to feed the Squad's snorkel." (The time span from my arrival to this point was about three to four minutes.)

Standing in the street outside, still in just my uniform baseball jacket, I began directing the remaining still companies while I waited for another chief officer to arrive. Once the RIT Chief was on scene, I asked him to keep an eye on things while I moved my buggy out of the way into a strip mall parking lot across the street and put on my turnout gear. When I returned to the front of the building, I directed Tower 14 and Squad 2's Snorkel to set up at opposite corners of the building and start getting the plywood off of the second-floor windows. I also directed Engine 38 to feed water to Tower 14. I then heard a familiar voice approaching quickly and loudly, "Kev, Kev, Engine 76. We got a good hydrant on Madison. Whaddya need?!" It was Capt. Jim Steffen of Engine 76, a very aggressive captain with a very aggressive crew. In hopes of getting some work Jim had his guys find and secure an unfrozen hydrant before even coming to me. "Hey Jim, drop two to the rear. There's a load of fire on the second floor. DON'T, AND I MEAN DON'T try those wooden porch stairs!" "Got it Kev!" he replied and off he went. About this time Deputy District Chief Mike Wrobelinski arrived. After I gave him a quick briefing, he assumed overall command of the fire. Also, because of the extreme weather conditions and need for more engines, Chief Wrobelinski escalated the Still & Box to a 2-11 alarm.

From their respective baskets, Squad 2 and Tower 14 worked hard to remove what turned out to be several layers of plywood covering the second-floor windows in Side A. As each window was opened it provided a way to get water on the fire from the baskets and from handlines on the street.

It also gave the fire a fresh supply of oxygen helping it flare up and eventually burn through the roof. This is what we wanted. The building was structurally unsound when we arrived and was a write-off anyway. It was all about "surround and drown" and not getting anyone hurt.

For the next six hours, as the windchills dipped below zero, we stood outside and poured water on the fire through window openings and the partially collapsed roof until it was completely extinguished.

The final remaining companies left the scene around 9:30 p.m. I stayed another half an hour or so being interviewed by our fire investigators, getting the police reports, and speaking with the Water Department. Back in quarters just before 10:00 p.m., I had a sandwich and another bowl of soup before doing my paperwork and turning in for the night. I had no more runs for the rest of the shift.

> 01/15/15
> Assignment—Battalion 13 (Engine 95's Quarters, Pulaski & Madison)
> Primary Response Area—Westside
> Weather—Temperatures in mid 20s

The morning and afternoon parts of my shift were relatively normal. I had a few uneventful runs and around 4:00 p.m. I heard about ten gunshots outside my office window while doing paperwork.

"ALLEY GARAGE"

At 8:30 p.m. I responded to a still alarm for a fire in an alley garage. The first arriving companies reported light smoke from a garage across the alley from the given address. Engine

117 entered through the unlocked service door and found a small fire in a stripped-down automobile while Tower 14 worked on removing the overhead door. Using only a hand pump Engine 117 extinguished a small amount of fire inside the vehicle.

When the smoke began to clear Lt. Ryan Walton of Engine 117 called out to me, "Hey Kev! Come in here. There's blood all over the place." I entered the garage and met Ryan near the driver's side door. "Look. There, there and there," he said as he pointed out large amounts of fresh blood in several locations throughout the garage. You never know what you'll find or what you're getting into, even at normal everyday runs. In order to preserve evidence in what could be a possible crime scene, I immediately ordered all firefighters out of the garage. Before stepping out ourselves, I asked Ryan, "Did you pop the trunk yet?" "Yeah, there's nothing in there," he replied. Opening the trunk is standard operating procedure on ALL auto fires. Again, you never know what you'll find.

With everyone out of the garage I got on the radio to the alarm office,

"Battalion 13 to Main, the fire's out. Send me a CPD supervisor and OFI please."

"Battalion 13, Whadaya have there? The police are gonna ask."

"I have some information for them. I'll call you on the phone."

"Okay Battalion 13."

"I'm also releasing all companies except 117. They're gonna be here with me for a little while."

Whenever a fire unit makes a request for the police, the police dispatchers want to know the nature of the call. I knew this but didn't want to broadcast over the air that we have "blood all over this garage" or "a possible crime scene" as this would certainly draw a media response that I felt wasn't necessary at this time. Using my cell phone, I called the alarm office and explained the situation to the senior alarm operator on duty. He relayed the information to the police and also to our OFI investigators.

A police beat car arrived quickly followed by a sergeant and almost immediately by our fire investigators. Ryan and I briefed them all on what we found. Then, standing outside, we used our flashlights to point out the areas where we found blood. "You know, this address is a drug house," offered one of the police officers. By now several more uniformed and plain clothes officers began to arrive and scoured the yard, gangway and back porches on the property looking for any further evidence. "We got something," one of the officers called from the yard. Shining my flashlight from the alley gate I could see several officers in the yard hovering over a backpack with fresh bloodstains. "Thanks guys," said the sergeant, "we'll take it from here." With that I released Engine 117 and we both returned to quarters.

There was no mention of our find on the early morning news. Most of the time we don't get the end of the story. Sorry.

01/18/15
ASSIGNMENT—BATTALION 13 (ENGINE 95'S QUARTERS, PULASKI & MADISON)
PRIMARY RESPONSE AREA—WESTSIDE
WEATHER—TEMPERATURES IN THE LOW 30'S

"STILL ALARM"

At about 8:30 p.m. I responded to a Still Alarm for a basement fire. Just as I pulled up, Engine 76 held all companies and reported that they had a small rubbish fire in the basement and that it was "out on arrival." As I walked up, the officer of Truck 35, Doug Maki, told me there wasn't much of a fire and led me into the basement to show me what he found. When we got downstairs Doug pointed to a very small pile of ashes in the middle of the concrete floor. It looked like someone crumpled up a couple of sheets of newspaper and lit it up. "That's it?" I asked, "I've seen bigger fires on birthday cakes." "Yeah, we would have held you up but here's the twist." He then quietly told me that he had just spoken with a woman who lives on the second floor and that she told him a woman that lives on the first floor started the fire. She also added that the woman who allegedly started the fire had threatened her with a knife earlier, and that there was an outstanding warrant for her arrest. People say things all the time, but you can't be too careful, so I immediately requested CPD and OFI. Also, with the possibility that the threat was real, Doug and I left the basement and went back outside. If something went down, we didn't want to be caught in a basement with only one way out. Once outside I radioed the fire alarm office, "Battalion 13 to Main. I'm gonna keep 76 and the truck here with me until the police arrive. But they'll be in service and available if you need them for another run."

While waiting for the police the woman from the second-floor apartment, who made the original call, came outside, and told me that she was worried about her husband. She said that he inhaled a lot of smoke when he went into the basement to toss water on the fire. I followed her back inside her apartment where I found her husband sitting at the kitchen table smoking a cigarette. "What's wrong?" I asked. "Nothing, nothing, I'm okay! She worries too much," he answered. I asked him several times if he would like medical attention. He repeatedly declined. Judging from the size of the "fire" I was pretty sure he was okay. He probably took more smoke from a drag on his cigarette than he did in the basement. Regardless, as a precaution, we had two firefighters examine him and take his vitals. Everything was normal.

We waited about twenty minutes and there were still no police on the scene. Not wanting to broadcast the particulars of this incident over the radio, I called the alarm office from my cell phone and explained the entire situation. This time the alarm operator must have heard, and focused on, the word "knife," because within a minute a large police response showed up with lights and sirens. When I explained to the first arriving police officer that we were not in immediate danger, he held up all additional responding police cars.

With CPD now on the scene, I released Engine 76 and Truck 35 and thanked them for hanging around. After giving the police all the information, they thanked me and said they would handle it from here. They also added that they've been to this address several times before. Apparently, there is an ongoing feud between the tenants who were both in the process of being evicted. The police officers added that there was in fact an arrest warrant for the one woman, but it was old and not active. Our fire investigators arrived, and I turned the scene over to them.

> 01/21/15—01/22/15
> ASSIGNMENT—BATTALION 14 (ENGINE 109'S QUARTERS, 22ND & KEDZIE)
> PRIMARY RESPONSE AREA—WESTSIDE, LITTLE VILLAGE
> WEATHER—TEMPERATURES IN THE MID 30S, RAIN
> OTHER –WORKED A 48-HOUR SHIFT ON OVERTIME

I was supposed to be in the 13TH Battalion for a few more workdays. However, I was offered to work off-shift on overtime in Battalion 14. Rather than move another relief battalion chief around on my shift day, and so that I could do all forty-eight hours in one battalion, I told Manpower that I'd be okay with taking the 14TH for both days. It's not as complicated as it sounds. This swap worked out for everyone involved. Manpower does a good job of trying to accommodate all relief officers.

Both successive twenty-four-hour shifts were relatively quiet.

01/24/15—01/27/15—01/30/15
Assignment—Battalion 11 (Engine 119's Quarters, Avondale & Harlem)
Primary Response Area—Northwest Side
Weather—Temperatures between 20s and 40s
Other—Worked in B-11 three work shift days in a row

Battalion 11 is quartered with Engine 119 and Truck 55 in a firehouse located in a fairly quiet northwest side neighborhood, one that kind of resembles the suburbs. I was there for three shifts. Incident-wise, all three days were uneventful.

FEBRUARY 2015

02/02/15
ASSIGNMENT—BATTALION 14 (ENGINE 109'S QUARTERS, 22ND & KEDZIE)
PRIMARY RESPONSE AREA—WESTSIDE, LITTLE VILLAGE
WEATHER—BLIZZARD—TEMPERATURES IN THE LOW 20S—20" OF SNOW
OTHER—GROUNDHOG DAY!

The day before this workday was Sunday, February 1, 2015, Super Bowl Sunday. It was also the day that Chicago's fifth largest snowstorm on record began. The snow started falling Sunday evening and continued throughout the night until Monday morning around eight o'clock. When it was over, the blizzard dropped a total of twenty inches of fresh snow on the streets of Chicago. Sunday night, in anticipation of a difficult morning commute, I loaded three eighty-pound sandbags into my pickup truck bed for additional traction. I also moved it out of my garage and into a parking space on the street in front of my house. Chicago alleys don't get plowed, and I didn't want to take the chance of not being able to get out of my alley in the morning. You just can't call-in "snowbound" on the Chicago Fire Department. You have to go to work. Around 10:30 p.m., I mapped out what would be my route to the firehouse in the morning. My plan was to take Chicago's designated "snow route" streets. It would not be the straightest way to get to work but I knew the plows would be running up and down them all night. It was my best shot. At 11:00 p.m. I took one last peek out the window and saw that the predicted blizzard was in full swing. I set my alarm clock for 3:15 a.m., an hour earlier than usual and turned out the lights.

The thought of digging out my truck and getting to work kept me awake pretty much all night so about 2:30 a.m. I gave up and got out of bed. Looking out the front window I could see that my truck was buried in about fifteen inches of snow, and it was still falling hard. Foregoing any breakfast or coffee, I gathered all my fire gear, work clothes, bedding, and briefcase near the front door, grabbed a shovel and went outside. I have to admit the peaceful silence of a snowstorm at 3:00 in the morning was actually pretty nice. The only sound I heard was my shovel scraping the sidewalk. It took me about a half an hour to make a path from my front door to the truck and another fifteen minutes to brush it off. Then, with the truck running and warming up, I made a couple of trips back inside the house to grab my stuff and load it up. By the time I got the last of my gear in the truck, the sidewalk was once again covered with snow, as was my truck. It was coming down fast.

My assignment for the day was Battalion 14, located at Engine 109's quarters near 22ND and Kedzie.

My plan to get there was to use Chicago Avenue, a designated "snow route." As I set out, the two-block drive from my house to Chicago Avenue wasn't too bad. Driving my truck, in 4-wheel drive with the added sandbag weight, I slowly pushed down my street creating the first tire ruts in the deep snowdrifts. The drive west on Chicago Avenue wasn't too bad either. Once I turned onto Kedzie, I was lucky enough to get behind a city plow truck and followed it for three and a half miles all the way to the firehouse. What a break!

As I pulled up to Engine 109's house around 5:00 a.m., all members of the currently on-duty shift were already outside doing their best to clear the parking lot. Firehouse protocol is that whenever snow falls overnight, the member on last watch rings the house bells and announces over the PA system something like, "Gooooood morning! It's snow shoveling time! All hands-on deck!" With this announcement all members get up, get dressed and begin clearing snow from the aprons, sidewalks, and parking lot so that the rigs can get out, and so that the on-coming shift will have somewhere to park. Using shovels and one snow blower, the off-going crew had the front apron cleared pretty well, but the snow was still falling fast, and it was hard to keep up. I pulled around to the rear parking area and, with four-wheel drive engaged, ran my truck up into a snowbank. My thought was that I'd park it as far out of the way as possible leaving room for the other on-coming shift members to do the same. Once the off-going shift leaves for the day, we would worry about getting our vehicles situated. Opening my door, I stepped into about eighteen inches of snow and plodded my way to the back of my truck. From there I unloaded my gear and trudged into the firehouse.

A few minutes after my arrival more on-coming members began showing up. Still in the darkness of the early morning, we all grabbed shovels and went to work helping the off-going shift. Even with all of the snow and the work ahead of us for the day, everyone was in a good lighthearted mood, laughing and joking. After about twenty minutes of hand shoveling, a large city of Chicago snowplow pulled up. The driver rolled down his window and yelled to us, "I'm supposed to get all firehouses and police stations on my route. If you guys move those cars in the rear, I'll clear your parking lot after I do your apron." BINGO! We shuffled the cars out and within ten minutes this guy cleared out our entire parking lot. On his last pass one of the firemen yelled to him, "Come on in for a donut and some coffee!" "Thanks. I'm good. I've been drinking coffee all night," he yelled before driving off.

At 8:00 a.m. we had a brief roll call in quarters. We went over the usual cold weather and safe driving procedures as well as how we were going to handle fires on impassable side streets. (Extremely heavy snowfalls add a different dimension to firefighting tactics. Narrow, snow filled side streets sometimes make it impossible for our rigs to get through. Engine companies may have to deal with dragging hose hundreds of feet through knee high snow all the way down from the nearest large street. Trucks also have a hard time carrying long heavy ground ladders and tools under these conditions.)

After roll call I left the house to start my morning rounds. The city plows had done a nice job clearing the main arteries, but the side streets were still mostly buried. As I neared 22ND and Pulaski, I heard Engine 109 report on the scene of an ambulance assist on the 2200 block of Drake. At the exact same time, I caught a glimpse of thick black smoke in the air, back in the direction of my quarters. It appeared to be coming from just west of 109's house. Taking a detour from my intended route I began heading towards the smoke.

"Battalion 14 to Main, do you have anything coming in just west of 109's quarters?" I asked the fire alarm office.

"Yeah, we're on the phone with a caller now reporting an auto fire at 24TH and St. Louis. 109's tied up. We've got Engine 38 on the way."

"Message received. I'm gonna head over there."

In the past, I've had reports of auto fires that actually turned out to be cars inside of garages. Another time a van was totally involved in fire and parked next to a wood-frame house. With Engine 38 coming from a distance, and all the snow on the ground, I wanted to take a look.

As I went east on 22ND I passed Engine 109. They were on the scene of their ambulance assist run parked in the middle of the side street, Drake, facing north only about three blocks from the column of smoke I reported. Looking south, the opposite direction down Drake, I could see that the streets already had ruts in the snow, so I put my buggy in 4-wheel drive and continued heading towards the smoke. Before I got to the end of the block I heard 38 report on the scene, "Engine 38 to Main, we're on the scene at 24TH and St. Louis. We have an auto on the street." Already committed on Drake, I continued pushing my buggy through the snow and pulled up on Engine 38. "I just wanted to see what you had here. I'll catch you later at quarters," I said as I pulled off. No sooner than I cleared the intersection, I heard Engine 109 report that they were involved in a minor accident. Before the fire alarm office could call me, I reported over the radio, "Battalion 14 to Main, I'm taking the Accident Investigation with 109." The accident occurred when Engine 109's rear wheels slipped out of the snow ruts and clipped a parked car. No one was hurt. There was no damage to the rig and a minor scrape on the vehicle. I completed the investigation with the police and continued on my rounds.

The rest of the shift was uneventful. I had several runs but nothing out of the ordinary.

02/05/14—02/28/15

The remainder of my workdays in February were surprisingly slow. Nothing to note.

MARCH 2015

03/01/15
Assignment—5-1-5 (Special Operations—Engine 5's Quarters, DesPlaines & Jackson)
Primary Response Area—City Wide
Weather—Temperatures in the low 20s

Sunday March 1st was the day of Chicago's Polar Plunge. Temperatures were in the mid teens with a steady wind.

The Polar Plunge is an annual event where a few thousand people jump into the frigid waters of Lake Michigan at the North Ave. Beach to raise money for the Chicago Special Olympics. The Chicago Fire Department's Air Sea Rescue team works the event each year standing by in case of emergencies. Since I was working as the Special Operations Chief this day, and Air Sea Rescue falls under my supervision, I attended the event.

This year about 4,200 people signed up to take the "plunge" but many more than that showed up. Even though the reported air temperature was around twenty degrees, the North Avenue beach area was alive with a party atmosphere. There was music provided by a DJ, food concessions, vendors, and many of the "polar plungers" were walking around dressed in elaborate costumes. I was told by one of the event planners that the night before the "plunge," many of the participants held or attended private "plunge parties." "Yep...that looked like the case," I thought.

Things started early in the morning with a large front loader breaking a hole into the ice. I walked down to take a look at the "plunge" area and was surprised to see how small it was. It was only about 30 feet wide and about 20 feet out into the lake. Its deepest point was only about thigh high.

The event kicks off with a few celebrities taking the "plunge" first followed by the remainder of registered participants. All those waiting their turn are staged in a warming tent until their number is called. From there, they are sent in groups of fifteen to take the "plunge." It all happens kind of fast, with each participant only staying in the water for about ten to twenty seconds. Many dunk themselves completely while others only wade in. As they scamper out of the water, volunteers working the event hand them dry towels. As one group runs out the next runs in.

Prior to the start of the event a safety briefing was held by the CFD Air Sea Rescue Chief, Leo Bascom. Leo gave a quick presentation to all CFD and CPD members explaining the event and our action plan. We were briefed on the location of ambulances and the radio frequencies that would be used. Right after the meeting Leo, along with the CFD and CPD divers, entered the water wearing dry suits and began removing large chunks of ice creating a safe area for the "plungers." For the next few hours, the divers would stand in the water in a half circle around the inside of the hole to make sure anyone who needed assistance was tended to. Throughout the day there were a few scrapes and bruises but no major injuries. Some of the participants, especially ones wearing heavy costumes, did need assistance after floundering around and not being able to stand up.

This year's event started with bagpipers leading the "guest of honor," Vince Vaughn, into the water. Dressed in a Chicago Blackhawk jersey, Vince went in all the way over his head and like everyone else for the rest of the day was out in about ten seconds. The second group of VIPs to go in was the cast of the hit television show, *Chicago Fire*. About half of them wore CFD T-shirts. The others were shirtless with shorts, and one of the female cast members wore a blue CFD bikini. As the group got closer to the water, I noticed that a woman riding piggyback on one of the cast members was getting a lot of attention from the crowd. It was Lady Gaga. At the time she was dating the lead cast member on the show, Taylor Kinney. The rumor going around was that, so as not to take away from Vince Vaughn's "guest of honor" appearance, she did not make it known to the media that she was taking the "plunge." As the cast members entered the water the screams started. The guys tackled each other while Taylor and Lady Gaga went completely under. The cast, including one Chicago firefighter, were all laughing and shivering as they made their exit from the water. The third group of VIPs to enter the water was about one hundred Commonwealth Edison workers. (ComEd was a big sponsor of the event.) This group looked like they had the most fun! The last VIPs to take the plunge were a few local politicians.

I'm really glad I had the opportunity to work this event. I had a lot of laughs seeing the costumes and watching people's faces as they entered the frigid water. The rest of the day was pretty uneventful.

03/04/15
ASSIGNMENT—BATTALION 23 (ENGINE 72'S QUARTERS, 79TH AND STONY ISLAND)
PRIMARY RESPONSE AREA—SOUTHEAST SIDE
WEATHER—TEMPERATURES IN THE MID 20S

Battalion 23 is located on Chicago's southeast side and is another one of the busiest battalions in the city. Averaging about ten runs a day, Battalion 23 covers all types of neighborhoods from distressed areas to lakeshore high-rises. This was my first time in the 23RD Battalion and with wind chills around zero, I was expecting a pretty busy shift. I was wrong. My first run of the day didn't come until after midnight.

Around 11:00 p.m., after finishing up my administrative paperwork for the day, I laid down for what I hoped would be a peaceful night.

"STILL ALARM"

About twenty minutes after midnight, I was sent to a Still Alarm near 93RD and Cottage Grove. Knowing that Engine 82 and Truck 42's quarters were right around the corner from the given address, I walked to my buggy, turned on my portable radio and listened for their "on scene" report. No sooner than I turned the key in the ignition, Engine 82 and Truck 42 reported on the scene, "82 and the truck are at 93RD and Cottage, nothing showing on a 3-story brick building with a storefront on the first and apartments above." Many times, after midnight a "nothing showing" report in an apartment building turns out to be what we call a "pot of meat" or "meat on the stove." Traditionally, companies on the north side of the city use the term "pot of meat", while companies on the south side of the city use the term "meat on the stove."

This is where someone comes home late, many times intoxicated, and decides to heat something up on the stove, then falls asleep. The burning pot sets off a smoke detector or the smell alone wakes neighbors. The first companies to arrive to find a "pot of meat" or "meat on the stove" usually holds up everyone else responding and handles it themselves. Without hearing "hold the chief," I continued my response and made it all the way to the scene about three miles away.

When I arrived, companies were searching all three floors and the basement in an attempt to locate the source of a very light haze of smoke that was hovering on the first and second floors. It didn't smell like wood burning. It smelled more like something electrical. Our first thought was that the haze was caused by a bad ballast on one of the fluorescent light fixtures on the first floor. However, we still had to investigate to rule out any real fire.

The officers of Engine 82 and Truck 42 reported to me they were using their thermal imaging cameras and physically feeling walls for heat, but so far could not locate the source of the smoke. The only hint to where it may have been coming from was when Truck 42 reported a contrasting heat reading on their camera in the kitchen of the second-floor apartment. "Hold on truck...I'm on my way up," I told them over the radio. When I got upstairs, they showed me what their camera was picking up. After confirming with the back of my hand that there was definitely heat behind the wall, I instructed a firefighter from the truck to open a small inspection hole. What we found behind the plaster and lath was a hot radiator pipe running up from the basement to the third floor. No fire.

After about fifteen minutes the haze dissipated completely. Not being able to find a definite source, we all concluded that the smoke was most likely a ballast as we had initially thought. A burned-out ballast is pretty common and normally not a dangerous situation. As a precaution we instructed the tenants to leave the lights off and have an electrician check this out before turning them back on.

I picked up all companies and advised everyone in the building to call back immediately if they, again, smelled anything unusual. As I was walking out the door one of the tenants thanked me and added that he too thought it was the ballast on the first floor but called us just to be sure. He said the smoke made him nervous because last year he and his wife had a fire in their apartment when they lived in the building next door. I told him that I totally understand and to please call 911 if he sees or smells anything that he's not comfortable with.

While completing my paperwork back in quarters at around 12:45 a.m., I heard an engine company report over the radio, "We're on the scene with a fire in a 1½-story frame building." The address they were reporting was only a few blocks west of my battalion boundary. Knowing that I would be dispatched as the RIT Chief, I got up out of my chair and started putting on an extra sweatshirt. However, as I walked out of my room the computer dispatch tones went off sending me to a different fire at a different address. The fire I was being sent to was pretty close to the location of the confirmed fire.

"STILL ALARM"

As I was driving to my assignment, the chief on the scene of the confirmed fire escalated the alarm to a Still & Box. From the radio chatter I could tell that they had their hands full. The chief reported the original fire building was "totally involved" and the fire was communicating to two frame buildings on either side. He also reported having two frozen hydrants.

I was about a block away from my assigned run when the engine that arrived before me reported a "false alarm" and held everyone up. I immediately notified the fire alarm office that I was available to take in the Still & Box.

"Battalion 23 to Englewood...I'm available for that Still & Box."

"Okay...Battalion 23. It's covered. You can return to quarters."

"No way," I thought. The fire was only about a quarter of a mile away from where I was and close enough for me to hear some pretty hectic, on scene Fireground radio communications. 2-2-5, Deputy District Chief George Moran, was on the scene and from the intensity in his voice I could tell that things weren't going well and had a strong feeling that the alarm would soon be escalated to a 2-11. Knowing that if the alarm were escalated, I would be called to take it in, I pulled over to the curb and waited instead of heading back to quarters.

The next radio communication came over the air about two minutes later, "2-2-5 to Englewood...emergency...give me a 2-11."

I immediately got on the radio, "Battalion 23's taking in the 2-11." "That's right Battalion 23 ... take in the 2-11," the office replied.

"2-11 ALARM FIRE"

I was there within seconds and parked about a block away from the fire. While donning my gear at the back of my buggy, over the rooftops I could see that familiar pulsating orange glow and large embers popping in the sky. Both are telltale signs that a wood structure is heavily involved in fire. As I began walking towards the front of the fire building, 2-2-5 made an announcement over the Fireground radio channel, "All companies working at the 2-11 use caution. The original fire building has partially collapsed."

When I got closer, I could see the water spray from the exterior hose lines and one deck gun filling the air. The freezing temperature quickly froze the water and had already coated the street and firefighters outside with a layer of ice. As I approached Chief Moran, who was standing in the middle of the street, I reported, "Chief, I'm Battalion 23, one of your 2-11 chiefs. Whaddya need?"

Without hesitation he replied, "Kev, take the exposure next door to the north. I got Engine 101 and Truck 41 up in that attic trying to stop it from gettin' in there. Lemme know what ya got as soon as you get up there."

"Got it," I replied.

The wooden front porch and stairs of the one and a half story north exposure building were coated with a thick layer of ice. I grabbed a hold of one of the shaky wooden handrails and carefully made my way up the stairs. The front door had two hoselines going into it. One went through the first floor and out the back door to the yard and the second into the kitchen and up a very tight small set of stairs leading to the attic. The continuous flow of cascading water running down from the attic into the kitchen made the stairs and the entire first floor another sheet of ice. I turned on my flashlight and crawled up the stairs on all fours.

Once in the attic I did a quick size-up up and reported back to 2-2-5.

"Battalion 23 to 2-2-5. 101 made a nice stop up here in the north exposure attic. Most of the fire is out. Smoke conditions are moderate. Truck 41 already has a good part of the roof stripped. We got a good view of what's left of the original fire building from here. I can see a few hot spots. I'm gonna let 101 work their line on 'em."

"2-2-5 to Battalion 23, message received. Good work 101."

When things calmed down in the attic only two firefighters at a time were tending the line and the rest of us sat back for a breather. Talking through the light smoke that was still lingering, I heard one of the firemen say something about being at this address before. "You guys had a fire here before?" I asked. One of the firemen responded, "We had a call for a fire next door at the original fire building about two hours ago. The first engine checked it out but said they couldn't find anything and held everybody up." This, of course, reminded me of the similar situation I had earlier at 93RD and Cottage, the run with the overheated light fixture ballast. Could we have possibly missed something back there? Man, I hope not.

(One of the most uncomfortable situations a fire officer is presented with is one where there is no definite finding of where or what the problem is. It has to be in the officer's gut that he/she feels comfortable leaving the scene. This is not to second-guess the companies that responded here earlier. I once had a fire where an arsonist tried unsuccessfully to light up a building. Literally, minutes after we left, he tried again and succeeded.)

Hearing the radio report that the fire was struck out, I reported to Chief Moran that we were done up in the attic and were going to start picking up our line. As usual, while carefully making our way down the icy attic stairs, a couple of us took hard spills and slid down on our butts. Being the last one down, when I got to the kitchen, I called out, "Everybody okay?" Through the dark, ice castle looking kitchen I got the old grumbling response, "Yeah, yeah yeah..." With this, we all continued through the apartment slipping, sliding and dragging out our hose line.

Back out front, before leaving the scene, I spoke with 2-2-5, "Hey George, the attic looks good. We gave it a real good washdown and everybody's okay. With your blessing I'm gonna take off." "Okay," he replied, "thanks for your help Kev."

I got back to quarters about 5:00 a.m., made a fresh pot of coffee and completed my paperwork before being relieved at 5:30.

Okay, so that was my first time in the busy Battalion 23. I had no runs all day but was up all night!

> 03/06/15
> Assignment—Battalion 13 (Engine 95's
> Quarters, Pulaski & Madison)
> Primary Response Area—Westside
> Weather—Temperatures in the teens

Once again, due to a shortage of battalion chiefs, I was asked to work a double shift. My first twenty-four hours would be today in Battalion 13. My second would be at Battalion 4.

Each morning at shift change, firefighters, officers and chiefs of the off-going shift, brief on-coming members on anything noteworthy that occurred during their shift or the shift before. This is usually done at the kitchen table over coffee. After putting my gear in the buggy, I went to the kitchen and sat across the table from the chief that I was relieving.

"Morning Kev," he said. "Not sure if you heard this but, two shifts ago, they had a 2-11 on the 300 block of south

Albany. It was a vacant 3-story brick. Somebody lit it up good."

"Everybody okay?"

"Yeah, nobody got hurt but it sounds like they had a hell of a time. They had at least two or three frozen hydrants and had to go in-line to get water from a block away."

He then went on to tell me more about the fire. Late that night companies were stilled out to a fire at an approximate address of 300 S. Albany. Because of numerous calls for the same fire, the alarm office upgraded the response to a Still & Box. (The alarm office can and will escalate an alarm if there is a report of people trapped or if they are getting a lot of calls reporting the same fire.) Upon arrival the first engine and truck found a vacant 3-story brick building with a large amount of fire on the second and third floors. When the first two engines encountered frozen hydrants the battalion chief on scene quickly escalated the fire to a 2-11. Without water for a quick knockdown and with the help of high winds, the fire progressed rapidly making its way out of the second and third floor windows into both gangways and threatened to communicate to the occupied buildings on either side. Because of the frozen hydrants, the first four engines on the scene had to use in-line operations. This meant they had to hook up to, and pump water from, working hydrants more than a block away. Although the original fire building was a total loss, the quick thinking and experience of first arriving companies kept the fire from communicating to the occupied structures on either side.

After getting the whole story, I was also informed that Engine 44 and Truck 36 had been back to the scene on rekindles three times the day after the fire. (When a building burns so badly that collapse occurs, firefighters cannot get in to extinguish every bit of fire that is hidden under debris. Companies do their best but with fires of this magnitude it's not uncommon to be called back on rekindles as demolition crews find small hidden "hot spots.")

Firefighters are always looking for ways to improve both their hands-on and mental skills. With that in mind, it's not uncommon for companies who were not at a fire to return to the scene for a discussion drill. We try to picture what the first companies saw and walk through the decisions they made. We also discuss how we would go to work if another fire were set in the same building or same area.

After morning roll call Engine 95, Truck 26 and myself took a ride over to the 300 block of South Albany. There we found demolition crews working to remove the bricks, plaster and wood that was once a handsome old Chicago style building. While 95 was looking at hydrant locations and Truck 26 was talking about ladder placement, I spoke with the demolition crew. "We should have the site completely cleared by this afternoon," the supervisor told me. "There's no more smoldering so it doesn't look like you guys will have to come back."

During the remainder of my shift, I had about seven fire calls. All were false. The next morning, I got up around 4:30, took a shower and got my stuff together. My relief came in at 5:15 and after a quick briefing I was off to Battalion 4 to start my second twenty-four-hour shift.

03/07/15
ASSIGNMENT—BATTALION 4 (ENGINE 23'S QUARTERS, 20TH & DAMEN)
PRIMARY RESPONSE AREA—PILSEN, LITTLE VILLAGE, NEAR SOUTHWEST SIDE
WEATHER—TEMPERATURES IN THE LOW 30S

The 4TH Battalion is housed along with Engine 23 and Tower Ladder 5 in the Pilsen neighborhood at 20TH and Damen. This was my first time working in the 4TH battalion.

Throughout the day and evening, I had several runs including a "Still In A High-Rise" that turned out to be false. A resident mistook the odor of her neighbor's oven cleaner for smoke. A bit tired from the previous shift, and knowing that I'd lose an hour of sleep because of the daylight savings clock change tonight, I got in bed around 10:00 p.m. When I'm in or near a busy battalion like this one, I'll leave the scanner radio on low overnight. I don't usually sleep well at work but this time I fell asleep as soon as my head hit the pillow.

"STILL & BOX"

At about 3:00 a.m. I awoke to the dispatcher's voice on the scanner, "A Still and Box Alarm at 313 S. Albany. Companies responding to the Still & Box, we're getting a report of people trapped on the second floor." It's strange how this works, but from a sound sleep, within seconds of hearing the radio announcement, I was able to determine,

- That 313 S. Albany was on the same block as the 2-11 alarm arson fire two days ago.
- I knew this was most likely a "hit" because the fire alarm office boxed it.

- I would be responding because I was in the next battalion east of the fire address.

All of this was going through my mind as I got out of bed and threw on an extra sweatshirt. I was already walking to my buggy when the run came over the dispatch terminal in the firehouse,

"Battalion 4...Still & Box...313 S. Albany."

Pulling out of the firehouse, over the radio the alarm office gave me the assignment of RIT Chief and said Truck 26 would be my RIT truck. As I drove west on Roosevelt Road, I could already hear a flurry of radio traffic coming from the fire scene. In one of the broken communications, I thought I heard it said that people on the street were confirming that someone was trapped.

Upon arrival I put on my turnout gear and reported to the RIT staging area in Sector A where I met up with Truck 26. Doing a quick exterior size-up up I saw the fire building was a 2-story brick coach house located in the rear of a corner lot next to a small alley. Both floors were charged with thick black smoke. As the officer of Truck 26 and myself were discussing the scene, we suddenly heard the muffled sound of a firefighter speaking over the radio through his SCBA mask.

"This is Truck 36. We got two victims on the second floor. We're bringin' 'em to the front door!"

The chief in charge of the fire confirmed receipt of Truck 36's message and ordered companies outside to clear a path in the cluttered yard. He also waved to the ambulance crews standing by to move their stretchers closer to the alley gate.

To help the members of Truck 36 find their way back to the stairway through the smoke and to assist in removing the victims, several firefighters entered at ground level. One of them ascended to the top of the stairs and began waving his flashlight, calling out and banging on the floor. This was an attempt to help the rescuers find their way back to the stairway. Within seconds the firefighter at the top of the stairs could see the vague beam of light through the thick smoke. The lit flashlights dangling on the rescuing firefighters' belts told the guy on the stairs where they were. "HERE, HERE, HERE," he shouted through his SCBA facepiece while still banging on the floor trying to guide them out. Using these directions, the two members of Truck 36 turned and headed for the stairs, each of them dragging a victim. When they reached the stairs, the other firefighters inside helped bring the victims down and out of the building.

Everyone outside watched as the two lifeless figures were placed onto waiting stretchers and wheeled off to the ambulances.

When a victim is located during an interior search of a fire building the main objective of a firefighter becomes getting that person outside as quickly as possible. Sometimes we win and, unfortunately, sometimes we don't.

The following is an excerpt from the next day's *Chicago Tribune*:

> *"As a result of the fire, a 79-year-old woman was transported to John H. Stroger, Jr. Hospital of Cook County, and a man in his 40s was taken to Mount Sinai Hospital, said police and fire officials. Both were listed in critical condition. According to police, the woman, who suffered smoke inhalation, and her 45-year-old son are expected to survive."*

That night those two guys from Truck 36 risked their own lives to save those of a helpless mother and son ... and won.

Literally, within minutes of awakening from a sound sleep Truck 36 arrived on the scene. Armed with information of "people trapped on the second floor," the truck's crew of five firefighters split into two teams and went to work. One team of two carried a 200 lb, 38' ground ladder down an icy alley and raised it to the roof of the fire building. Then, with their axes in hand, they climbed to the roof and immediately began ventilation. Simultaneously, the officer and two other members forced entry at the front door and without a hoseline in place yet began a systematic interior search. The officer took the first floor and the remaining two firefighters ascended to the second where they crawled through dense smoke and intense heat searching blindly for victims. Enduring brutal conditions created by bottled up heat, the two firefighters continued their search on the second floor until they came across two bodies. After a quick radio transmission indicating that they found the victims, each firefighter grabbed one victim by their clothing and began dragging them in the direction of where they remembered the stairs to be. Through the smoke they could see faint flashlight beams ahead of them. They could also hear their fellow firefighters calling the way out. Just before they reached the top of the stairs the smoke began to lift, and the intense heat became a little more bearable. This was because the two firefighters on the roof did a great job of getting a ventilation hole cut. This was an excellent example of how quick thinking, teamwork and fast accurate roof ventilation saves lives.

Regarding the possible cause of the fire, investigators on the scene found that an accelerant was used.

I got back to the firehouse about 4:30 a.m., made some coffee and was relieved of my forty-eight-hour shift at 5:00.

Updated information: On March 23, 2015, it was

reported online in *A Chicago Sun-Times Publication, Homicide Watch Chicago*, that the 79-year-old woman rescued from the fire above succumbed to her injuries and died. The fire was ruled "suspicious" and the woman's death, a homicide.

> 03/10/15
> ASSIGNMENT—BATTALION 8 (ENGINE 125's QUARTERS, NARRAGANSETT & FULLERTON)
> PRIMARY RESPONSE AREA—WEST AND NEAR NORTHWEST SIDES
> WEATHER—TEMPERATURES IN THE HIGH 20s

Shutout—No runs –No hits—No errors

> 03/13/15
> ASSIGNMENT—BATTALION 9 (ENGINE 70's QUARTERS, CLARK & PETERSON)
> PRIMARY RESPONSE AREA—ROGERS PARK, UPTOWN, LAKEFRONT
> WEATHER—TEMPERATURES IN THE HIGH 40s

Fire companies in the 9TH Battalion respond to every type of incident imaginable and must always expect the unexpected. They cover the north end of Lake Michigan's shores, Lake Shore Drive, CTA elevated trains, high-rises, hospitals, senior living homes, nursing facilities, colleges, bars, theaters, concert venues, and tens of thousands of apartments.

Throughout the day and night, I had quite a few runs but nothing of consequence.

"AUTOMATIC ALARM IN A HIGH-RISE"

While I was gathering up my things to go home at 5:00 a.m., I was dispatched to an "Automatic Alarm in a High-Rise" at an address near the lakefront. Upon arrival I reported that I had "a 12-story residential high-rise with nothing showing." Entering the lobby, I noticed that the power failure backup lighting was on. Indicators on the alarm panel, located behind the unattended front desk, confirmed a power failure, and also showed that no fire detectors had been activated. Directly across a small courtyard was another residential building about the same height. Via radio Truck 47 notified me of the same situation there.

With this information I reported to the fire alarm office that neither of the building's alarm panels indicated a fire alarm and that we were, instead, dealing with a power outage.

I then assigned Truck 47 to one building and Engine 59 to the other. Their initial responsibilities were to locate all elevator banks and make sure no one was trapped in an unmoving car. They were also to locate and review each building's emergency action binders and report back with any special needs information. (Every high-rise building should have, in their lobby, an emergency action binder that contains emergency information specific to that building. For example, these binders contain floor plans, locations of entrances and exits, number of occupants, phone numbers for building maintenance personnel, etc. Especially helpful to us in this particular situation, these binders also have a list of any residents with special needs. This would include the physically restricted and or those who have oxygen machines requiring electrical power.)

While in the lobby, two men approached me. They introduced themselves as a maintenance crew responsible for several other buildings in the area and said they were responding to a reported power surge and outage. One of them informed me that their buildings briefly lost power, but most of them came back on within a few minutes. He also said, at this time, only two of their buildings were without power. This gave me a total of four high-rises with no power, all on the same block.

(Many high-rises are equipped with in-house public address, or PA, systems that run on backup power. This is very helpful to first responders. Using this communication asset, we can provide information and directions to residents regarding the issue at hand. This provides them with comfort just knowing that the fire department is on the scene and working on the situation. In more dire incidents, such as a fire, a PA system can help us control the movement of evacuees if necessary. Take for instance a fairly common situation. Let's say someone in a senior home accidentally leaves a pot on their stove with the burner on. The heated metal and contents of the pot would set off a smoke detector. The odor could make its way out to the hallway and into other apartments alarming residents. With the use of an in-house PA system, we could provide residents with information like, "The fire department is on the scene and checking out an alarm on the 8TH floor. Please stay in your apartments. We will update you very soon." Then, a subsequent announcement might be, "This is the fire department. We investigated and found an overheated cooking pot. There was and is NO EMERGENCY. All is well." In this example, without a PA system, we may have had elderly people wandering halls and stairwells self-evacuating for no reason.)

Protocol dictates that when power is out to multiple high-rise buildings the on-scene Incident Commander must request a Type II Power Outage Response. This is a standardized response that brings more resources to the scene including a chief officer above my rank. As per protocol, I notified the fire alarm office, "Battalion 9 to Main, I have at least four residential high-rise buildings without power. Give me a Type II Power Outage Response and set the staging area at Broadway and Rosemont. Also, get me an immediate ComEd response."

With the possibility that there still may be more than just the four reported buildings down, I radioed the captain of Truck 47 and told him I was going to take a quick drive around the block to try and determine the extent of the outage. Driving slowly around a two-block area, I could see lights on in the windows of the other surrounding high-rises. It didn't take long to conclude that only the original four buildings were without power. I then radioed back to Truck 47,

"Battalion 9 to Truck 47. I'm back. We only have the original four buildings on this block down. Any report for me?"

"Truck 47 to Battalion 9. I met with those maintenance guys and sent a few of my crew down to their buildings with them. They already came back. Here's the report on all four buildings. All elevators have been located and are empty, we checked the books at the front desk, no one is on oxygen or in need of assistance at this time."

"Nice job Cap. Thanks."

When 2-2-2, Deputy District Chief Herb Norris, arrived on scene, I briefed him on the situation and the actions we had already taken. He then notified the alarm office that he was assuming command. Only a few minutes later a full ComEd crew arrived. They informed us they had already surveyed the situation and they would have power restored to all four buildings in a couple of hours. It's always good news when ComEd finds and can fix the problem quickly. When they're done, we can leave.

It was now about 5:40 a.m. My usual relief at the firehouse would have taken place at 5:30. (Normally, if a chief gets stuck at a scene near relief time, the on-coming chief will drive over in his/her private vehicle and make the relief switch there. After providing a briefing of the situation, the off-going chief will leave the buggy at the scene and drive back to the firehouse in the other chief's personal vehicle.) At about 5:45, I called the firehouse to let my relief know that we were in stand-by mode and that we could be released shortly. I added that I had no personal plans for this morning, so I was not in a hurry to get home. I also said I'd call him if this thing was going to go past 6:30.

Just moments before 6:30 the power came back on to all four buildings. With that came the order for all companies to pick up and return to quarters. All in all, this wasn't a very difficult run. No one needed special assistance, and no one got hurt.

As I was walking back to my buggy daybreak had begun on what would be a nice cool Saturday in March. Looking east through the forest of high-rises, I caught glimpses of a beautiful dark blue sky over the expanse that was Lake Michigan. The sun would be rising soon and I kinda wished I had time to take a ride to the shore to watch it, but I had to get back to the firehouse so that my relief could get in-service. As the sky became brighter another thing struck me, the calmness of daybreak. There were no pedestrians in sight and only a couple of cars had passed. I was really appreciating this sereneness when suddenly I heard a loud CRUNCH! Looking behind me I saw 2-7-2, our Command Van, pulling away from a bent parking meter. The driver apparently backed into it while making a U-turn and now, not realizing he hit it, he continued to pull away. Before I had a chance to call him on the radio 2-2-2's voice came over the air, "2-7-2 come on back to the scene." He then radioed to the fire alarm office and informed them that 2-7-2 was involved in an accident. "Oh man," I thought. I now would have to do the investigation and all required paperwork. This included waiting for the police to arrive, gathering all the information and going to the police station for copies of their reports when the investigation was over. Grrrrrr! Then, literally within seconds, my cell phone rang. It was my relief, Chester Sola. Hearing the announcement of the accident over the radio from the kitchen table at the firehouse he called me, "Kev, stay there. I'm heading over now. I'll handle the accident investigation. You can go home." Whew! Chester arrived about ten minutes later and we made the switch. He was now on-duty, and I was free for the next forty-eight hours.

> 03/16/15
> Assignment—Battalion 3 (Engine 14's Quarters, Milwaukee and Chicago)
> Primary Response Area—Near Westside, West Loop
> Weather—Unseasonably warm. Temperatures reaching the 70's

It's always nice to work in the neighborhood where I grew up, where I spent six years as a firefighter and where I still live as of this writing. I know the streets, the area and the surrounding fire companies well. It's also fun to work with old friends, especially the captain of Engine 14, Bill Haddon. Bill and I were firemen together years ago on Engine 30. (Engines 14 and 30 are both in the third battalion.)

The day started out pretty normal. All battalion chiefs working in the First District today were to report to District Headquarters by 10:00 a.m. for a special meeting and a drill. The meeting covered mostly administrative stuff and the drill was on high-rise fire operations. Nothing new was presented in the drill, but it's always good to go over what the bosses expect, especially at a high-rise fire where things can get pretty intense.

During the day I had only one run. I was sent to a nearby hospital to "check the well being of an injured member." This is an administrative run where a battalion chief responds to a hospital where an on-duty member was transported. The chief's duty is to investigate how the member was injured, to make sure he/she is getting proper care, and to make notifications to the proper CFD bosses about the patient's condition. No big deal this time, the investigation was for a member with a broken rib.

After dinner I left quarters to do my regular night visits. I first stopped at Engine 22 in Lincoln Park, and then went to my old house, Engine 30. I was a firefighter on 30 from March of 1988 to November of 1994. I left when I was promoted to lieutenant. One of my favorite things to do at 30's house was to sit out front with other firefighters on a nice evening. Even though we were located on a main street this firehouse had a "neighborhood" feel. People, many with dogs, would often stop by to chat and visit with our appropriately named Dalmatian, "30." We knew many of the neighbors by name and would always have a box of treats on hand for their dogs. This night I hung out in front of the firehouse with the officer for an hour or so enjoying the first nice weather of the year. Around 9:00 p.m., while still in front of 30's house, I heard over the radio there was some type of incident going on near

Addison and Sheridan. I missed the first part of the transmission so I wasn't sure what it was, but I could tell it wasn't a fire. The officer and I stopped our conversation trying to hear more of what was going on. No sooner than we stopped talking my number was called, "Battalion 3, take an Accident Investigation involving Truck 44 at 520 W. Belmont." I confirmed my assignment with the fire alarm office and headed north. The address I was assigned to was actually in Battalion 5's district. This made sense. I was covering for him while he was handling the incident creating all the radio chatter.

"ACCIDENT INVESTIGATION"

While en route to my run, I heard Battalion 5 request a Type I Power Outage Response to Addison and Sheridan. He reported having a fairly large residential area without power. Now, all that radio chatter made sense.

Heading east on Belmont, and still a few blocks away from my run, I could see Truck 44's light's flashing up ahead. As I got closer, I noted that the streetlights were out. This made Truck 44's emergency strobe lighting seem exceptionally bright.

Upon arrival I parked behind Truck 44, reported on the scene, and started getting my paperwork ready for the investigation. My responsibilities included interviewing both drivers and completing a narrative of what happened. Before I could get out of my buggy, Truck 44's officer came to my window.

"Anybody hurt?" I asked.

"No, the only guy in our rig was the driver, he's okay. The rest of us were inside the building getting people out of an elevator. There were three younger guys in the car that hit us. They're all okay too. There's minor damage to our bumper and minimal damage to their car. Our rig was parked when these guys hit us. We weren't moving."

"All right...I got it."

"Hey Chief, before you go over there, I just want to tell you that the driver of the car is being really belligerent. When my driver went to see if anybody was hurt, he started waving his arms, yelling, and lecturing him on how our rig shouldn't have been parked the way it was and that we're the blame."

"Okay, you wait here. I'll go talk to him."

Armed with this information and looking to calm things down, I walked over to the driver of the car and politely introduced myself. However, before I could get three more words out, I, too, was loudly lectured on how to park a fire truck. At first, I was kinda offended being schooled by a twenty-something-year-old guy wearing shorts, flip-flops and a long-sleeved button-down shirt with the sleeves rolled up and driving his mom's Audi with Wisconsin plates. My initial thought was to explain to him that he just hit a non-moving, 40-foot-long fire truck with more flashing lights than the Las Vegas strip...but I bit my tongue and walked away.

Within a few minutes two police cars and my boss, 2-2-2, Deputy District Chief Rich Gallagher, arrived simultaneously. The street was now super lit up with flashing blue, red and green lights. I briefed Chief Gallagher and the police officer on what happened so far. We then all walked over to speak with the driver of the car. This time the interview went a lot better. The driver was very apologetic and cooperative. It appeared to me that he might have been convinced by the two passengers in his car to tone it down and cooperate with the investigation. Maybe it was all the flashing lights? Who knows?

As 2-2-2's driver was taking pictures and I was getting my

accident paperwork together, we heard over the radio that the incident a few blocks away was elevated from a Type I to a Type II Power Outage. With that, the fire alarm office called to see if I was available to take it in. I looked at Chief Gallagher. Before I could ask, he sent me on my way, "Go ahead Kev, I'll handle the rest of the investigation. Just email me your report when you get back to quarters later." "Thanks boss," I replied before confirming my status to the alarm office..."Battalion 3 to Main, I'm available and taking in the Power Outage."

"POWER OUTAGE"

Upon arrival I was given an assignment by 2-2-1, Deputy District Chief Bob Hagen, to check out a few high-rises on the 500 block of Cornelia. I was told to see which ones had power and which ones didn't. After walking the block and reporting that all buildings were up and running, Chief Hagen assigned me to the lobby of a building on North Lake Shore Drive. It was without power and running on its own limited backup generator. My assignment was to stand by in the lobby with Engine 78 in case anyone in the building needed assistance. The building manager, who was called in from home, was on scene and provided us with the building's emergency action binder. He also assured me that there was no one needing any special attention in his building. I then asked him to make an announcement over the building's PA system informing the residents of the situation and to instruct anyone needing assistance to please call the lobby.

About a half hour later another fire company came into the lobby and told us that the word from ComEd was that a rat got into a transformer vault outside and shorted out the power to several high-rise buildings. They added that ComEd was sending over a very large generator to get power up while they worked to replace the transformer. It turned out to be a long night of sitting around. Several hours later, when it was determined that we were in good shape as far as people needing assistance, I was released from the scene.

I went back to quarters, completed my Accident Investigation Report, and emailed it to Chief Gallagher along with another "thanks" for handling my investigation. I got to bed around 2:00 a.m. and was happy to sleep, uninterrupted, all the way to 5:00 a.m.!

> 03/19/15
> Assignment—5-1-5 (Special Operations—Engine 5's Quarters, DesPlaines & Jackson)
> Primary Response Area—City Wide
> Weather—Temperatures in the mid 40s

Besides fire and EMS runs, the CFD is routinely called upon to mitigate many different types of emergencies. From entrapments in underground sewers and trenches to rope rescues on high-rise buildings, the CFD must be prepared to respond quickly and perform efficiently. As the old saying goes, "always expect the unexpected." To be ready for anything, the CFD maintains a fleet of special purpose apparatus (i.e., smoke ejectors, high powered lighting apparatus, jump bags, collapse rescue equipment and an auxiliary snorkel). These rigs are housed throughout the city in various firehouses and can be called upon to respond to any incident in a moment's notice. All members of a firehouse, where a special purpose rig is quartered, are responsible for its cleanliness and readiness. They also must become certified and proficient with the equipment carried, and they must know how to safely drive and operate the apparatus. One of the responsibilities of 5-1-5, Special Operations Battalion Chief, is to oversee all special purpose rigs throughout the city. On a rotating schedule, 5-1-5 must conduct inspections and drills with all members who will be operating these specialty rigs.

I started this day's shift by conducting an inspection and drill on the special operations apparatus located at Engine 109's quarters. The inspection consisted of a walk around the apparatus with the firefighter who was assigned as the driver/operator for the day. In most firehouses members take turns in this position. This helps keep each member fresh on the operation of their assigned rig. During the inspection the driver and I walked around the apparatus while he went through an inventory checklist and explained how each item worked. After this, we took the apparatus outside where he put it to work demonstrating his ability to safely and efficiently handle its operation. When we were done, the house captain invited me to stay around for breakfast. Having worked in this firehouse many times before I knew everyone on shift. They were a good crew, and I knew they always put out an awesome breakfast spread. After a great meal, some good conversation and fielding questions about what I'm going to do when I retire, I threw five dollars in their lottery club for the day and went on my way.

My next stop was Special Operations field headquarters where I was scheduled to meet Squad 1 for a drill on another piece of Special Ops equipment, the Rescue Vac. The Rescue Vac is basically the same vacuum truck you would see cleaning out a street sewer. It has a large diameter hose that is connected in the rear and hangs over the front windshield making it look something like an elephant's trunk. The idea of using this type of equipment on the fire department was introduced and implemented by Assistant Deputy Fire Commissioner and Chief of Special Operations, Ed Nagle, during an incident a few years ago where a man was trapped chest high in gravel. ADFC Nagle requested a Chicago Department of Sewers vacuum truck to respond to the scene to "suck" the gravel out from around the man in order to release him. After that incident the fire department was given a Vac truck of its own.

The drill today was conducted by Special Operations Lt. Ted Kroll. Before demonstrating the rig in operation, he told us of its exceptional power and of the dangers of using it improperly. He warned us that it's powerful enough to deglove someone. (Look up deglove! Actually, on second thought, you might not want to do that!) After this drill the rest of the day was quiet.

After dinner I visited Engine 7 and Truck 58's quarters. I was the captain of the truck there for a few years and knew everyone on shift. We had a few laughs over coffee before I headed back to quarters. It was still early so I decided to make one more stop at Engine 106 to see Lt. Adam Volkmann. Adam was my old partner back when I was the captain of Engine 42 downtown. Same deal here, we had a few laughs and did some catching up. I wasn't there long when at about 9:00 p.m., our conversation was interrupted by a radio transmission indicating that a fire was about to be reported. The southside fire alarm office called over the air, "Englewood to Battalion 16 and all companies responding to the approximate address of 4000 S. Pulaski, we're getting a lot of calls on this. People are calling from the Stevenson expressway reporting a large volume of fire just south of the expressway near Pulaski."

We listened intently as the first companies arriving on the scene reported, "Office, we're up on the bridge at Pulaski. We have a fire, but we can't make access from here. We're gonna have to find another way in. We got the train yard on one side and the expressway on the other." The alarm office replied, "We're looking at maps up here. It looks like you're gonna have to go back to Kedzie and go west on 38TH street." Battalion 16 was first to report in front of the building. "Battalion 16 to Englewood, I have a 2-story ordinary constructed factory building with fire going through the roof. This is an emergency, gimme a box."

In anticipation of the fire being escalated to a 2-11 alarm, I said goodbye to the guys at Engine 106 and began heading south. 5-1-5, Special Ops takes in all 2-11's within the city limits.

"2-11 ALARM FIRE"

I didn't even make it five blocks to the Kennedy Expressway when the following radio transmission from Battalion 16 came over the air, "Emergency. Emergency. Emergency. This building is totally involved, and we have no hydrants near the fire. Give me a 2-11...and also give me a Level 1 Hazmat response. There are known chemicals in this building." Battalion 16's next transmission followed quickly, "Battalion 16 to Englewood, start in the hose wagon and the auxiliary snorkel too." The hose wagon is another Special Operations rig. It carries over a quarter mile of large diameter hose and is used to supply water long distances. The snorkel would be used to apply water down in through the already collapsed roof. As I came down the ramp from the Dan Ryan onto the Stevenson expressway, I could see the glow of the fire from as far east as

Ashland Ave., about three miles away. I knew this was going to be a long night.

Following the directions given earlier over the radio, I took Kedzie south and drove in west on 38TH. As I got closer, I could see the flames were twice as high as the roof and I could hear the Fireground radio transmissions indicating that getting water to the fire was going to be an issue. I parked my buggy and reported via radio that I was on the scene. No sooner than I reported, Deputy District Chief Bob Hagen came over the radio and gave me the assignment of Water Officer. My job was then to locate hydrants in the area and oversee in-line operations.

The objective of an in-line operation is to get water from a far away working hydrant, under correct workable pressure, to a master stream nozzle near the fire. In this case, the master stream was a snorkel. Using this incident as an example here is how the set-up works:

- The snorkel is set up in front of the fire building.
- Engine A backs up to the snorkel and drops one end of a large diameter supply hose.
- Engine A then drives slowly, with the hose flaking off the rear bed, in the direction of a hydrant that has been identified as "working."
- When Engine A has dropped all their large supply hose, it stops.
- Engine B then drops its large supply line to Engine A and drives off in the same manner.
- This continues until one engine (in this case Engine C) reaches the "working" hydrant and connects to it.

- When all engines and the snorkel are connected, Engine C will start flowing water at a very low pressure to Engine B, then B to A and A to the snorkel.
- When there is water flowing from the nozzle on the snorkel all engines in line will slowly, and in coordination, increase their pressure until a pre-determined nozzle pressure is reached.
- In order to overcome friction loss in the hose, and to prevent damage to fire pumps, it is important that each engine is operating within a pre-determined discharge pressure range.

Things can get sort of chaotic during the initial phases of an operation like this, and they did. Just as I located a good working hydrant, my assignment was modified. I was now ordered to make my way around the railroad yard to 40TH and Pulaski to assist Battalion 2, Chief Stan Saganowski, in setting up an in-line operation through the opposite side of the rail yard. I walked about a block back to my buggy then drove about a mile around the rail yard to get where Battalion 2 was.

While driving to my new assignment, I heard Deputy Fire Commissioner Glenn Dempsey on the radio directing engines to 41ST and Pulaski. From what I heard it was apparent that Chief Dempsey knew the area well. I soon found out he did. About three years ago he was in charge of a fire right next door to this address and remembered how to get water back to where we needed it.

As I pulled up to 41ST Street, Chief Dempsey gave me my assignment, "Kev, take this street to the end then go left through the train yard. Check on Engine 88, they said they found a hydrant back there. See if it's usable. Also get Engine

25 connected to that hydrant they're parked next to. They're gonna be the first engine in line."

On the way down the street, I passed Engine 25 and told them to start connecting their hard suction hose to the hydrant. I then proceeded down the street to find that the hydrant Engine 88 found was in fact usable, meaning that we would be implementing two in-line operations. I radioed this information back to Battalion 2 who then had 88 pull a line to Engine 127 who was in turn feeding a Tower Ladder in front of the fire building. (88 and 127 were going "in-line to the Tower Ladder.") When I drove back to Engine 25, I found them struggling to connect their hard suction hose to the hydrant. (Making a hard suction connection can be difficult. The hard suction hose itself is 6" in diameter by 10' long and is very rigid and heavy. Two of these pieces must be connected together, and then attached to the hydrant on one end, and a pumper on the other. It doesn't bend easily and usually takes four to five firefighters to get the job done.)

After a minute of watching them struggle, I asked one of the young firefighters to let me have a try at it. He did, and after a couple of attempts we were able to get the suction hose connected to the hydrant. Also, while working on this with Engine 25, I noticed that they had not yet connected the required gate valve to the hydrant. "Hey, make sure you put your gate valve on that hydrant before we start sending water," I directed before walking back to my buggy to put on my gear.

When I returned, I found that the gate valve was still not on the hydrant. I called over to the officer and told him to see to it that a gate valve was put on that hydrant NOW. It then occurred to me that when I first gave the order to the young firefighter I was dressed in a blue sweatshirt and didn't have my white helmet on. He probably didn't see my buggy parked in front of his engine and wasn't expecting a chief to help connect hose to a hydrant. Maybe he didn't hear me, or maybe because I wasn't dressed like a chief, he wasn't okay with taking an order from "some other firefighter." Whatever .... the gate valve was put on the hydrant.

With Engine 25 now ready to go, I jumped in my buggy and drove back to meet Battalion 2. After a brief discussion, we opted to have the hose wagon back up to Engine 25 at the hydrant and drop their hose from there to Engine 109 (over three blocks), then from Engine 109 to Engine 43, then a short distance to the auxiliary snorkel. When everything was hooked up and ready to go the order was given to "send the water." We all watched as the hose began to fill. Water was being sent all the way from 41ST and Springfield to 38TH street and then to the nozzle on the snorkel basket.

After about ten minutes Chief Saganowski informed me of a problem. "Hey Kevin, we're not getting any pressure at the snorkel's nozzle. 109 and 43 are telling me that they're getting 0 psi on their intake gauges. Go see what's goin on down there."

Driving back towards the hydrant I first confirmed that both 109's and 43's intake gauges were reading zero. I then made my way back to Engine 25 at the hydrant. As I got close, I saw the engineer of Engine 38, who was previously standing by without an assignment, walking away from Engine 25. I then heard a radio transmission say that the issue was found, and that the in-line operation was now ready to go. It appeared to me that the engineer of 38 must have heard there was a problem and went over to Engine 25 to see if he could help. As I pulled up, I yelled to him from my buggy, "What was the problem?" "It's all good chief." he replied. "What was the problem?" I asked again. His reply again was, "We're all good." At this point I presumed that the engineer from 38 did some troubleshooting and found the problem but humbly didn't want to upstage anyone. That was good enough for me. I then radioed back to Chief Saganowski telling him we were ready to pump water.

At fires of this magnitude, once things are set up and working, we transition to "surround and drown" mode. Some of us call these "reunion fires." With water being applied by large appliances the need for manpower is not as great. Some firefighters man the appliances and some supervise, while others are kind of free to walk around and talk with people they haven't seen for a while.

In my sector, 2 snorkels and 2 tower ladders were now pouring water into the building from where the roof used to be. This was a good time to grab a cup of coffee and a granola bar from the Salvation Army canteen. (The Salvation Army canteen is a truck manned by volunteers. They respond to extra alarm fires and other long-term emergency incidents where they provide first responders with drinks and light snacks. Their service is really appreciated, especially on those extremely hot days and long cold nights.)

In front of the canteen truck, a couple of my bosses and I were discussing the early part of the operation when Bill Ripken, the captain of 5-1-1, our Hazmat Team, came over. Earlier, because there were supposedly chemicals in this building, Bill was given the task of testing the water from our fire hoses that was overflowing out of the structure. 5-1-1 has a mini lab on board their rig. I don't recall the exact names of the chemicals but what I do remember is Captain Ripken reporting that their IDHL (Immediately Dangerous to Life and Health) numbers were on the moderate to high side. With that information a radio announcement was made ordering all companies operating near the fire building to continue wearing their air masks. No one at the scene reported illness or required medical attention.

Surprisingly the fire was struck out or "under control" fairly quickly at about 11:30 p.m. I was released at 1:00 a.m. but most companies remained on the scene pouring water on the structure until the next morning. On the way back to quarters I stopped for fuel and was in bed by 2:30 a.m. My alarm clock woke me at 5:00 a.m....YES! 2 ½ hours of sleep...IN A ROW!!

Due to the continued manpower shortage, I had not had a Daley Day (five days in a row off) in quite a while. My first Daley Day in months began when I left the firehouse this morning.

03/25/15
ASSIGNMENT—BATTALION 23 (ENGINE 72'S QUARTERS, 79TH AND STONY ISLAND)
PRIMARY RESPONSE AREA—SOUTHEAST SIDE
WEATHER—TEMPERATURES IN THE LOW 40S

My assignment for the day was Battalion 23. After not having a Daley in months, the past five days off felt like an extended vacation. Feeling refreshed, I reported for work early and ready to go. Battalion 23 is quartered with Engine 72 and Tower Ladder 34 near 79TH and Stony Island. It's one of the busiest firehouses in Chicago.

An old friend of mine, Joe Moretti, was on duty as the captain of Tower Ladder 34. Joe and I go way back to 1985. He, several others, and I worked out together for the physical exam to come on the job. Joe is a lot of fun and I was looking forward to working with him for the next 24 hours.

The day and evening parts of my shift were pretty ordinary.

I had about five runs, all of them false alarms. Two of the five calls were an overheated self-cleaning oven and someone cooking bacon that set off a smoke alarm in a high-rise.

I got into bed at about 10:30 p.m., just as Engine 72 and Tower Ladder 34 were dispatched from quarters to a Gas Leak Investigation on the street at 80TH and Crandon.

(From my experiences over the years, I've found that many gas leaks reported "on the street" around this time of the night tend to be false. I've had many runs where people walking their dogs or walking home from work will catch a whiff of gas and call it in. It's kind of complicated but there is a correlation between outside temperature inversions, cool calm nighttime air and the smell of gas. Basically, on clear cool nights with high pressure a natural gas odor can be prevalent. Let's just leave it at that. Regardless, our response doesn't change. We treat every run as confirmed until we can determine otherwise. When we arrive on the scene, we check the area with our meters and noses, and more often than not these runs are classified as "a mistaken citizen.")

Before turning out the lights I put my radio on low and waited to hear Engine 72 and the Tower report on the scene.

About a minute after pulling out of quarters Tower 34 reported, "Tower 34 to Englewood we're on the scene. We have a large gas leak in the street. Give me a Level I Hazmat Response. We're gonna assist the people who are self-evacuating from an apartment building on the corner of 80TH and Crandon. Also be aware that this incident is kitty corner from a hospital." I jumped out of bed immediately and threw on my jacket. As I was heading downstairs to my buggy, the alarm dispatch terminal in our firehouse sounded sending Ambulance 22 and me to the scene of the Level I Hazmat. While en route, the fire alarm office announced over the radio, "Companies on the Level I Hazmat at 80TH and Crandon, the wind direction is out of the west." On all Hazardous Material runs, the wind direction is given to responding companies so that they can approach from, and set a staging area, upwind from the incident.

"LEVEL I HAZMAT–GAS LEAK"

Upon my arrival I parked my buggy about a block away near 79TH and Crandon and reported to the alarm office,

"Battalion 23 is on the scene at 80TH and Crandon. Set the Staging Area at 79TH and Paxton. I'll get back to you in a second."

As soon as Joe heard me report on the scene, he called me on the Fireground radio frequency.

"Tower 34 to Battalion 23, we have a large flow of natural gas coming out of a construction hole at the intersection of 80TH and Crandon. We got the police helping us evacuate two apartment buildings downwind and we're blocking off the area...Kev, you got my message about this being next to the hospital, right?"

"Battalion 23 to Tower 34, yeah, I got it. I'm walking down now, where are you?"

"I'm at 80TH and Crandon by the giant dust cloud."

As I walked quickly down the street I began my initial size-up. From almost a block away I could see the dust cloud that Joe described and could hear the loud hissing sound of escaping gas. As I got closer, I saw that the hole from where the gas was leaking was covered with large steel plates. In each of the plates were a couple of holes about three to four inches in diameter. These holes are used by heavy equipment to grab and move the plates during normal use. The leak under the steel was so great that it was pushing through the small holes, kicking up and blowing dust into the air about 20'. What also caught my eye were two vehicles parked near the hole, not at the curb but in the street as if they were driving by and stopped. Neither of the vehicles was running or occupied. Still surveying the scene, I set my sights on potential exposure problems. Across the street and downwind was a 3-story apartment building about 100' by 100' with a light wind blowing in its direction. Next to the 3-story was a bungalow and next to that was another apartment building. Behind me on the southwest corner was a hospital. With this initial size-up I gave my first progress report to the alarm office, "Battalion 23 to Englewood. I've got a large natural gas leak in the street from a construction hole. We're in the process of evacuating several buildings downwind."

After another review and quick processing of all the information in my mind, I began setting things up.

"Battalion 23 to Engine 72, come around the block and back down 80TH from Luella. Only back down halfway and lead out from there to 80TH and Crandon. Charge your line and stand by."

This would put them upwind of the leak and in position with a charged line in front of the hospital. I had them back down only halfway because I didn't want any running vehicles near the site. "Battalion 23 to Tower 34, send a couple of your crew into the hospital emergency room with a meter and see if you're getting anything. Battalion 23 to Squad 5, get me some readings at street level on the downwind side." In less than a minute both companies reported back that they were not getting any readings on their meters.

(Natural gas is lighter than air and dissipates rapidly when a leak is outside. My thought was that even though there was a large amount of gas escaping, it was blowing high enough and strong enough into the air and far enough away from any buildings that the chance of an inadvertent ignition was minimal. But you never know.)

While Joe's crew took readings in the street, the lieutenant of Squad 5, Reggie Boyko, walked over to where I was standing and said, "Hey Kev, you know that sometimes these gas leaks travel through the sewer lines and into surrounding houses. You want us to check on that?" "Yeah, good idea, lemme know what you find," I replied. Reggie then directed his crew to take readings in several street sewers near the scene.

My next progress report was, "Battalion 23 to Englewood, the gas is still flowing. I have the area cordoned off. 72 is standing by with a charged line. We're not getting any readings downwind or in the hospital."

"Message received Battalion 23."

"Battalion 23 to Englewood, get me an ETA on the gas company and also start in a warming bus for the people we evacuated. Have the bus respond to 79TH and Crandon."

"Message received Battalion 23."

I then told Ambulance 22 to grab their gear and go to the corner and let me know when the bus got there. Their job would be tending to the evacuated residents.

At this point I was only on scene for about 5 minutes and just getting ready to escalate the alarm to a Level II Hazmat when I saw a gas company representative on the scene. Sometimes these leaks can be stopped with a few turns of a nearby valve, so I held off on pulling the Level II. The gas company worker was an older looking man wearing a white helmet. He was carrying a long hook tool and walking quickly across the street from where we were standing. His mannerisms projected a sense of confidence and focus as he removed a manhole cover across the intersection from the leak and began to climb down. My first thought was to get some info from him and an estimate on how long it would take to get the gas shut down, but as I approached, he sternly waved me off saying, "Gimme a second!" His white helmet, that of a supervisor, and his apparent age told me that this guy knew what he was doing so I backed off and watched as he descended below street level. At this point Reggie, the officer of Squad 5, came over and we both shined our flashlights to help the gas company guy see as he climbed down a ladder affixed to the walls of the manhole. When he reached the bottom, he immediately began turning a steering wheel type valve. After about what seemed like twenty deliberate and very strenuous turns, the leak from the hole in the street began to subside.

With this, I radioed in another progress report, "Battalion 23 to Englewood, a supervisor from the gas company is on the scene, in a nearby manhole and working on shutting the gas down now."

Just as I released the talk button on my radio, two more gas company workers arrived, raced to the hole, and yelled down, "Whaddya need?" Climbing up the ladder and looking very spent, the supervisor guy yelled back to them, "There's another shut-off across the street! Get that one!"

The second two guys immediately ran across the street and removed the sewer lid. While one quickly climbed down the ladder into the hole, the other held a flashlight from above.

Now out of the hole, the man in the white helmet reported to me that the leaking main was 24 inches in diameter and was at 20 pounds of pressure. (As a comparison, the gas that comes into your house is only ¼ pound.) He also said there were two more valves in the area that needed to be closed and his crews were working on that now. "We should have this shut down completely in about five minutes," he added. I relayed his information to the alarm office and told them we would be continuing to monitor explosive readings on the street and in the sewers and that all companies on the scene were standing by.

Almost exactly five minutes later there was a second noticeable reduction in escaping gas. A minute after that, silence. With a nod from the gas guy in the white helmet, I radioed another report to the alarm office, "Battalion 23 to Englewood, the gas is shut down. We're going to continue to take readings in the area. All companies are standing by. You can secure the Level I on my orders."

About 30 minutes later companies reported to me that all meter readings were at zero and all evacuated residents were back in their homes. We were done! Well, there was one thing left that I needed an answer to. What was the deal with the two cars parked next to the hole? As the remaining crews on scene were helping Engine 72 bed their hose, I walked over and asked randomly, "Hey, did any of you find out what those two cars were doing parked by the hole?" One of the firefighters who had been questioning witnesses earlier said he was told both cars belonged to women who were on their way to work at the hospital across the street. Not realizing there was a gas leak in her path, the lady in the first car tried to go around the hole. The escaping gas was apparently strong enough to deplete the airflow into her engine and shut down her motor. I've never heard of this before but, hey, I guess anything's possible. The driver of the second car smelled the gas and bailed out.

With all companies finally picked up, I took one last look around the scene and saw the older gas company guy with the white helmet talking to a couple of his co-workers. I walked over, introduced myself, and complimented them on their work.

"Nice job guys. I was really glad when I saw you on the scene so fast."

"Yeah, thanks," said one of the workers. Then, pointing at the guy in the white helmet he added, "This guy's gonna have a story to tell about his last day on the gas company."

"What?" I replied as I turned to the supervisor.

"Yeah, in about two hours I'm gonna be retired!" he laughed.

With that I shook his hand, thanked him again for his help and congratulated him on his retirement. Man, I hope I have the same gusto as this guy on my last day.

> 03/28/15
> ASSIGNMENT—BATTALION 23 (ENGINE 72'S QUARTERS, 79TH AND STONY ISLAND)
> PRIMARY RESPONSE AREA—SOUTHEAST SIDE
> WEATHER—TEMPERATURES IN THE HIGH 20S

Another day in the 23RD Battalion.

While doing my morning rounds, I noticed a large group of police vehicles and a small crowd at the corner of 88TH and Cottage Grove. It didn't appear that there was any urgency at the scene, so I didn't stop. Later that day I read the following report online of what happened just one hour before I passed by.

> *"Saturday morning, a 26-year-old man was shot in the 8800 block of South Cottage Grove Avenue in the city's Chatham neighborhood, police said. Officers responded to the scene*

about 9:15 a.m. and found the 26-year-old man with a gunshot wound to the head."—Chicago Tribune

My day was pretty uneventful. At about 8:00 p.m. I had a run for a fire in an alley garage that turned out to be only a garbage can next to the garage. Most of the fire was out by the time we arrived. Companies used a couple of hand pumps and a neighbor's garden hose to extinguish what was left of the fire. Just as we were getting ready to leave the scene, we were dispatched via radio to another alley garage fire about three blocks away. I was first on the scene at the second run and found several tires burning inside a frame garage with no overhead door. The first engine pulled up right behind me. Their crew was able to pull the burning tires into the alley and extinguish them before they got the garage going.

A few more false alarms throughout the night and my shift was over.

The following morning before going home, I read online about a separate shooting that occurred in the same area only a day earlier than the one I saw while doing my rounds. This incident and the one I came across at the start of my shift, are sad reminders of just how many bullets are flying around this city, many of them in the 23RD Battalion.

APRIL 2015

04/03/15
Assignment—Battalion 14 (Engine 109's Quarters, 22nd & Kedzie)
Primary Response Area—Westside, Little Village
Weather—Temperatures in the high 40s

Nothing too unusual today, only two runs.

"STILL ALARM"

About 6:00 a.m. just after reporting for work, the computer dispatch tones went off and everyone in quarters was sent to a Still Alarm at an address that was just a few blocks west of our firehouse. Engine 109, Truck 32 and I arrived first and reported "nothing showing" on a 3-story brick apartment building. As we exited our rigs, we were approached by a man who told us, "I was sleeping and I heard a smoke alarm going off in the apartment above me. I went into the hall and smelled smoke and heard people coughing so I called 911. I heard the people from that apartment coming home around 4:30 this morning. I knocked on their door, but nobody answered."

I waited outside with the tenant while Engine 109 and Truck 32 went to the third floor to check this out. Seconds later the captain of Engine 109 radioed down, "Hey Chief, we don't smell anything up here or hear a smoke alarm. We're knocking on the door now and there's no answer." After about a minute or two the captain radioed back a second time, "Chief, there's still no answer. Whaddya want us to do?" Before taking any further action, I turned to the tenant and asked, "Are you absolutely sure that you heard the alarm, people coughing and smelled smoke?" "Yes," he answered.

"Battalion 14 to 109, go ahead and force entry but try to do as little damage as possible."

"109, message received."

Seconds later 109 reported back, "Chief, we're in the apartment. The smoke smell is weed and incense. We got four people sleeping in the living room that have no idea we're even in here. We're stepping over them."

"All right, wake 'em up and see if they're okay and open up some windows. The police are here and on their way up to do the damage report on the door. They said they'll handle it from here."

"Battalion 14 to Main, Mistaken Citizen, we're all in service returning to quarters."

"STILL ALARM"

Just before lunch I was heading back to quarters when I was sent, via radio, to a Still Alarm for a house fire. I confirmed receipt of the run and told the alarm office to notify companies that I was responding from a distance. About a minute after I was dispatched, Engine 107 reported on the scene with "light smoke showing." Their follow-up report came quickly, "Engine 107 to Main, hold up the second companies but let the chief come in. We had rubbish in a closet. We got it with hand pumps. Truck 32 is with us."

I arrived several minutes later and was briefed by the officer of Engine 107. He reported that on his arrival he saw light smoke coming out of the front door and a woman with several kids on the front porch. Pointing inside the door, the woman directed them to a first-floor bedroom where they found some paper on fire and some clothing smoldering in a closet. Using their hand pump they extinguished the fire, bundled up the remains and took it to the backyard where they were now soaking it with a garden hose. He also added that, because his thermal imaging camera was showing elevated heat levels around the light fixture in the closet, he had Truck 32 open the ceiling and walls around it to check for fire, but it was clear. "Okay," I said, "let's have a look." I entered the bedroom to find heavy soot on the walls but the fire itself had been contained to the closet. I also saw that Truck 32 had their ventilation fan in the window and were cleaning up the wet lath and plaster on the floor.

With the apartment now well ventilated, I told the woman and children out front to come back inside and have a seat in the living room. It was kind of cold out and none of them were wearing jackets. Even with all the doors and windows open the apartment was warmer than the front porch. In an attempt to determine the cause of the fire, I began interviewing the woman who identified herself as the grandmother of the six children. She told me she was in the living room when she thought she smelled smoke and immediately went to check on the children who were playing in the bedroom. When she opened the door to the room, she saw a haze of smoke and two of the older children trying to open a window. She then entered the room and said she saw flames in the closet near the light bulb on the ceiling. She immediately got all the kids out and called 911.

Because young children were involved, and because of the possibility of them starting the fire, I had to notify our Office of Fire Investigation. When the investigators arrived, I filled them in on the grandmother's story then watched as the investigator professionally and calmly questioned the children. After about ten minutes the youngest child innocently and remorsefully admitted to putting a shirt over the light bulb in the closet to see the light change colors. He explained that he'd seen the older kids put a blue shirt over the bulb to see the light turn blue and a green shirt to see it turn green, so he tried it. OFI determined the cause of the fire was "accidental."

Before leaving, the investigators and I gave a quick lecture to the children and grandmother on fire safety and the importance of smoke alarms. The grandmother then walked us to the door and graciously thanked us for our quick response, our cleanup of the scene and for speaking with the kids.

"Battalion 14 to Main, I'm in service returning to quarters."

> 04/06/15—04/09/15—04/12/15
> ASSIGNMENT—BATTALION 22 (ENGINE 62's QUARTERS, 114TH & STATE)
> PRIMARY RESPONSE AREA– FAR SOUTH, ROSELAND, PULLMAN
> WEATHER—TEMPERATURES IN THE HIGH 40S

Battalion 22 is located in the Roseland area of Chicago. In the 1950's and 60's Roseland, and the neighboring Pullman area, were heavily populated with middle class blue-collar workers employed by steel mills to the east, a very large paint factory and The Pullman Car Company. (Side Note: In 1962 the rock band Styx was formed in Roseland.) Today, much of Roseland and its surrounding areas are full of abandoned buildings, vacant lots and burned-out storefronts. There are also many street gangs around and it's not uncommon for Engine 62 and Truck 27 to respond to "gunshot victim" calls.

The chiefs in the 22ND battalion aren't the busiest as far as the number of runs. However, they have what I call a high "run to fire" ratio. Basically, Battalion 22 does not respond to a lot of the more common false alarm runs like Check the Box, or Automatic Alarm in a High-Rise. When the 22ND battalion goes out the door on a Still Alarm, there's a very good chance it will be an actual structure fire.

My three successive workdays in the 22nd, however, were slow and uneventful.

04/18/15
Assignment—5-1-5 (Special Operations—Engine 5's Quarters, DesPlaines & Jackson)
Primary Response Area—City Wide
Weather—Temperatures in the mid 60s

"CAR INTO THE BUILDING"

At around 9:00 a.m. I was dispatched to a Car into the Building on the far southwest side. I didn't make it in. The first arriving chief held all companies.

"PERSON IN THE WATER"

Sometime mid-morning I responded to a Person in the Water at 2700 S. Damen. The first arriving companies positioned themselves on the Damen Ave. bridge over the Chicago River and reported a body floating face down in the water below.

This was not going to be a rescue. It would be a recovery and possible crime scene. Our primary objective was to figure out a way to gain access to the shoreline below the bridge and secure the body so that it wouldn't float away. Police divers would make the removal.

A few minutes after I arrived, one of the fire companies on scene reported finding a large gate and gravel path leading to the area we needed to access. After they cut the lock on the gate, I walked down to the riverbank with my boss, Deputy District Chief Andy Bajorek and the CFD Dive team (6-8-7). Surveying the scene, we found the victim tangled in some weeds near the shore and secure enough so he wouldn't float away. Not wanting to disturb what might possibly be a crime scene, we decided to stand by and wait for the police.

When CPD arrived we briefed them on what we found and turned the scene over to them. While speaking with the police, a call came over our fire department radios for a Still & Box in a High-Rise downtown. Chief Bajorek and I jumped in our buggies and responded. Our dive team stayed behind with the police.

"STILL AND BOX IN A HIGH-RISE"

The fire turned out to be some overheated electrical equipment in the basement of a high-rise building. It was contained and extinguished quickly. However, a large volume of smoke made its way into the first-floor atrium and several floors above. My assignment was to meet Battalion 2 in the basement and assist in figuring out a way to get the smoke up and out of the building. We decided to use 9-2-3, our Mobile Ventilation Unit.

The MVU is a small truck equipped with a very large,

mounted fan that is capable of creating hurricane force winds of around 85mph. Often mistaken for a Smoke Ejector, a unit that "sucks" smoke out, the MVU operates on a different principal, positive pressure. Using the MVU a high-pressure wind is blown into a structure at one location and vented at another. By opening and closing doors and windows within the structure smoke can be "channeled" out via a chosen opening. Think of blowing into a straw full of holes. A lot of the pressure is dissipated because of the many openings. Now consider blowing into a straw of the same length with only one opening at the opposite end. The force at the exhaust end is greater and much more efficient. The MVU can also be used to ventilate buildings of carbon monoxide and other dangerous elements.

After surveying the areas of the basement and first floor where smoke was still lingering, we devised a plan that would have the MVU blow into the front doors of the atrium and exhaust out a basement door to the alley. When the radio announcement was made confirming that our path was set up and ready to go, the order was given to start the fan. After about ten minutes, companies in the basement began reporting that the smoke was starting to move. Twenty minutes later the basement was clear.

All three of my runs for the day happened before noon. The rest of the day and night were quiet.

> 04/24/15
> ASSIGNMENT—BATTALION 11 (ENGINE 119's QUARTERS, AVONDALE & HARLEM)
> PRIMARY RESPONSE AREA—NORTHWEST SIDE
> WEATHER—TEMPERATURES IN THE MID 40S

Slow day.

04/27/15
Assignment—Battalion 12 (Engine 57's Quarters, Division and Western)
Primary Response Area—Humboldt Park, Logan Square
Weather—Temperatures in the low 50s

Normally a Working Fire response is not dispatched until a fire company or chief officer reports on the scene with a fire. One exception is when the fire alarm office gets numerous calls at one time for the same address. In addition to the original still alarm companies, a Working Fire response adds a Squad, Command Van and Rapid Intervention Team (RIT). The RIT's job is not to fight the fire but to standby ready to go to work in case a firefighter gets in trouble and calls a Mayday. If a Mayday is called, it's the RIT's duty to locate and remove the firefighter.

"RIT"

Shortly after lunch I was dispatched from quarters to a Working Fire at Chicago and Harding. The dispatch of a Working Fire Response was an indication that the fire alarm office must be getting a lot of calls on this. Pulling out of quarters, I received my assignment.

"Battalion 12 you're gonna be RIT with Truck 36."

"Battalion 12 RIT. Message received."

As I turned west on Chicago Ave. from Western, I could see a large volume of black smoke in the sky up ahead. I was about a mile away when Battalion 13 arrived on the scene and gave his report, "Battalion 13 to Main, I'm on the scene at Chicago and Harding. I have heavy fire in a 3-story ordinary constructed building. Gimme a box and make the staging area

Chicago west of Pulaski." Upon my arrival I parked my buggy about a block east of the fire and got dressed. Once in my turnout gear, I grabbed my flashlight and walked to the front of the fire building where I met up with Jerry Dawson, the officer of Truck 36.

Per department protocol, as the RIT officers, Jerry and I walked around the entire structure while his crew stood by near the front of the building. Our objective was to take note of doors, windows and hazards that might help or hinder our RIT operations in the event a Mayday was called. When we got to the rear of the building, we noticed smoke pushing out of two boarded up basement windows. We also saw the hydrant man from Engine 95, by himself, dragging a 2 ½" line down the middle of Harding toward the fire building. "Kev!" Jerry yelled to me, "I'm gonna give 'em a hand." "Okay, why don't you have him bring that line here. We'll help him strap it to this tree," I yelled back. Together the three of us got the hoseline set up and secured to the tree so that the one firefighter could manage the high-pressure line by himself. Jerry and I then continued our survey of the fire building.

Walking towards a gangway that led back to the street, I was hit by a spray of water. The stream that just soaked me had come from inside the fire building on the first floor where an engine company was operating. Looking at the structure from the alley, I was able to see something the crew inside couldn't. From my vantage point, I saw not only the entire back porches totally involved, but also a heavy volume of fire consuming the entire room directly next to them. Taking into consideration the smoke pushing from the basement windows and the heavy volume of fire in the rear, my concern was that more fire was under them, in the basement, causing structural damage. I immediately grabbed my radio microphone,

"Battalion 12 to the engine company working on the first floor, BACK OUT!" Unfortunately, radio traffic on the scene was so heavy that my message kept getting cut out. Standing in the backyard, I began waving my arms and yelling, "BACK OUT! BACK OUT NOW!" But they couldn't hear me.

I had to get their attention somehow. "95," I yelled to the firefighter holding the hose in the alley, "knock down some of that fire, then splash some water at those guys on the first floor!" (Getting hit with a hoseline always gets your attention, as it did mine a few seconds earlier.) Jerry had rejoined the firefighter in the alley and was now helping him manage the line. He knew what I was thinking: as soon as those guys inside get hit with a stream of water, one of them is going to come to the window and start yelling for us to stop. The firefighter in the alley immediately directed his hose stream onto the burning back porches and simultaneously splashed water into the first-floor window at the crew inside. Sure enough, as soon as they got hit with the spray of water, one of the firefighters inside poked his head out of the window. Before he could start cussing me out, I yelled to him, "GET EVERYBODY OUT OF THERE NOW." No sooner than I communicated my message to him, a loud series of short air horn blasts began to sound around the entire building. This is the signal for emergency evacuation. It means "all firefighters GET OUT immediately!" The evacuation order was given by the Incident Commander out front who then escalated the alarm to a 2-11. Heeding my warning, and hearing the sound of the air horn blasts, the crew quickly backed out of the building. With the evacuation order given, this meant we were going defensive.

Now, for the time being, the possibility of a firefighter being lost or trapped inside was not a concern. Jerry and I still reported what we found in our RIT survey to his crew. Doing this ensured they would be ready in the event another company might later be ordered to re-enter the building to completely extinguish any hot spots.

For the next three hours, companies poured water on the fire from the outside until it was completely extinguished. In the end, no firefighters re-entered the building.

No more runs for the rest of the shift.

MAY 2015

05/03/15
ASSIGNMENT—BATTALION 16 (ENGINE 127'S QUARTERS, 63RD & LARAMIE)
PRIMARY RESPONSE AREA– MIDWAY AIRPORT, SOUTHWEST SIDE
WEATHER—TEMPERATURES IN THE LOW 70S

"STILL ALARM–ALLEY GARAGE"

About 2:00 p.m. I was dispatched to a Still Alarm for an alley garage. While en route I heard the first engine report on the scene with a garage fire. As I pulled up, I looked down the alley from the cross street and saw my first engine, Engine 34, in the alley working their rubbish line on what appeared to be a small amount of fire on the exterior of a garage. I immediately got on the radio and had my second engine, Engine 88, go to the street address out front and secure a hydrant.

When I got down the alley, I saw the melted remains of a large plastic garbage container right up against the corner of a 20'x 20' wood frame garage. Damage to the structure's siding and roof was moderate. At this point Engine 34 already had the fire pretty much out and was starting to wash down the exterior while Tower 54 worked on opening the overhead door.

"Engine 88 to Battalion 16, we're out front and hooked to a hydrant. You want us to lead out?"

"No, 88, just stand by for now," I replied.

A few minutes later Tower 54's crew rolled open the overhead door. Now, visible through a haze of smoke, was the interior of a garage filled from top to bottom with a very large amount of smoldering trash. The fire, that originally started in a garbage container next to the garage in the alley, made its way up the siding, through the eaves, and into the attic where it ignited mounds of paper, cardboard and rags stored inside. Even though the fire was "out," we still needed to overhaul, which meant all that rubbish in the garage had to be pulled out and washed down thoroughly so it wouldn't reignite after we left. Everyone knew immediately that what remained of the 500 gallons of water in the engine's tank wasn't going to be enough to finish washing this down. So, since this was going to be only a clean-up job, I had two options. I could let Engine 34 handle it or I could have Engine 88 drive around to the alley and use their tank water. I wasn't too keen on using 88 because if I did, I'd have two engines in the same area with empty tanks, at least for a little while. Also, 88 is an Advanced Life Support (ALS) engine, and I preferred getting them back in service ASAP.

"Battalion 16 to Engine 88, we're good. You can pick up and get back in service."

As expected, only a few minutes later Engine 34 ran out of tank water. After a resourceful attempt to finish the job using a neighbor's garden hose proved to be too much, the officer had his crew disconnect their hoseline, drive around to the street, hook up to a hydrant, refill the tank, and return to the alley to complete the wash down.

After dinner I did one of my evening visits at 34's house.

Over coffee, the engine officer and I had a chat about garage fires and how you never know what you'll find.

> 05/09/15
> ASSIGNMENT—5-1-5 (SPECIAL OPERATIONS—ENGINE 5'S QUARTERS, DESPLAINES & JACKSON)
> PRIMARY RESPONSE AREA—CITY WIDE
> WEATHER—TEMPERATURES IN THE MID 60S

At 10:00 a.m., after completing my morning administrative duties, I drove over to Monroe Harbor for a drill with our SCUBA team, Engine 13, Truck 6 and Battalion 1. The drill was on tossing a rescue "rope bag" to a drowning victim. One of the divers, dressed in full SCUBA gear, floated around in the water about twenty feet offshore while we all took turns tossing the rope bag to him. It's not as easy as it may sound. Trying to judge distance while looking out from the shore at Lake Michigan and attempting to hit a target that is bobbing up and down in the waves, can be a little tricky. Everyone took a turn at this carnival game until he or she was able to get the bag to the diver. The second part of our drill was a refresher on the basic duties of land companies at water rescue incidents. Topics covered included helicopter landing assistance, locating access points to waterways, determining a credible "last seen point," getting a ladder into the water and other tasks necessary to get a scene ready for responding divers. The drill lasted about 90 minutes.

The rest of the day was pretty uneventful...until the middle of the night.

"PERSON IN THE WATER"

About 3:45 a.m. I was dispatched to a "Person in the Water" at the Wells Street Bridge and the Chicago River. While I was en route Battalion 1 reported on the scene,

"Battalion 1 to Main, I'm on the scene with 42, Truck 3, Squad 1 and 6-8-7. We don't see anything. Do you have any more information on this?"

"Main to Battalion 1, the caller said he saw two people jump into the river from the Wells St. Bridge and didn't see them come out. That's all we have."

"Battalion 1 to Main, call that guy back and have him come out to the bridge so he can show us exactly where they went in."

When I arrived minutes later, I saw the fire companies and a few civilians on the Wells Street bridge looking and pointing west. I communicated my arrival to Battalion 1,

"5-1-5 to Battalion 1, I'm on the scene. I'm gonna go over to Orleans St. to see if I can see anything from there."

"Okay, 5-1-5, lemme know what you find."

When I got to the Orleans St. Bridge, I took a position on the north end and began scouring the water and shoreline with my flashlight. The CPD Marine Unit and the CFD Fast Boat had also just arrived and were checking the area using their thermal imaging cameras (TIC) and forward-looking infrared (FLIR) cameras. A few minutes later the CFD helicopter, 6-8-1, arrived and was hovering above using their high-powered spotlight to assist in the search. The light worked well but the noise and wind created by the helicopter's rotors was quickly becoming a hindrance. Knowing that our dive team and squad were on the scene suited up and ready to go into the water, I figured we wouldn't need the helicopter's two divers. Before I had a chance to call them on the radio, the helicopter called me,

"6-8-1 to 5-1-5, we have two divers suited and ready."

"5-1-5 to 6-8-1, your light is helping but your rotor wash is kicking up a lot of debris down here and the noise is making radio communications tough. Go to a higher altitude and pull back a couple of blocks. I'll get back to you in a minute."

"6-8-1, message received."

With that, the helicopter backed off to a position high enough and far enough away that the rotor wash and noise subsided. After about 15 minutes, with no indication this incident was bona fide and because we had divers at the scene ready to go, Battalion 1 and I decided to release the helicopter.

Experience has shown that when two people are reported "in the water" the usual possibilities are:

- One of them fell into the water accidentally and the second went in as a would-be rescuer.
- One of them intentionally entered the water after a pet or personal item, and then found themselves in trouble, and the second went in as a would-be rescuer.
- The jumpers are "thrill seekers" and entered the water intentionally. (Try searching "Chicago River Jump" on *YouTube* and you'll find several videos of people jumping from bridges into the river.)

With the information we had it was my assumption that the #3 possibility was more likely what we were dealing with. On Saturday nights after the bars have closed, young partiers fueled by alcohol have been known to become reckless "thrill seekers." Most of the time these daredevils are out of the water and gone by the time we get there. However, we still have to investigate thoroughly. Scenarios have played out in the past where "thrill seekers" have jumped into the water and either can't stay afloat or hit something below the surface and are injured or knocked unconscious. These incidents have also caused a second jumper to enter the water to rescue his/her friend.

Still on the north end of the Orleans bridge, I grabbed my thermal imaging camera and crawled over a short stone wall and down a long set of concrete stairs that led from the bridge to the riverbank. (A thermal imaging camera is designed to detect heat and display a contrasting image of what you're looking at onto its screen.) If someone recently exited the water, there's a possibility that even though the water dried up, their cold footprints might still be visible on the camera. Sure enough! As soon as I turned the camera onto the stairs, I saw two sets of footprints leading from a wall mounted ladder at the riverbank right to where I was standing and up the stairs I had just come down. With this new information, I radioed my findings to Battalion 1, "5-1-5 to Battalion 1, I went down to the riverbank with my camera and found footprints from that ladder on the north wall going up the stairs. I think we had thrill jumpers."

With that information Battalion 1 relayed my report to the fire alarm office. He informed them that we now had good evidence to believe this incident involved thrill jumpers who were out of the water prior to our arrival. Battalion 1 then released all companies.

I got back to quarters around 4:45 a.m. This gave me enough time to complete my paperwork for the day, go down to the kitchen, have some coffee and check out the Sunday sales papers before getting relieved at 5:30.

05/12/15
ASSIGNMENT—BATTALION 18 (ENGINE 54's QUARTERS, 71ST & PARNELL)
PRIMARY RESPONSE AREA—ENGLEWOOD
WEATHER—TEMPERATURES IN THE LOW 60S

"STILL ALARM"

At around 1:00 p.m. I was sent to a Still alarm on South Peoria. The first arriving company reported a fire on the second floor and in the attic of an occupied 2½-story frame building, 20'x 40'. Everything went smoothly. Engine 116 led out to the second floor through the front door. Engine 84 led out to the attic via the back porch. Truck 51 put a nice hole in the roof and threw a 20' ladder in Side A. Truck 18 raised a 38' ground ladder in Side B and shut off the gas and electric meters in the basement. Both trucks and Squad 5 performed searches and ventilation. The fire was extinguished quickly, and extensive overhaul was performed safely. What more could a chief ask for?

"STILL ALARM"

At 4:35 p.m. I was dispatched to a fire in the 6400 block of South Laflin. Upon arrival, Engine 116 reported smoke from a 2-story Red X brick building. (As mentioned earlier, a Red X Building is a structure identified by the Chicago Building Department as having significant structural damage. To warn firefighters, these buildings are affixed on all four sides with large white placards each displaying a Red X. If a fire company reports a fire or smoke in a Red X Building, all firefighters are to be kept out until two chiefs can perform a bottom to top inspection and agree that it is safe for firefighting operations. The second chief is dispatched automatically as soon as a confirmed fire in a Red X Building is reported. Important to note is that if the building is determined to be unsafe to go IN, it is also considered unsafe to go ON. This means no roof operations. Also, important to note is many buildings marked by a Red X have been found to be in fine shape. For example, I had a small fire in a Red X building once that was very structurally sound. The only thing I found that may have indicated the reason for the Red X was a couple of crooked window frames. The marking system used by the building department was kind of new and still not perfected.) In addition to the automatically dispatched second battalion chief, a higher-ranking chief was also responding. In this case the second battalion chief was Battalion 20, and the higher-ranking chief was 2-2-5, Deputy District Chief Bob Hagen.

When I arrived on the scene, I parked my buggy out of the way at the end of the block. As I was walking towards the building my initial assessment of the structure from the outside was that it looked in pretty good shape. However, the interior would still have to be checked out. I also saw that Truck 20 had already raised their main ladder to the roof. Being that this is a Red X building, I figured they put it there just in case it might be needed later. Apparently, this wasn't so, because seconds later I heard the sound of a saw starting on the roof. (This is an exceptionally aggressive group of seasoned firefighters. I'm sure their initial assessment of the structure's exterior was the same as mine, however, for everyone's safety, we still had to follow Red X protocol.) I immediately got on my radio and using the Fireground channel (a channel that can only be heard in close proximity to the scene), announced, "Battalion 18 to Truck 20, get off the roof now." With that, the sound of the saw stopped, and two firefighters stepped onto the main ladder and made their way down.

Focusing my attention back on the building, I began my size-up. At this time the volume and movement of the smoke puffing out from behind the boarded-up windows indicated the fire inside wasn't much. Regardless, per protocol, we couldn't make an interior attack because of the Red X. This is where it gets tough. Firefighters are an aggressive bunch. Like me, I knew these guys were chomping at the bit to get in there and put this fire out. I also knew that both the second responding chief and the DDC were only minutes away. With that in mind I thought to myself, "As soon as one of the other chiefs gets here we can check out the structure and if all is good, we can turn these guys loose."

Firefighters don't like standing around, especially in front of a building that's on fire. So, for now, I had to keep everyone busy outside.

"116, lead out a line and get ready to go in through the front door."

"Engine 101, help 116 then get ready to take a second line off their rig."

"Squad 5, open that rear basement door. When 116's line is charged start getting the plywood off the windows from the outside."

"Truck 20, throw a ladder to the second-floor window."

"Truck 41, throw your 38' to the roof in the rear."

I figured keeping everyone busy would stop them from inching their way into the structure when I wasn't looking. It worked. Each crew quickly took to their assigned tasks. When the plywood was removed from the first window and fire was visible, I had Engine 116 hit it from the outside through the opening.

A few minutes later Battalion 20 and DDC Hagen arrived. By the book, Battalion 20 and I did a bottom-up structural survey starting in the basement. When we reported to DDC Hagen that we found no apparent structural deficiencies, he unleashed the companies. Engine 116 took their line into the first floor and 101 took a line to the second. I entered the building and bounced between floors checking things out. The fire was extinguished quickly, and all searches were reported complete and negative.

As companies were backing their lines out of the building, I did a final walk-through and then exited via the back door. Walking through the gangway back towards the front, I could see DDC Hagen intently staring at me with a smirk on his face. I approached and asked,

"Yes Chief?"

"Nice job Kev."

"Thanks Bob."

"Oh...and the next time you have a fire in a Red X Building and want to 'secretly' tell companies to get off the roof, do it on the Fireground channel, not Englewood where everyone in the whole city can hear you."

Apparently, I mistakenly had my radio set on the Englewood frequency, a citywide channel, when I sent my message telling those guys to get off the roof. Oh well. I knew what was coming next. For at least the next few weeks I'd have to endure some good-natured ribbing about my "secret" radio transmission, and boy did I.

05/15/15
ASSIGNMENT—BATTALION 16 (ENGINE 127'S QUARTERS, 63RD & LARAMIE)
PRIMARY RESPONSE AREA– MIDWAY AIRPORT, SOUTHWEST SIDE
WEATHER—TEMPERATURES IN THE MID 60S

No runs.

05/18/15
ASSIGNMENT—BATTALION 16 (ENGINE 127'S QUARTERS, 63RD & LARAMIE)
PRIMARY RESPONSE AREA– MIDWAY AIRPORT, SOUTHWEST SIDE
WEATHER—TEMPERATURES IN THE HIGH 70S

No runs.

05/24/15
ASSIGNMENT—5-1-5 (SPECIAL OPERATIONS—ENGINE 5'S QUARTERS, DESPLAINES & JACKSON)
PRIMARY RESPONSE AREA—CITY WIDE
WEATHER—TEMPERATURES IN THE LOW 70S

The 5-1-5 Special Operations buggy is equipped with many special pieces of equipment that are not carried in a regular battalion chief's vehicle. Each time I am assigned to 5-1-5, I take some extra time to re-familiarize myself with these specialized tools and meters.

At 5:30 a.m., just after reporting for work and feeling exceptionally invigorated this Sunday morning, I immediately began an extensive inventory and complete cleaning of the 5-1-5 buggy and all of its equipment. Using a pre-printed checklist, I removed each piece of equipment from the buggy, cleaned it thoroughly, and did a re-familiarization drill on it for myself. By 7:00 a.m. my brain was overflowing with knowledge and my nostrils were filled with the refreshing smell of cleaning solution. After putting everything back in place, I grabbed a cup of coffee and went upstairs to my room to wash up and get my paperwork started.

"2-11 ALARM FIRE"

At 7:20 a.m. I heard the following report over my fire radio, "Engine 54 is on the scene at 67TH and Marquette. We got a large 2-story frame totally involved. It's gettin' into the building next door."

Knowing that 67TH and Marquette Rd. is the same street I waited to hear a corrected address. Seconds later Battalion 18, who arrived right behind the first companies, requested a Box at 67TH and Union. With that, the alarm office made the announcement over the radio, "A Still and Box 67TH and Union."

I quickly got my stuff together and started making my way downstairs to my buggy. If the alarm were to be escalated one more level to a 2-11, I would be automatically dispatched. Being that I had citywide response privileges as Special Operations Chief, I figured I'd start heading that way just in case. Sure enough, just as I got into my buggy a 2-11 alarm was requested by Battalion 18. Out the door I went. While en route heading south on the Dan Ryan expressway, I could already see a plume of heavy black smoke miles away.

When I arrived on the scene companies had already been put into "defensive mode." The original 2-story frame was totally involved, and the fire had spread to a second frame building next door that now, too, was heavily involved in fire. I reported to 2-2-5, acting Deputy District Chief Sandra Koats,

"Chief, I'm 5-1-5 today. What can I do for you?"

"Kev, take a walk around the whole scene and give me a progress report."

"Got it."

Chief Koats was covering the A Side of the scene, so working counterclockwise, I started my survey of the D, C and B Sides:

- The D Side was a large vacant lot where Squad 5's snorkel was in position and setting their stabilizing jacks. An engine company had already dragged a 4" supply line to the snorkel and was in the process of hooking that up. Together they'd have the snorkel up and applying water in a few minutes.
- The C side (rear) was a busy scene with engine companies working three handlines from the backyards. Because of several large trees, overgrown shrubs and an old burned-out garage, these companies originally had a tough time positioning their lines but were all now lobbing water into the structures through several window openings.
- The B Side also had a vacant lot between the fire buildings and the next exposures. There too, companies were working handlines. I did see one engine crew working a line in the B sector within the collapse zone. (The collapse zone is an area around the fire building equal to one and a half times the height of the structure. Operations are not conducted within this zone to protect firefighters from the possibility of

> a wall collapse.) Waving my arms, I got the attention of the engine crew and told them to move back. They shut down their line temporarily, gave me the thumbs up and backed up immediately.

I reported back to 2-2-5 and Battalion 18 that everything looked like it was going smoothly.

Back at the command post in Side A, I saw that 2-1-21, District Chief Mike Dillon, was now on scene and in command of the fire. Standing next to him was the captain of Tower Ladder 34. Before I had a chance to ask the chief for another assignment, he grabbed my sleeve and said, "Set up Tower Ladder 34 in front of the building."

At this point most of the fire was extinguished and there wasn't a super urgency to get the tower working. Once set up, its job would be to get the basket up near the attic windows and apply water to the hard-to-reach hot spots. The most important part of this operation was backing this mammoth rig down a couple of narrow streets past other fire apparatus and into place without hitting anything. These Tower Ladders are HUGE! With our assistance, the driver skillfully maneuvered the giant apparatus into place where an engine company was waiting to supply it with water. Once everything was set up and water was flowing to Tower 34's basket, the remaining fire was extinguished quickly, and the fire was "struck out." I was released from the scene a few minutes later at about 9:00 a.m. and headed back to my quarters.

Traditionally, Sundays in the firehouse are pretty laid back. Just some basic house and apparatus cleaning, a drill and the rest of the day is pretty much open. After cleaning up from the fire and completing my paperwork, I went downstairs to the kitchen where I paid the cook for the day's meals and hung around chatting with the officers and crews of Engine 5 and Truck 2 for a bit. Their house and rig work were done, and they were now waiting for their battalion chief to stop by for a drill on high-rise tactics.

Being assigned to 5-1-5, I was on my own for the day with citywide boundaries and a full tank of fuel. With the thought that Sunday morning traffic on Lake Shore Drive would be light, I decided to drill myself on harbor and lakefront access points. My drill would consist of riding up and down Lake Shore Drive and, using maps carried in the Special Ops. buggy, I would make note of roads, gates, and pathways that fire companies could use in case of a water rescue assignment.

As I approached Michigan Ave., I noticed that the Chicago Department of Transportation had Balbo St. closed off. I then remembered that this day was Chicago's annual Bike the Drive. Bike the Drive is an annual charity event that *Wikipedia* describes as, *"a recreational, non-competitive bicycle ride held each year in Chicago, in which Lake Shore Drive is cleared of motor vehicle traffic and opened exclusively to bicyclists for several hours beginning at dawn."*

The event draws over 20,000 participants and runs from 5:00 a.m. to 11:00 a.m. The temporary "bike path" on Lake Shore Drive goes about 15 miles from 57TH street on the south to Bryn Mawr on the north. Also, a part of this event is a mini festival held at Grant Park where participants sign in, visit vendor tents, and listen to live music.

With Lake Shore Drive blocked off I couldn't do my access familiarization drill, so I thought I'd do a "walk-thru" preplan of the park just in case CFD services happened to be needed for the remainder of the day. I parked my buggy and notified the alarm office that I would be at Grant Park doing a "site familiarization drill." Walking around the park I took note of entrances and exits and also introduced myself to the event coordinator. When the music kicked up, I walked over to the main stage. There, I caught a few songs performed by one of Chicago's well-known party bands before returning to quarters for lunch.

Still in "Sunday mode," after lunch I took a ride to visit an old friend of mine at Engine 78's quarters, the firehouse across the street from Wrigley Field. On my way there I came upon another large event, the Belmont/Sheffield Festival. While waiting in traffic I could hear some pretty good classic rock music coming from the stage about a half a block in. "Oh well," I thought, so I pulled my buggy to the curb and did another "site familiarization drill." The band was very good but exceptionally loud. This made it difficult to hear radio transmissions, so I left after only a couple of minutes. When I got to 78's quarters I chatted with my friend about our upcoming retirements, mine in November and his in the following year. I then returned to quarters for dinner.

"PERSON IN THE WATER"

After dinner I headed for Squad 2's quarters at Diversey and Pulaski for a scheduled evening visit. While en route I was dispatched to a "Person in the Water" at Harrison and The River. I turned on my lights and siren, jumped on the Kennedy Expressway and headed southeast. Engine 5 arrived on the scene first and reported over the radio that a Water Taxi had already picked a man out of the water and was now docked with him on board. Battalion 1 and I arrived just about the same time. We made our way down to the riverbank where we found the Water Taxi moored with what appeared to be a homeless man sitting in a chair covered with a blanket. While Battalion 1 gave his report on the radio I confirmed with the boat's captain that there was, in fact, only one victim in the water. I then held the responding helicopter and dive teams. When the ambulance arrived, members of Truck 1 carried the victim in a stair chair up the bank and assisted in placing him in the ambulance.

The article below is from the next day's on-line *Chicago Tribune*:

MAN RESCUED FROM CHICAGO RIVER

A homeless man who is believed to have lived along the South Branch of the Chicago River was rescued by a passing water taxi Sunday night after he fell in the river, according Chicago Fire Department officials

The man fell in the water near Wacker Driver and Harrison Street about 8 p.m., Battalion Chief Steve Little said.

A passing water taxi helped the man out of the river a few minutes later.

"All of the water taxis are trained to perform water rescues, so they just reached down with their net and fished him out," Little said.

The man was taken to a local hospital as a precaution but is expected to be fine, Little said.

From the Harrison Street bridge, a small blue tent was visible under the bridge.

Copyright © 2015, Chicago Tribune

After this run, I filled up my fuel tank and returned to quarters. No more runs on this shift.

> 05/27/15
> ASSIGNMENT—BATTALION 7 (ENGINE 91'S QUARTERS, DIVERSEY & PULASKI)
> PRIMARY RESPONSE AREA—WEST LOGAN SQUARE, NEAR NORTHWEST SIDE
> WEATHER—TEMPERATURES IN THE MID 70S

No runs.

> 05/30/15
> ASSIGNMENT—BATTALION 7 (ENGINE 91'S QUARTERS, DIVERSEY & PULASKI)
> PRIMARY RESPONSE AREA—WEST LOGAN SQUARE, NEAR NORTHWEST SIDE
> WEATHER—TEMPERATURES IN THE MID 70S

A couple of routine runs. Nothing of consequence.

JUNE 2015

06/02/15
Assignment—5-1-5 (Special Operations—Engine 5's Quarters, DesPlaines & Jackson)
Primary Response Area—City Wide
Weather—Temperatures in the mid 60s

No runs.

06/08/15
Assignment—5-1-5 (Special Operations—Engine 5's Quarters, DesPlaines & Jackson)
Primary Response Area—City Wide
Weather—Temperatures in the low 80s

A couple of routine runs, held up on all.

06/11/15
Assignment—5-1-5 (Special Operations—Engine 5's Quarters, DesPlaines & Jackson)
Primary Response Area—City Wide
Weather—Temperatures in the low 70s

My shift started as usual. I reported for work at 5:15 a.m. and began making my relief. Relieving a battalion chief is loosely completed in two parts. First, the on-coming chief removes, from the buggy, all the gear and belongings of the chief who worked the shift before and replaces it with his/her own. At this time an operational check is also completed on the breathing apparatus, radios, meters and other tools. This part of the relief is usually completed while the off-going chief is still in his/her room finishing up their paperwork before going home. The second part of the relief is receiving a briefing from the off-going chief on the previous day's activities. This is usually done in the kitchen over coffee and could include a casual talk about an incident and or a reminder of something on the calendar, such as a scheduled drill or maintenance needed on the buggy.

At about 5:30 a.m., while putting my gear in the buggy, a man in civilian clothing entered the firehouse and approached me. In a heavy Eastern European accent, he introduced himself as Erik, a professor from a university in Amsterdam, who was doing a study on fire departments throughout the world. He told me he had permission from our Department to ride along with me for the day and observe daily operations. This is not unheard of, so I welcomed Erik and asked him to have a seat while I confirmed he had "ride along" permission from District Headquarters. After confirming that he did have Department approval, I cleared out the passenger area and gave Erik his seat for the day.

As far as runs and incidents, it was a pretty uneventful day. I did however keep Erik busy by attending several drills and giving him a tour of different parts of the city.

At 9:00 a.m. we met the SCUBA team (6-8-7) at the CFD drill pool where they were doing preventive maintenance on some of their equipment before heading over to the lakefront to do a rescue drill.

The drill pool is in an old school building that was converted into a training facility for both the Fire and Police Departments. The large indoor pool is set up to be used for many types of underwater rescue operation drills. Through a donation from a major automobile manufacturer, the city was able to get a shell of an automobile that can be submerged in the pool and used to train divers on how to extricate victims from vehicles underwater. In order to replicate decreased visibility, as one would find in a lake or river, a lot of the pool training is done with darkened facepieces to mimic zero visibility. In a submerged automobile drill, a diver must locate the vehicle, find the victim inside, release them from some sort of entanglement, remove them from the vehicle and bring them to the surface, all without being able to see.

When 6-8-7 was done with their maintenance tasks, we followed them to the lakefront at North Ave. where they did a full out rescue dive drill with their 150 lb mannequin. While two divers were suiting up inside their truck, the Chief of Air Sea Rescue dropped the large mannequin in the water near the shore wall. He also tossed in a smaller "baby" mannequin about twenty feet away. The drill began when the divers emerged from the truck. In sort of a role-play manner, the chief told the two divers a baby had fallen into the lake and the parent went in to save it. Neither had surfaced. Both divers were then taken to the "last seen point" and instructed to enter the water and find the victims.

Two rescue divers always enter the water and work as a team. The search diver will descend and do a systematic search pattern. The backup diver remains nearby on the surface ready to assist in recovering the victim, or to provide help in case the search diver gets in trouble. The team uses a two-way communications line. One end is connected to a speaker/microphone box on shore. The other end is connected to the divers' facepieces. Using this communication system, the officer on shore instructs the divers on where to search and what type of pattern to use. This system also allows divers to communicate "hands free" by simply speaking into their masks.

Once in the water, and only a few minutes into the drill, the search diver reported that he found the adult mannequin and was bringing "him" to the surface. The second diver, who was on stand-by, began to swim over to the last seen point. Just before he got there the search diver popped out of the water with the "victim." Both divers then swam to the shore wall where the Air Sea Rescue Chief and I were standing by with nylon webbing. When a handcuff knot was securely tied on the mannequin's arms, the chief and I lifted it out of the water. The ASR Chief then gave the order, "Now go find the baby." Being familiar with the area where the first victim was found, the search diver went back down and immediately found the baby mannequin. It too, was brought to shore and handed off to us. My ride-along, Erik, was very impressed at the efficiency of our SCUBA team. The dive drill finished up around noon, so I took Erik back to the firehouse to grab a quick lunch before heading over to Engine 16's quarters to see the CFD Hazmat Unit (5-1-1).

We arrived at Engine 16 around 1:30 and were met by the captain and crew of the Hazmat Unit. They welcomed Erik and gave him a thorough tour of their apparatus and equipment while I sat and chatted with the engine officer.

When the Hazmat tour was finished, Erik and I drove to a junkyard on the southside where training was being given to truck companies on a new, battery-powered Jaws of Life. This tool was soon to be issued to all truck companies in the city and would be replacing the gas generator-powered models we had been using for years. The advantages of going from gas generator power to battery are numerous. The battery tool is much lighter, there are no connection hoses to get tangled, two tools can be used simultaneously without being tethered to a power unit, and battery tools do not give off exhaust fumes. Another very nice feature of the battery-powered tool is that it eliminates the noise emitted by a gas generator. The quiet nature of the battery tool over the loud generator makes it easier for rescuers to communicate with each other and with victims. It also keeps patients calmer during extrication operations. Erik and I sat in on the lecture part of the drill, then watched as firefighters used the new tool to dismantle a few junk cars.

On the way back to quarters I stopped at Exchange Ave. and Peoria to show Erik The Chicago Stockyard Fire Memorial sculpture. This piece of art was completed in 2004 and dedicated to the 21 firefighters who lost their lives on December 22, 1910, while fighting a fire at the Chicago Stockyards. Prior to Sept. 11, 2001, this was the deadliest fire, for firefighters, at a single location.

Our last stop before heading back to quarters was Engine 18, the home of the television show *Chicago Fire*. Since production of the television series began, Engine 18's quarters has become a well-visited tourist attraction. On days when filming is not taking place, firefighters assigned there welcome visitors and allow them to take as many pictures as they want. When Erik was done with his tour of the "TV firehouse," we returned to quarters.

(Side Story: The TV Firehouse, Engine 18's quarters, is also District 1 Headquarters. When working in any battalion in the First District, chiefs have to visit there at least once a shift for administrative purposes. Sometimes, during actual filming of the show, I would be stopped by someone from the production crew and asked to wait outside until hearing the word "cut."

Once, while dropping off my daily paperwork and before heading to the district office, which is in another part of the building, I stopped in the kitchen to steal a cookie or two. Sitting in a lounge chair, between me and a bag of Oreos, was a young woman from the production crew.

"Excuse me." I said politely before attempting to reach past her to get at the cookies.

"Oh, I'm sorry!" she said as she started to get out of the chair.

"No, you're fine. I just want to grab a cookie from that bag behind you."

We exchanged smiles and with a couple of Oreos in hand, I was off to the district office. About 30 minutes later while sitting around the conference table chatting with the other chiefs, I was made aware that the woman I had the brief cookie encounter with in the kitchen was Lady Gaga. At the time she was dating one of the stars of *Chicago Fire* and would sometimes hang around the set during filming. Well, that was my big brush with fame. I reached past Lady Gaga to get at a bag of Oreos.)

After dinner and before heading back to his hotel, Erik expressed his gratitude to all the members of Engine 5 and Truck 2. He thanked them for their hospitality and me for a very entertaining day. He left and the rest of my shift was quiet.

> 06/14/15
> ASSIGNMENT—BATTALION 1 (ENGINE 13'S QUARTERS, WACKER AND COLUMBUS)
> PRIMARY RESPONSE AREA—DOWNTOWN
> WEATHER—TEMPERATURES IN THE LOW 80S

Battalion 1 covers most of the downtown area and, as far as the numbers of runs go, is the busiest battalion in the city. During today's shift I had 18 runs in 24 hours. This is fairly common for a lot of engines and trucks. However, for battalion chiefs who don't respond to runs such as EMS, Rubbish, Autos and Carbon Monoxide Investigations, 18 runs is a busy day.

It was a warm Sunday, and the downtown area was alive. All day and into the evening hours, the sidewalks were crowded, and the streets were jammed with heavy traffic. Not being too used to working downtown, navigating my buggy all day through the swarms of people and cars proved to be a little nerve-wracking. Between my emergency responses and administrative duties, I was on the street throughout most of my twenty-four-hour shift.

In addition to many false "Automatic Alarms," I had one "Still in a High-Rise" (no fire, mistaken citizen), one "Fire in the Subway" (no fire, burning footwear on the third rail) and one "Person Threatening to Jump."

"PERSON THREATENING TO JUMP"

About 4:30 a.m., while still wide awake, I got a run for a "Person Threatening to Jump" from a hotel roof on Michigan Avenue. On arrival I remained downstairs while two police officers, two paramedics and 5-1-5, the Special Ops. Chief went up. Within a minute or two, 5-1-5 radioed down that the scene was secure and there was no one threatening to jump. A subsequent transmission said everyone was on their way down. With this information, I released all fire companies on the scene.

When the elevator door opened the paramedics wheeled out a young girl in a stair chair. "She was at the Spring Awakening Festival in Soldier Field all day and she's not feeling so good," one of them said, "we're gonna take her over to the hospital to get checked out." Apparently, the girl felt ill and found her way to the roof to get some fresh air. For some reason her friends called 911 saying she was threatening to jump.

Around 5:00, as the ambulance pulled away, the sky was beginning to turn from night black to pre-dawn blue and there was an eerie quietness on Michigan Avenue. It was a calm Monday morning and there was almost no foot or vehicle traffic. The only ones who remained on the scene were Special Operations Chief 5-1-5, Matt Oakes and me. Sitting on the rail of an elaborate Michigan Avenue planter box, Matt and I chatted for a while about the busy shift we both just had and how glad we were that it was almost over.

"Hey, you're in 5-1-5 next day right Kev?" asked Matt.

"Yeah, I'll be YOU next day."

"Well, I hope you have a good shift."

"Thanks Matt. Take care."

With dawn now fully breaking I walked back to my buggy

and thought, "I haven't even made my bunk yet." I was working on zero hours of sleep. Thankfully, my shift would be over in an hour and I'd be going home.

On my way back to quarters, before being relieved of duty, I had two more runs! Both were false alarms.

> 06/17/15
> Assignment—5-1-5 (Special Operations—Engine 5's Quarters, DesPlaines & Jackson)
> Primary Response Area—City Wide
> Weather—Temperatures in the high 60s

On my previous workday I had a discussion with another battalion chief about helicopter operations. The discussion centered around communicating with the pilots and a review of what they need from us on the ground. Today, being assigned to 5-1-5, Special Operations, I thought, "What better way to get the correct answers than to speak with the pilots themselves?" So, around 7:00 a.m., I called Air Sea Rescue and told them I was coming out for roll call and a drill. The Air Sea Rescue firehouse is located in a desolate area at the south end of the lakefront. I took the scenic route down Lake Shore Drive and arrived a little after 8:00 a.m.

As I walked in the door the lieutenant sitting at the front desk rang the house bells to summon all members for roll call. When everyone was present, I introduced myself and explained that I was there to have a review chat with the officer on helicopter protocol. While I stood by, the lieutenant, who doubles as the helicopter pilot, went through his usual formal roll call with his members. When he finished, he had his crew give me a full tour of the hangar and two helicopters while he completed his morning paperwork.

The guys were great! I got a very informative 45-minute drill on the choppers themselves, and what goes on in the air before and after the divers are deployed over water. It was obvious that these guys loved their job. When we walked back to the front desk, I complimented the officer on his crew and told him that beyond giving me a thorough tour, they eagerly answered all of my questions. The officer and I then continued the drill over a cup of coffee where he got more specific on the helicopter itself and provided me with a good overview of what information a pilot needs from companies on the ground.

After the business end of our talk was done, the lieutenant asked if I would be relocating out of the city after I retired. I told him that I have always lived in the city near Chicago and Ashland and that I had no immediate plans on leaving after retirement. With a surprised look on his face he replied, "I grew up at Grand and Noble!" The intersection of Grand and Noble is only blocks away from where I grew up. We talked for quite a while finding out that he and I both knew a lot of the same people from "the old neighborhood." It was really a fun chat! After about an hour I got up to leave and thanked him for his hospitality. We shook hands, he wished me luck in my retirement years, and I left.

Just as I was pulling out of the security gate in the parking lot, another chief's buggy was pulling in. It was Chief Tim Elliot, of Air Sea Rescue. Tim and I came on the job together almost thirty years ago. We haven't seen much of each other since then, but recently, he and a few other guys from our candidate class were in the process of planning a formal banquet to recognize our "29 and a day" milestone.

(Along with Tim and I, one hundred and forty-eight others entered the Chicago Fire Department on July 16, 1986.

This July 16TH marks the completion of our 29TH year on the job. The way things are written, we have to work 29 years and 1 day to be fully vested in our pension. Reaching "29 and a day" is a big thing. A few months earlier, when solicited by members of the party planning committee, I told them I wouldn't be attending the banquet. I'm not really a big banquet kinda guy and would have preferred a more informal gathering.)

In our buggies, passing each other through the gate, we exchanged waves and Tim recognized me. Rolling down his window he asked, "Kev, are you going to the party?" "I'm sure it'll be a great time, but I think I'm gonna take a pass," I replied.

Not taking "no" for an answer he asked me to park my buggy and come into his office. He said he had something he wanted to show me. I kinda felt this was going to be like buying a car. Once they get you to sit down inside, you're gonna sign on the dotted line. Out of respect for Tim and the work he put into this event, I re-parked my buggy and went back inside. In his office he showed me a list of everyone who confirmed they were attending and a large class picture we had taken back in 1986. I could see how excited and sincerely passionate he was about this, so I caved in and signed up. I took his contact info and told him I'd send him the payment in full tomorrow. While writing down his address he asked, "So, what brings you here to Air Sea Rescue today?" I explained that I had come to do a refresher drill with his crew on helicopter operations.

"You ever been up in the fire department helicopter?" he asked.

"No, I haven't." I replied.

"Do you have time for a quick ride? It would be a good

drill for you to see firsthand what it looks like from up above when you're on the ground directing us at incidents."

"Actually, I do have the time, and that would be great!"

Being responsible for all air operations of Air Sea Rescue, and an expert helicopter pilot, Chief Elliot was, within reason, able to take the helicopter up at his discretion. We left his office, and he instructed the crew to get the chopper ready. While donning his flight suit, he handed me a radio headset and explained that he'd been flying helicopters as both a pilot and instructor for many years.

Sitting in the idling chopper on the helipad Tim ran through a pre-flight check of the machine and explained each step as he went along. Cleared for takeoff, he radioed to an air traffic controller telling him that the CFD helicopter would be in the air for a brief flight near quarters. With takeoff cleared, we lifted off the pad and ascended high over the firehouse. As we flew over the south shores of Lake Michigan, through the headsets, Tim continued to explain the workings of the helicopter and pointed out things that he looks for from the companies on the ground at different incidents. (The CFD helicopter is not only dispatched to water rescues, but to several other types of calls including high-rise fires and incidents involving trains.) It was both interesting and enlightening to see the perspective of the pilot and to learn a few small tips on how best to utilize the helicopter when it responds to one of my runs. The entire flight lasted only about 20 minutes. Once the chopper landed and was shut down, we got out and started walking towards the firehouse.

"Let me know if you ever wanna go for another ride," Tim offered. "I own my own helicopter. I can take you up anytime you wanna go."

"That's a very generous offer! I may take you up on that." I replied.

"Any time Kev. You know where to find me."

"Thanks again…I'll see you at the party!"

We shook hands and I was on my way. It was a very interesting and informative morning with the Chicago Fire Department Air Sea Rescue team!

The rest of the day was calm … no runs.

06/20/15
ASSIGNMENT—BATTALION 14 (ENGINE 109'S QUARTERS, 22ND & KEDZIE)
PRIMARY RESPONSE AREA—WESTSIDE, LITTLE VILLAGE
WEATHER—TEMPERATURES IN THE HIGH 70S

"STILL ALARM"

I was working on a trade with another chief today. It was a very slow shift. My first run came in at 9:30 p.m. We had a fire in the attic of a 1½-story brick home that was hit by lightning. The occupants reported they heard a loud "boom" and then smelled smoke five minutes later. Engine 99 extinguished the fire with one line. We were done and picked up in about 40 minutes.

06/23/15
Assignment—Battalion 14 (Engine 109's Quarters, 22nd & Kedzie)
Primary Response Area—Westside, Little Village
Weather—Temperatures in the high 70s

Slow day, only one false run.

06/26/15
Assignment—Battalion 4 (Engine 23's Quarters, 20th & Damen)
Primary Response Area—Pilsen, Little Village, Near Southwest Side
Weather—Temperatures in the high 60s

About 10:00 a.m. I was dispatched to an accident investigation involving a CFD vehicle. There were no other vehicles involved. There was only minor damage to the vehicle and no injuries. No big deal.

The rest of the day was pretty uneventful. I got into my bunk around 9:30 p.m., worked a crossword puzzle and turned out the lights around 10:00. A half an hour later the phone in my room rang. It was my boss calling from District Headquarters. Apparently, the accident investigation I did earlier was missing the required police report. So, it was out of bed and off to the police station.

"AUTOMATIC ALARM IN A HIGH-RISE"

While on my way to get a copy of the police report I was dispatched to an "Automatic Alarm in a High-Rise." There was no fire. The alarm was caused by a faulty smoke detector on the 8TH floor. However, while investigating the cause of the alarm, a couple of violations regarding the operation of the elevators in Fire Service Mode were found. Elevator keys were missing from the fire department lock box, and the ones that were there didn't work. Before leaving the scene, I took notes on the violations then radioed to the alarm office, "Put me back on previous."

I then continued on to the police station, picked up the accident report and delivered it to my boss at headquarters around 11:30 p.m. In addition to providing him with the police report, I told him about the elevator issues I had just run into. I told him I'd be doing a referral form and making a phone call to the Fire Prevention Bureau in the morning. He took down the information and said he, too, would make a call to the Bureau as well.

When I got back to quarters, I completed the referral form, and the remainder of my shift was quiet.

> 06/29/15
> ASSIGNMENT—BATTALION 14 (ENGINE 109'S QUARTERS, 22ND & KEDZIE)
> PRIMARY RESPONSE AREA—WESTSIDE, LITTLE VILLAGE
> WEATHER—TEMPERATURES IN THE HIGH 70S

Nothing all day.

JULY 2015

07/2/15
ASSIGNMENT—BATTALION 7 (ENGINE 91'S QUARTERS, DIVERSEY & PULASKI)
PRIMARY RESPONSE AREA—WEST LOGAN SQUARE, NEAR NORTHWEST SIDE
WEATHER—TEMPERATURES IN THE HIGH 60S

"STILL ALARM–ALLEY GARAGE"

At 7:00 p.m. I was dispatched to an "Alley Garage" fire in the Logan Square neighborhood. First to arrive on the scene, and with "nothing showing," I drove around to the alley. There, I found two teen-aged kids watching their mom spraying water from a garden hose onto the smoldering corner of their garage. I could see the small fire was out, so I held the second companies and had Engine 91 and Truck 13's crews report to the rear. I wanted them to make sure the fire was completely extinguished while I interviewed the family.

"What happened?" I asked. The very nervous mom apologetically told me that, with her permission, her teenaged son was burning some old documents in a small metal bucket in the backyard. She said she had allowed this before and she was very strict about fire safety. She assured me her son always kept a garden hose nearby to wet down the burnt ashes and he is extremely careful. From her account, my determination was that the kid must have accidentally thrown some still smoldering ashes into the plastic garbage can in the alley. This, in turn, started the alley container on fire and it spread to the siding on the garage. After speaking with the family a bit more, I told them and the police who were now on the scene, that my official determination of the cause of the fire was "accidental."

While Engine 91 and Truck 13 were picking up their tools, a car turned into the alley and slowly approached. I watched as the mom excitedly ran up to the vehicle and through the rolled down driver's window, began explaining what happened and why the fire department was there. The driver in the car was dad coming home from work. He parked in front of the garage next door and then came up to me and began apologizing for his son's carelessness. "No problem," I told both the mom and dad, "that's what we're here for." The mom then explained to the dad that the "nice fire chief" had a wonderful calm demeanor and that if it weren't for him, she would have "freaked out." They then called their son over and had him apologize to me and shake my hand. "No worries," I said, "but if I were you, I'd rethink this document burning thing and buy a shredder." The mom and dad, both nodding in agreement, thanked me again as I walked to my buggy. There was minimal damage to the garage, no one got hurt and everyone learned a valuable lesson. I guess you could say it was kind of a heartwarming family run.

"STILL ALARM"

The rest of the evening and night were quiet until around 5:00 a.m. when, just before going home, I was dispatched to a Still Alarm on North Milwaukee Avenue. The comment section of the run sheet and the computer in my buggy both read: "Smoke From a 2ND Floor Window."

On arrival we found a large, old, corner, brick building with stores on the first floor and apartments on the 2ND and 3RD. As I parked across the street, I could see light smoke emitting through a screen on a 2ND floor, front apartment window, and through my open driver side window I could hear the beeping sound of a smoke detector. I also smelled that distinct odor of burnt food. I've had a million of these runs. It's usually a case where someone comes home late, sleepy, intoxicated and hungry. They decide to heat something up on the stove and then fall asleep. Routinely, these "pot of meat" or "meat on the stove" runs are handled by simply gaining entry, turning off the stove, carrying the pot to the sink, soaking it with water, ventilating and making sure occupants inside are okay.

The street level entrances to the apartments above the stores were not very obvious. This was a huge building and there were about five entry doors, all were locked. A gate leading to the rear porches was also chained and padlocked. "Okay," I said, "Truck 13 throw your 20' to that window and go in through the screen. Squad 2 take a walk around and see if you can find an open door to the second floor. Everybody else just stand by."

After the ladder was positioned to the window, FF Jesse Diaz of Truck 13 climbed up, raised the screen, and entered the apartment. Once inside he went directly to the kitchen where he found the smoldering remains of a pizza in the oven. With gloved hands he took the pizza to the kitchen sink, soaked it with water, then radioed down to me, "Burnt pizza Chief." At almost the same time Squad 2 also radioed, "Squad 2 to Battalion 7, we're in the hallway now and knocking on the apartment door. No one's answering. Do you want us to force entry?" "No," I replied, "we got a guy in there now." After shutting off the stove and soaking the pizza and hot pan, Jesse went to the front door and let Squad 2 in. Together they began opening a few windows to vent the light haze in the apartment.

Jesse then began checking all the rooms in the apartment. The first bedroom door he got to was locked. Knocking loudly, he announced, "Fire Department!" He announced this several times before the doorknob began to slowly turn from the inside. When the door opened Jesse was met by what appeared to be an intoxicated young woman dressed only in underwear. "What's... going... on?" she slooowly and calmly asked. Jesse explained that the pizza she put in the oven burned and caused her smoke alarm to activate. He went on to add that the alarm woke a neighbor who smelled smoke and called the fire department. "Ohhhhhh..." she said. Then, without another word, she gave Jesse a soft smile, waved goodbye and slowly closed the door in his face.

I was still outside waiting for Jesse's report when he poked his head out of the window laughing. From above he called down, "Chief, you're gonna have to come up here." Not knowing what to expect, I climbed the ladder and entered the apartment through the window. "There's a girl in that bedroom who looks like she's been drinking...a lot. I tried to talk to her, but she closed the door on me," Jesse explained. "Is there anyone else in here?" I asked. The lieutenant from Squad 2 answered, "We checked the whole apartment. There's no one else here."

Well, we couldn't leave without making sure that the young lady was all right, so now I knocked on the door. While waiting for the door to open Jesse said, "Oh yeah Chief, I forgot to tell you, she doesn't have a lot of clothes on." No sooner than the last word came out of his mouth, the door opened and there stood the young woman in possibly the skimpiest underwear ever made. "Ma'am, are you okay?" I asked. With a smile and slurred speech, she replied, "I'm fine officer...and I'm so sorry about the pizza." She then gently closed the door in MY face.

Before I could turn around, I heard one of the police officers standing behind me say, "Hey Chief," we just spoke with the neighbor across the hall who is a friend of this young lady. She said she'd check on her throughout the morning to make sure she's okay. I think we're all good here." I thanked the police and released the remaining companies, then gave my final radio report to the fire alarm office, "Battalion 7 to Main, we had burnt pizza in the oven. We woke up one sleeping occupant and vented the apartment. I'm handing this over to the police. All companies are in service returning to quarters."

> 07/8/15
> ASSIGNMENT—BATTALION 17 (ENGINE 60'S QUARTERS, 60TH AND UNIVERSITY)
> PRIMARY RESPONSE AREA –UNIVERSITY OF CHICAGO, HYDE PARK, SOUTHSIDE
> WEATHER—TEMPERATURES IN THE HIGH 60S

Slow day, only a couple of false runs.

07/11/15
ASSIGNMENT—BATTALION 16 (ENGINE 127'S QUARTERS, 63RD & LARAMIE)
PRIMARY RESPONSE AREA– MIDWAY AIRPORT, SOUTHWEST SIDE
WEATHER—TEMPERATURES IN THE HIGH 70S

Slow day. We investigated one small electrical fire at a banquet hall that was out on arrival. The fire did minor damage to an exterior wooden awning but didn't get inside the building.

7/14/15
ASSIGNMENT—BATTALION 20 (ENGINE 15'S QUARTERS, 81ST & KEDZIE)
PRIMARY RESPONSE AREA—FORD CITY, MARQUETTE PARK
WEATHER—TEMPERATURES IN THE LOW 80S

No runs, no hits, no errors!

07/17/15

I was off on a trade this day so that my wife and I could attend my "29 and a Day" banquet. As explained earlier, this means a member has been on the Chicago Fire Department for 29 years and one day. This marks the day a member is fully vested and can retire. Reaching this point in one's career is a big deal! Exactly 29 years and one day ago our class entered the CFD. Most of us were in our twenties back then and this day seemed soooooo far away.

The banquet was held on the 80TH floor of the AON building in downtown Chicago. It was a warm and beautiful clear night making the city and Lake Michigan the perfect backdrop. I didn't get an exact number, but the turnout was great. I believe around 120 of the 150 members of my candidate class of July 16, 1986, attended the event. After dinner there were speeches, group photos, lots of laughter-filled reminiscing and the DJ kept the dance floor filled all night.

Earlier in my journal I noted that one of the organizers of this reunion, the chief at Air Sea Rescue, had to talk me into attending. I'm so glad he did. I had a great time!

07/23/15
Assignment—Battalion 1 (Engine 13's Quarters, Wacker and Columbus)
Primary Response Area—Downtown
Weather—Temperatures in the mid 80s

A usual day in Battalion 1. I had about 12 runs, mostly automatic alarms in high-rises that turned out to be false. No fires.

NOTE: ON JULY 16TH OF 2015, THE CHICAGO FIRE DEPARTMENT UNDERWENT A DISTRICT REORGANIZATION. AS A RESULT, MANY BATTALION NUMBERS WERE CHANGED.

07/25/15

Assignment—Battalion 12 (Engine 55's Quarters, Diversey & Halsted)...the old 5th Battalion

Primary Response Area—Lincoln Park, Wrigleyville

Weather—Temperatures in the low 90s

"STILL ALARM"

At around 11:00 a.m. I was dispatched via radio to a fire at an address near Wrigley Field. While I was en route, Engine 78 and Truck 44 arrived on the scene first and reported a fire in the rear of a 3-story condo building 25' by 75'. 78's crew quickly led out down the gangway and extinguished a pile of rubbish that was burning just outside the building's basement door. When the smoke cleared, heavy char marks could be seen on the doorframe indicating that fire might have communicated to the inside of the structure. Once fire gets inside it can travel up walls and spread throughout a building rapidly. Crews needed to get inside quickly to check for extension. To avoid unnecessary damage (and work), firefighters are taught early in their career to "try before you pry." So, before using a bar and sledgehammer to force entry, the officer of Truck 44 tried turning the doorknob and found it unlocked. The crews then entered the basement and found only minor fire extension to the interior.

I pulled up on the scene just as Engine 78 reported to

the fire alarm office, "Engine 78 to Main, hold the Working Fire Response and all other responding units but let the chief come in. The fire's out." I parked my buggy out front and reported, "Battalion 12 is on the scene. I'll give you a report in a second." Following the hoseline down the gangway to the rear I was met by the officer of Engine 78 who briefed me on what he had,

"Chief, we had a big pile of cardboard burning down here in the basement stairwell. It got the doorway going and a little got inside, but not much. Truck 44 checked the walls with their camera, everything's good. We're just washing down now."

"Okay," I said, "shut your line down for a minute and let me take a look." I entered the basement and, as described by 78's officer, I too found very little evidence that fire got inside. However, there was still quite a bit of smoke lingering in the unit.

"Did you guys force entry?" I asked.

"No, the door was unlocked," the officer of Truck 44 responded.

"Okay. Looks good to me. Truck, do me a favor and set up your fan. Let's get rid of this smoke."

Why a rear basement door with fire just outside of it was unlocked was something I would have to question while making my determination of the cause of the fire.

It was a warm summer Saturday morning, not a normal workday, so many people were around when the fire started. Back out front I began interviewing tenants and next-door neighbors. The first person I spoke with was the owner of the condo where the fire occurred. His duplex unit included both the first floor and basement. He explained to me he was on the first floor of his unit doing some house cleaning when a basement smoke alarm activated. He then went downstairs to investigate and smelled a light odor of smoke. Looking further, he opened the rear basement door leading to the yard and saw flames about waist high in the exterior basement stairwell. With that, he slammed the door shut, and not taking the time to lock it, he immediately called 911. He also reported that while waiting for the fire department to arrive, he went around the back through the side yard to the rear and snapped a few pictures of the flames. The interview continued.

"My guys said they found a lot of cardboard burning. Is there any reason why there would be cardboard stacked by your back door? Recycling maybe?"

"No, we never keep our recycling stuff near the building. We've been having problems with some homeless people around here. They've been sleeping in our yards and under our porches. We have to remove cardboard from our yards all the time. We also find condoms and feces."

"Do you call the police?"

"Yeah. They kick them out, but they just keep coming back."

"Okay, thanks. I'm gonna talk with your neighbors. I'll be right back."

I got the same story from other residents of the building and neighbors next door. They, too, reported that homeless people had been hanging around their yards. One resident told me when she asked a small group of homeless people to move along, they became confrontational. Another told me that just this morning, someone defecated right outside the basement door where the fire was. Because of these circumstances, I requested a response by our Office of Fire Investigation. When OFI arrived, I gave them a briefing and introduced them to the tenants and neighbors. The police were also on the scene. The official cause of the fire would be determined by OFI.

"STILL IN A HIGH-RISE"

At 3:30 a.m. I was dispatched to a "Still in a High-Rise" at an approximate address of LaSalle and Maple. My assignment was Fire Attack Chief. (On a bona fide fire in a high-rise, the Fire Attack Chief reports to, and directs operations on the fire floor.)

I was still en route when the first arriving companies reported "nothing showing." Seconds later Battalion 1's voice came across the radio,

"Battalion 1 to Main, I'm on the scene. Do you have any more information or a better address on this?"

"Main to Battalion 1, we're getting several calls reporting a large fire on a roof somewhere in that area. We're on the phone with one of the callers now trying to get it pinpointed for you."

"Okay, we'll keep looking but we don't see anything right now."

(Fairly often people in high-rises will call in what they think is a fire, but many times turns out to be a barbeque grill or chimney. Because these runs are called in from hundreds of feet above street level, the locations given are usually approximate.)

"Main to Battalion 1, one of the callers is saying that it's on the roof of the building with the green sign on it."

"Battalion 1 to Main, message received. We see the building with the green sign. We're gonna check it out."

"Battalion 1 to Battalion 12, take a couple of companies up top and let me know what you have."

"Battalion 12, message received."

Carrying hose, hand pumps and forcible entry tools, two fire companies and I entered the reported fire building. We put the elevators in Fire Service Mode and went up to investigate. Following procedures, we stopped the elevator three floors below the roof and walked up the rest of the way. Once at the top we exited the stairway into a short hallway. About twenty feet away, at the end of the hall, was a glass door leading to the rooftop. I knew we had something because the hall was lit up with a bright orange glow. At exactly the same time another company, who took a different set of stairs on the opposite side of the building, reported over the radio, "We're up on the roof now. We got a wooden deck totally involved. We're not sure if it's coming through the roof. We're gonna go down a floor and check it out."

By this time, I had already jogged down the hall towards the fire and stepped out onto the roof. From there I saw a large deck, about fifteen feet from where I was standing, totally involved in fire. The wooden structure was built about two feet above the roof itself and had a couple of steps leading up to it. From my vantage point I was able to get on all fours and look under the deck. It was clear. All of the fire was on top and burning upward.

"Battalion 1 to Battalion 12, are you up there yet?"

"Battalion 12 to Battalion 1, I'm up here. I got a rooftop deck 25' by 25' totally involved. Right now it looks like just the deck, not the roof. We're gonna need more than the 200' of hose Engine 4 has with 'em."

"Battalion 1 message received. I just pulled a Box on this.

I'll send up more hose and another company to help Engine 4 with their lead out now."

"Battalion 12 to Battalion 1, we're gonna be here a while."

With flames now reaching about twenty feet into the warm night air, crews scrambled down below and up in the stairwell to get water on the fire. At street level an engine needed to connect to a hydrant, then pump the water from the engine through a hose, to the standpipe and up to the roof. Up top the line had to be connected to the standpipe in the stairwell and stretched to the fire.

(A standpipe is a solid pipe built into a building that runs from street level to the highest floor, usually within an enclosed stairwell. Each floor landing has a hose outlet and a valve where firefighters can connect the hose they carry up.)

I knew we could knock this out quickly once we got water. I also knew this was going to need extensive overhaul to make sure there was no fire extension to the roof below.

After a minute or so, two firefighters emerged from the stairway pulling a dry hoseline. Everyone on the roof jumped in and helped them stretch their line into place. When they were ready, I radioed down, "Battalion 12 to Battalion 1, send the water." It took a few seconds for the water to make its way up, but once it was flowing from the nozzle, the fire was knocked down in less than a minute.

Now the real work started. In order to ensure that the fire was completely extinguished, we were going to have to remove all of the decking to inspect the roof itself. With a 4:30 a.m. temperature of about 80 degrees, and lots of hard labor in front of us, I requested a cooler of bottled water be brought to the roof.

Firefighters then methodically took apart the decking that was separated into 4'x 4' sections. We set up a system where truck and squad firefighters pulled up the sections of decking and passed them to an area where the engine company washed them down. Then, another truck piled the fully extinguished sections in an adjacent area. We continued this operation until the entire burned-out area of decking was removed. All members worked extremely hard. There was no fire extension to the roof. It was a job well done.

I got back to quarters around 6:00 a.m., just in time to get relieved and go home. With about only two hours of sleep prior to waking for the fire, I thought I'd go home this Sunday morning and take a nap. However, while on my way home from the firehouse, I remembered I had to play a "concert in the park" band job that afternoon from 2:00 p.m.—3:00 p.m. (I haven't mentioned this, but I play keyboards in a classic rock hobby band. It's something I've done since I was about seventeen years old.) This meant that I'd have to start loading my music gear around 11:00 a.m. There wouldn't be time to get in a good nap, so I loaded up on coffee and water and played the show on two hours of sleep. (Hey, it still beats my early years on the job when I worked construction on my off days after nights like this!)

07/29/15
Assignment—Battalion 2 (Engine 8's Quarters, 22ND & Wentworth)
Primary Response Area—Chinatown, South Loop, Bridgeport, Near South Lakefront
Weather—Temperatures in the low 90s

"AUTOMATIC ALARM IN A HIGH-RISE–RESIDENTIAL"

I was on the street doing my morning rounds about 9:00 a.m. when I was dispatched, via radio, to an "Automatic Alarm in a High-Rise—Residential." The location was a senior citizen building that I've been to many times before on false runs.

First to arrive on scene I reported "nothing showing" and walked into the lobby. Before I had a chance to look at the fire alarm panel, I was met at the front door by a security guard who told me there was construction work being done in the 5TH floor laundry room. He added that the building's maintenance man went up there and had just reported that dust from the construction work set off the smoke detector. He then offered me a look at a live security camera picture of the 5TH floor laundry room. I did but all I could see was a haze of dust. (False alarms from construction dust are very common. We get them just about every day. However, even if a representative from the building assures us there's no fire, we always send at least one company up to check things out.) While awaiting the arrival of Engine 29 and Truck 11, I walked over to the alarm panel and found something unusual. Instead of showing the expected location of a tripped smoke alarm, a light on the panel indicated a "Carbon Monoxide" alarm activation.

Knowing which companies were in route, I contacted them via radio,

"Battalion 2 to Truck 11 and Engine 29. When you get here bring in your CO detectors."

"Truck 11, message received. We just pulled up. We're on the scene."

"Engine 29, message received. We're two blocks away."

When Truck 11's crew entered the lobby, I explained the situation and sent the lieutenant and one firefighter up to investigate. When Engine 29 came into the lobby, I sent them up with a second CO meter. Arriving at the fifth floor, the lieutenant of Truck 11 radioed down that his initial CO reading in the hallway was 30 ppm but just outside of the laundry room it was 212 ppm. My initial thought was, although not life threatening, this is a fairly high amount of CO, especially when it's in a building full of senior citizens. Because of this, I decided to request a Level I Hazmat Response. Just as I was reaching for my radio microphone, I got a second report from the fifth floor,

"Truck 11 to Battalion 2, the source of the CO was a gas-powered saw being used to cut the concrete floor in the laundry room. We have the saw shut off and we opened all the windows in the room. Our readings are starting to drop."

With that information I decided to hold off on requesting a Level I Hazmat.

"Battalion 2 to Truck 11, sounds good. Get everyone out of the laundry room then close the door to the hallway. Let's try to keep this contained to the work area."

"Truck 11 to Battalion 2, it's already done."

"Okay Truck, I'm on my way up. You keep monitoring the hallway and 29 you take your CO meter to the 4TH, 6TH, 7TH and 8TH floors and lemme know what you got."

Before getting on the elevator, I told the remaining members of Truck 11 to get their exhaust fan and take it upstairs ASAP. On the ride up I got the following reports,

"Truck 11 to Battalion 2. Readings in the 5TH floor hallway are all down to around 20 ppm. A maintenance man just showed up with a large fan. We're setting it up now."

"Okay, point the fan out the window then open the hallway door."

I then called Engine 29, "Battalion 2 to Engine 29, how's it going?"

"Engine 29 to Battalion 2, zero readings on 4, 6, 7, and 8."

When my elevator opened on the 5TH floor, I could see that all the apartment doors, and the two doors leading to the stairwells, were closed. This was good, but I still wanted to make sure all the tenants on that floor were okay. With readings now below dangerous levels, I had firefighters knock on each door on the 5TH floor and speak with every tenant. All residents were fine and were instructed to stay in their apartments until we were done.

With the CO and construction dust confined to the 5TH floor, our task was now to completely and efficiently ventilate. In order to get the readings down to zero and clear the lingering light dust cloud, I instructed the firefighters to use our fan in conjunction with the maintenance man's fan that was already working. The plan was to use our fan to suck the CO from the hallway and channel it into the laundry room where the maintenance man's fan blew it out the window. Once both fans were running, to increase airflow, I instructed a firefighter in the lobby to open the doors to both stairways at ground level. Once those doors were opened on the first floor, I had firefighters open the stairwell doors on 5. This created an updraft in the stairwells from ground level that, combined with our fans, created a nice airflow path up the stairs, down the fifth-floor hall and out the window of the laundry room. After only a few minutes all the construction dust was gone, and we had zero CO readings throughout.

Before returning to the lobby, I huddled the construction workers and building maintenance people together for a quick lecture. I explained that what they did was very dangerous, and they should have known better than to operate a gas-powered saw inside a structure without any mechanical ventilation and monitoring meters...especially in a high-rise full of senior citizens! I further drove home the point by adding, "This had the potential of being BAD...VERY BAD. Bad enough to make the lead story on the news!" They all nodded in agreement, and I left.

Once outside I gathered the crews of Truck 11 and Engine 29 together for a quick critique. First, I commended the officers and their crews on a job well done. I then stressed the importance of not taking anyone's word on Automatic Alarms or any other runs. "Always look for yourself!" I told them, then added, "If I accepted the security guard's account that it was only construction dust that set off the alarm, we would have attempted to reset the system and left...and things could have been a lot different."

"FUEL SPILL"

Sometime in the mid-afternoon I was dispatched to a "Fuel Spill" on the Dan Ryan Expressway. Apparently, a car ran over some debris in the roadway causing a piece of metal to flip up and puncture its gas tank. When I arrived, companies were trying to stop the leak using a commercial leak stopping putty carried on all fire rigs. From experience, I knew that this stuff doesn't work very well while the fuel is still leaking. I exited my buggy, went to the rear and from my firecoat pocket pulled out a wooden golf tee. Handing it to one of the lieutenants I said, "Try jamming this in the hole. It's wood so it won't cause a spark. Then when the leak stops or at least slows down, you can use the putty." The lieutenant explained my idea to one of the firemen and handed him the tee. The firefighter crawled under the car, wedged the golf tee into the hole and the leak stopped. IDOT then spread some sand over the area and towed the vehicle away.

When I was a young kid on the job an older chief once handed me a wooden golf tee and told me to keep it in my firecoat pocket. "You'll know when you need it," he said. Thinking this was some sort of joke or a good luck piece of some kind, I carried it for years. One day, back when I was a lieutenant, I had a car leaking fuel. That was my "ah ha" moment. I reached in my pocket, pulled out that golf tee and stopped the leak. After that, I too, handed out a few wooden tees. I'll bet at least a few of the firefighters who were at this run now carry a couple in their pockets.

Throughout the rest of the afternoon, I had several automatic alarms, nothing out of the ordinary.

"PUBLIC RELATIONS EVENT"

This evening was the annual Chicago Police vs. Chicago Fire Department baseball game at US Cellular Field, home of the Chicago White Sox. Earlier in the day, while at District Headquarters, I was told to report to parking lot B an hour before the 7:10 game time. There, I was to meet a CFD rig that would be positioned outside the stadium for public relations. I arrived at the park about 6:15 p.m. and was a bit surprised to find the turn out for the game was way bigger than I expected! My guess was there were about three to five thousand people. (Okay Cub fans, go ahead and insert some joke here about how this is more people than the Sox regularly draw...ha ha...very funny...I'm a Sox fan.)

Outside we greeted families and let kids take pictures with the fire truck. About 7:00 we heard the start of the National Anthem. Everyone in the parking lot stopped what they were doing and faced the stadium. All fire department members stood at attention and saluted the flag. Just as the anthem was ending, both the Chicago Fire Department and Chicago Police helicopters did a synchronized stadium flyover. THAT was pretty cool! When the game started, I left to do my routine scheduled night visits to a couple of firehouses in my battalion.

"PERSON IN THE WATER"

Tonight, in addition to many other public summer events throughout the city, Soldier Field was host to a highly publicized international soccer game between Manchester United and Paris Saint-Germain. I'm not a soccer fan, but from what I was told, this was a HUGE event.

Around 8:00 p.m. I was dispatched via radio to a "Person in the Water" at Burnham Harbor, right behind Soldier Field. Responding from only about a mile west, even with lights and siren, I was only able to creep slowly in bumper-to-bumper traffic towards the incident. While en route, the first arriving fire company reported they were on the scene and had one male in the water clinging to a dock. Listening to subsequent radio reports, I began to realize that the closer I got to the harbor the less of an emergency this became. The next radio transmission came from my boss, 2-2-1, Deputy District Chief Andy Bajorek who somehow beat me to the scene. His report was, "2-2-1 to Main, the victim is out of the water. Hold all companies still responding. The ambulance on scene will handle it from hëre." By this time, I was only about a block away, so I continued in.

When I arrived at the harbor, 2-2-1 told me he happened to be close by at Soldier Field when the call came in. He said the police received a report of a young man and his girlfriend screaming at each other just outside of Soldier Field, and that the argument appeared to be reaching the point of physical contact. When police arrived, the guy took off running through a park, down a hill and towards Burnham Harbor. The officers, who were giving chase, said the guy ran down a hill towards the harbor and ran right off the pier into the water. Then, after surfacing, he hung on to the dock and wouldn't come out. The police, along with the CFD dive team, convinced the man there was no where to run and that he should just come out on his own. A few minutes later, realizing the police were right, the man surrendered and was assisted out of the water by fire department personnel. Once on land, and handed over to the police, the man became very combative and verbally abusive towards everyone. It took two paramedics and three police officers to handcuff and tie the man to a stretcher...all the while he yelled to his girlfriend, "I love you!!"

The rest of the night was quiet.

AUGUST 2015

08/01/15
ASSIGNMENT—BATTALION 14 (ENGINE 109'S QUARTERS, 22ND & KEDZIE)
PRIMARY RESPONSE AREA—WESTSIDE, LITTLE VILLAGE
WEATHER—TEMPERATURES IN THE HIGH 80S

The weather on this summer Saturday in August was beautiful. Temperatures were in the mid 70's with plenty of sunshine. The area I was covering included Chicago's Little Village neighborhood, home to one of the city's largest Mexican populations. It's a very family-oriented area, and from experience, I knew that throughout my travels today I would see plenty of house party celebrations going on in the neighborhoods. I got my first fire run of the day around 11:00 p.m.

"STILL ALARM"

At approximately 11:00 p.m. I was dispatched to a fire on South St. Louis. The notes on my computer screen read "possible fire in the attic." Engine 99 was the first to arrive on scene and reported, "Smoke showing."

This area is densely populated and has very narrow streets. So as not to hamper accessibility of the responding fire companies, I decided to attempt parking in the alley. The address

I was given was an even number. So, knowing that even numbered addresses are on the north side of the street, I took the north alley. As I approached, I could see the backyard of the fire building was decorated with colored lights and filled with people. Apparently, there was a party going on outside when the fire broke out in the house.

I got out of my buggy and made my way through the crowd of people to the back porch where I met the captain of Engine 99. "I was just up the back stairs and got a good look," he said. "The fire is all in the front of the attic. There's a door about halfway back that's open just a crack. The fire is behind it now, but it's coming through and making its way to the rear. The smoke is heavy and it's pretty hot up there. We're not gonna be able to get to the fire until the roof is opened. If we try to hit it from the porch our water will push that middle door closed. We got a line led out now and are waiting for water." Knowing that Truck 32's roof team was already on their way up, I replied, "Okay. Stay down here at the back stairs and listen for me on the radio."

In order to safely extinguish this fire, we needed to get a ventilation hole cut in the roof to release the hot gasses that naturally rise. This would make the attic more bearable for Engine 99's crew. We also wanted to keep the attic window at the gable end intact. Breaking that window too soon without good roof ventilation could possibly create a "flow path" of fire, heat, and smoke, that could travel out of the attic, to the porch and down the stairs towards the firefighters making their way up.

I then did a quick once around the building and confirmed that two firefighters from Truck 32 were on the roof with their chain saw, and the second truck was in the process of throwing a ladder to the rear of the roof. I then radioed in my first progress report, "Office, we have a 2-story frame with fire in the attic. Roof ops are under way and ladders are thrown in Side A and C. 99's led out at the back stairs. We should have water on it in a minute." "Message Received Battalion 14," replied the alarm office.

Standing in front of the building, I grabbed a couple of truck firefighters who were on their way to the rear. I told them to reposition the ladder in front of the building from a second-floor window to the small attic window just under the roof's peak. When the ladder was in place, I told one of them, "You're gonna take out that attic window, but don't climb up until I tell you."

A minute or so later the captain of Engine 99 radioed to me,

"Engine 99 to Battalion 14, we got water. We're ready to go."

"Battalion 14 to 99, I can hear Truck 32's saw now. They should have a hole in a second. Don't go up yet. I'll turn you loose as soon as I see the roof venting. And, when you do get up there, make sure you check those knee walls before you go in and along the way."

"99, message received."

(Knee walls are short, wood framed walls in peaked roof attics. They are usually covered with drywall and run the length of the building on either side of the attic. The space behind them is usually used for storage. Firefighters are taught to open a hole in each knee wall prior to entering an attic and along the way as they advance. This ensures that the fire is not getting behind them and cutting off their egress.)

With roof ventilation in progress and knowing that Engine 99 had water and was ready to go, I told the firefighter standing next to me to climb the ladder up to the attic window and wait for my instruction before taking it out. Seconds later I heard the saw stop. This indicated that the hole was cut, and they were probably now picking at the roofing and wood with their axes. Sure enough, I looked up and saw a billow of smoke push out from the hole in the roof. Perfect! With that I gave a nod to the firefighter on the ladder, and he took out the attic window. I then radioed, "Battalion 14 to 99 it's all yours...go get it." It only took about two minutes when Engine 99 radioed down that the fire was out, and they were now washing down. "Good job 99," I radioed back.

While companies were picking up, to determine the cause of the fire, I began interviewing a group of people in the backyard. I was told that the large crowd was celebrating a "going away party" for a family member and her children. When I asked if there was anyone in the house at the time the fire started, everyone collectively shook their head "no." I posed my question again, this time asking if any kids might have been alone in the house. One of the residents of the building stepped up and told me that several children were inside the house, unsupervised, and that one of them came out to the yard and told the adults they heard a loud noise inside. When the adults went to investigate, they encountered smoke at the attic door and called 911. Because the fire was possibly started by children, I requested a response by our Office of Fire Investigation.

A few days later I happened to run into one of the investigators who worked on this fire. He told me that it started accidentally from a religious candle that was left unattended in the attic apartment.

08/04/15
ASSIGNMENT—BATTALION 14 (ENGINE 109'S QUARTERS, 22ND & KEDZIE)
PRIMARY RESPONSE AREA—WESTSIDE, LITTLE VILLAGE
WEATHER—TEMPERATURES IN THE HIGH 70S

FROM NBC NEWS CHICAGO
FIREFIGHTER CRITICALLY INJURED IN BRIDGEPORT BLAZE

The firefighter was "overcome by the stress of the fire"

PUBLISHED AUGUST 1, 2015 • UPDATED ON AUGUST 1, 2015 AT 10:18 AM

A Chicago firefighter was critically injured while battling a fire in the Bridgeport neighborhood Saturday morning.

The fire broke out around 8 a.m. at a building in the 500 block of West 31st Street, fire officials said in a tweet.

One of the firefighters was "overcome by the stress of the fire" and transported to a hospital in critical condition, according to Chicago Fire Department spokesperson Larry Langford.

Langford said in the heat and humidity of the summer, the department often rotates firefighters to prevent such injuries.

(When a firefighter suffers a severe on-duty injury, battalion chiefs from throughout the city are assigned 4-hour "special duty" shifts at the hospital. This is done to support the family of the injured firefighter and to keep headquarters informed of the patient's condition.)

I reported for duty around 5:30 a.m. The off-going chief

informed me that the condition of the firefighter, who had been injured three days ago, remained critical. He added I would probably soon be getting a call from District for my assigned special duty time at the hospital. Fifteen minutes later I was notified that I would be taking the 2:00 a.m.– 6:00 a.m. rotation.

"LEVEL I HAZMAT"

While on my morning rounds, I was dispatched via radio to a Level I Hazmat for a Gas Leak on the 2600 block of South Keeler Avenue. The comment section on my computer screen read, "Water Dept. Hit a 2-inch Gas Main."

Engine 99 arrived on the scene first and reported a small gas leak, and that a gas company crew was already there. When I arrived minutes later, gas company workers were in the process of repairing a damaged line located only a few feet under the parkway in front of a small church. As a precaution, Engine 99 stood by with a charged 2 ½" line and dry chemical extinguisher while the gas company worked on the leak. After only a few minutes the leak was stopped. With the escaping gas issue mitigated I secured the Level I, released all companies and returned to my morning administrative work.

The rest of the day was pretty normal. I only had a few false alarms and completed my usual administrative business.

Around 10:00 p.m., I set my alarm clock for 1:00 a.m. and laid down hoping to close my eyes for an hour or two.

At 1:00 a.m. my alarm clock went off. This gave me forty-five minutes to clean up, straighten my room, gather my personal stuff, and get to the hospital for my 2:00 a.m. assignment. Before leaving the firehouse, I phoned the alarm office to let them know I was heading to the hospital on special duty. The fire alarm office operator confirmed my assignment, "Okay Chief, we'll put you on special duty."

Two blocks from the firehouse was a 24-hour donut shop. I stopped there to grab a cup of coffee before heading to the hospital. About five minutes from the hospital, the alarm office called me on the radio, "Main to Battalion 14, return to quarters and give us a call on the phone." "Battalion 14, message received. I'm returning to quarters." When I got back to the firehouse I called the alarm office,

"This is Chief Stawiarski in the 14TH, what's up?"

"Chief, we don't have you on the schedule for the hospital today. Who gave you that assignment?"

"District told me I was on schedule from 2:00 a.m. to 6:00 a.m."

"Nope. Must have been a miscommunication. We have another chief on the way. You stay home."

"Okay, the 14TH is staying home."

I was relieved at 5:30.

08/07/15
ASSIGNMENT—BATTALION 14 (ENGINE 109'S QUARTERS, 22ND & KEDZIE)
PRIMARY RESPONSE AREA—WESTSIDE, LITTLE VILLAGE
WEATHER—TEMPERATURES IN THE LOW 80S

I reported for work about 5:15 a.m. After getting all my gear in the buggy, I sat in the kitchen for about a half an hour chatting with Phil Connor, the chief I just relieved. Phil informed me that the injured firefighter was still in critical condition and that I was scheduled to be at the hospital today from 2:00 p.m. to 6:00 p.m. He also told me today was the annual "Shake the Boot" day for the Muscular Dystrophy Association. As a battalion chief, I don't actively stand in the street and "shake the boot." However, I do have administrative duties relating to the fundraiser that have to be completed by 7:00 p.m. During our chat, Chief Connor also added that he took a ride past the address where I had the "gas leak" on my previous shift. He said, while there, he noticed a building directly across the street with its entire brick facade removed. I made a mental note of this and decided to take a casual ride by the building after morning roll call.

About 6:30 a.m., while doing my daily paperwork, I received a phone call from Special Operations Battalion Chief Matt Oakes. Matt needed a day off the following week and asked if I would work a trade with him. "Yeah, I'll work for you," I said, "and hey, as long as I have you on the phone, I'm going over to the 2600 block of South Keeler about 9:00 to take a look at a building with its facade removed. You interested?" (As Special Operations Chief, if this building were to collapse, Matt would be in charge of the technical end of the search and rescue.) "Yeah, I have nothing planned for the morning," Matt answered, "I'll see you there at 9:00."

Matt got to the Keeler address before me and was sizing things up when I arrived. The building in question was a 3-story brick with scaffolding in front from the sidewalk up to the roof. As an apparent attempt at securing the structure from trespassers, 4 x 8 foot sheets of plywood were affixed loosely to the scaffolding. Peering inside through the gaps in the wood, we could see the entire front of the building had been dismantled and the first-floor joists had all been removed. The second-floor joists were still in place, but with no flooring affixed to them. We also saw that an old, heavy wooden stairway leading to the second floor was suspended by a rope tied to a joist above. Also, visible through the plywood, was a gas meter with its valve in the off position but without a cap. This meant that one simple turn of the valve could release a large volume of gas into the structure and surrounding street and sidewalk. While walking around the outside of the building, we also noted that the top of the scaffolding was very close to the highest voltage power lines in the alley.

Matt and I decided to call for an immediate response from the Building Department and the police. While waiting for CPD to arrive, with the safety of fire department members in mind, I phoned District Headquarters and each firehouse in the immediate area to warn them about this building.

As we started to affix yellow caution tape around the perimeter, we were approached by two young men. Presenting us with approved building permits, they informed us the building belonged to a small church in the area and they, along with other volunteer church members, were working on the building with a local contractor. They were very cooperative when we asked for further information and were also very understanding when I explained that our concern was their safety. I told them I didn't want to be dispatched later this evening to dig them out from under two tons of bricks.

When the police arrived, we gave them a thorough briefing. I then notified the fire alarm office via radio, "Battalion 14 to Main, CPD is on the scene. I'm turning it over to them. They'll stay here and wait for the Building Department to arrive."

Later that morning, after completing my daily rounds and delivering my paperwork to District Headquarters, I spun back past the dangerous building to see if the Building Dept. had arrived yet.

5-1-5, Chief Oakes, was still there and the gas company

crew was in the process of capping off the open pipe. It was now getting close to 1:00 p.m. so I ran back to quarters, grabbed a sandwich, and left for my hospital rotation assignment.

At the hospital I took the elevator up to the injured firefighter's floor and was greeted by his family and the battalion chief who I was there to relieve. At this point, the firefighter had been in critical condition for seven days. There was an empty room next to his that was available for the chiefs on special duty. When the family assured me they didn't need anything, I went to the room next door. Soon after, a few of the CFD top brass showed up and we all spoke with the family for about an hour. When the big bosses left, I went back to the room next door and read the paper until being relieved at 6:00 p.m.

There was no time for dinner just yet. I still had to run around to all the firehouses in my battalion to take care of "Shake the Boot" business. When that was done, around 8:00 p.m., I got back to my firehouse and reheated a plate of fish the cook set aside for me. After my late dinner, I went back to my room, put on the Sox game, and started all the paperwork I hadn't been able to get to during the day. I turned out the lights around 10:30 p.m.

Occasionally, at work, I'll leave my fire radio on very low volume overnight. This was one of those nights. At around 4:30 a.m., while in a drowsy half-sleep, I thought I heard something over the radio that sounded weird. So weird, I thought I might have been dreaming. The transmission I thought I heard was, "Battalion 2 to Main, I'm on the scene. If companies don't show up fast I'm going in!!" After that the radio was silent. I waited to hear more but must have dozed off, because about fifteen minutes later, I woke up to hear more radio traffic. This time the report was that one victim was being transported to the hospital and one battalion chief was also going to the hospital for testing. Further radio transmissions, and the *Channel 9 Morning News*, confirmed that BC Stan Saganowski had jumped into the Chicago River at 21ST street to save a drowning woman. Stan was first to arrive and found several people pointing at a woman about twenty-five yards out who was "going under." Two other people, friends of the woman, were also in the water but safe near the shore. Stan kicked off his shoes, put on a life jacket, swam out to the woman, and brought her to shore. Nice.

> 08/10/15
> ASSIGNMENT—BATTALION 14 (ENGINE 109'S QUARTERS, 22ND & KEDZIE)
> PRIMARY RESPONSE AREA—WESTSIDE, LITTLE VILLAGE
> WEATHER—TEMPERATURES IN THE LOW 80S

At this morning's relief briefing, the off-going chief informed me that the injured firefighter was still in the hospital and there was no change in his condition. He also told me the dangerous building I reported last workday was deemed "okay" by the building department after several of the violations were corrected. With this in mind, I decided to hold a drill today with each company in my battalion, on the dangers of buildings under construction or demolition.

My first stop of the day was roll call at Engine 99's quarters. In addition to the usual roll call topics, we had an open discussion on dangerous buildings. During the drill the captain told me there was another dangerous building in his still district on Ogden Avenue. He said he had written several referrals to the Building Department on this very large, abandoned structure but hadn't got a response. I told him to meet me there after lunch.

About 1:00 p.m. Engine 99 and I met on Ogden. The building in question was an old, 3-story, vacant, mill constructed factory. It was about 150 feet wide by 100 feet deep and was showing several signs of possible collapse. The parapet walls were buckling, there were several deformed lintels and broken windowpanes that looked like they were ready to fall out of the building onto the street any minute. With this being a direct danger to passing pedestrians and vehicles, I requested an immediate response by the Building Department and the police. I also had Engine 99 block off one lane of vehicle traffic using their orange traffic cones.

Within an hour a Building Department inspector arrived. As soon as he got out of his car, he walked over and told me he was very familiar with this building. He said he had already submitted it for demolition once and that it was probably still on the list. With today's call and the obvious dangers it still posed, he said he would immediately submit a request for a "fast-track demolition." That was good enough for me. I handed the scene over to the inspector and the police.

"AUTOMATIC ALARM IN A HIGH-RISE"

About 4:00 p.m. I was dispatched to an "Automatic Alarm in a High-Rise" on West Maypole. This was not within my battalion boundaries. I got the run because the chief who would have normally handled it was on another assignment.

As I got close to the address a very heavy rain began to fall. Halfway into my right turn from Homan onto Maypole, I was stopped by a back up of cars. With my windshield wipers on high, I could just barely see that Engine 44 and Truck 36 were parked at the address up ahead with their lights on. The traffic jam was being caused by cars that had followed them down this narrow street. I then heard Engine 44 report via radio, "Engine 44 to Main, hold all responding companies but let the chief come in. We had burnt food in apartment #903. We're ventilating now. We're also giving medical attention to an elderly woman. She seems fine, just a little shaken up by all the excitement. Start us in an ambulance as a precaution." Unable to drive closer, but less than 100 feet away, I followed 44's report with, "Battalion 14 to Main, I'm on the scene. Gimme the police here for traffic control."

The downpour had now turned to a steady, heavy rain. Up ahead I could see that Engine 44 and Truck 36 were positioned just beyond the building's driveway. Directly behind Truck 36 were a delivery truck, several cars and then me, halfway into my turn at the corner. Now I'm thinking, "The delivery truck and these cars had to have seen the flashing lights of both fire apparatus but still pulled up behind them anyway."

As I was trying to figure out how to move these vehicles, out of my driver side window I caught a glimpse of ANOTHER car nosing in trying to get past me and onto the street with the jam-up! "You've got to be kidding!" I thought. Fortunately, I had enough room to nose my buggy up and block the street completely. No other cars could get in, and the ones that were there were going to be stuck until I moved allowing them room to back out. Puzzled as to why no one was paying attention to my emergency lights, I thought maybe they weren't working. This wasn't the case. I was able to confirm that my lights were on because I could see them in a reflection in the windows across the street.

Okay...I had to get these cars moved. There was only one

way to do this. Get out of my buggy, stand in the rain, and speak to each blocked-in driver. I told the drivers of the first two cars, "There is an ambulance on the way that has to get in here. I'm gonna move my vehicle and block traffic on Homan. When I do, you have to back out." They apologetically nodded their heads. The truck driver was another story. When I approached and motioned for him to roll down his window, and after explaining my traffic abatement plan, he began frantically banging on his steering wheel and yelling at me,

"You can't block the street like this! I gotta get down there. I got a job to do!"

"Look man," I said calmly as I stood in the pouring rain soaking wet, "I got an ambulance that's gonna show up any minute. We gotta make room for it. You gotta back out now."

"There's a lotta traffic behind me. You gonna back me out?!" he shouted.

"Absolutely," I replied.

I then jumped in my buggy, backed onto Homan, stopped traffic, and allowed all three vehicles to back out. Then, just as I was pulling forward with the intention of completely blocking Maypole, ANOTHER car tried to get past me. WHAT the hell was going on here?!! After fending this vehicle off, I parked diagonally across the street so that no other traffic could turn in. NOW, I was finally able to walk the one hundred feet to the entrance of the building and do what I was called here to do.

Drenched from head to toe, I entered the lobby and handed my keys to one of the firefighters standing by, "Do me a favor," I said, "go down to my buggy now and move it when the ambulance gets here so they can get through, then park me out of the way somewhere."

As I approached the lobby desk, I saw two firefighters

tending to a woman and waiting for the ambulance and asked,

"Is she okay?"

"She looks fine, and her vitals are good," answered one of the firefighters, "she's just a little excited. We're gonna let the ambo take a look at her. Then she'll decide if she wants to go to the hospital or not."

I then turned to one of the other firefighters in the lobby and asked,

"What's going on?"

"They're still upstairs ventilating the apartment but we're having trouble resetting the alarm system."

"Battalion 14 to Truck 36, how's it going?"

"The apartment is clear, but we think the smoke detector is bad."

"Okay, come on down. I have a maintenance man here. We're gonna put the building on 911 until they can get the system fixed."

At this point Ambulance 33 arrived and took over patient care.

When all crews were picked up and ready to leave, I called the fire alarm office and told them, "I'm putting this building on 911 till further notice." (This means the alarm system is out of service and will not automatically notify the fire department. If there is a fire in the building, someone will have to call 911 manually until the system is repaired.)

As the ambulance pulled away transporting the elderly woman to the hospital as a precaution, companies upstairs reported that all stairwells and hallways were clear. Done!!

08/13/15
Assignment—Battalion 14 (Engine 109's Quarters, 22nd & Kedzie)
Primary Response Area—Westside, Little Village
Weather—Temperatures in the mid 80s

Not much happened this day. I did take a ride back to that dangerous building on Ogden to see if anything was being done since last workday. It was. Demolition crews were at the site and already had most of the structure razed.

08/16/15
Assignment—Battalion 14 (Engine 109's Quarters, 22nd & Kedzie)
Primary Response Area—Westside, Little Village
Weather—Temperatures in the high 80s

Slow day.

08/17/15 thru 08/24/15

With my Daley Day and one Payback, I was off for eight days in a row!

08/25/15
Assignment—Battalion 9 (Engine 70's Quarters, Clark & Peterson)
Primary Response Area—Rogers Park, Uptown, Lakefront
Weather—Temperatures in the mid 70s

Ten runs, nothing notable.

08/28/15
ASSIGNMENT—BATTALION 8 (ENGINE 125'S QUARTERS, NARRAGANSETT & FULLERTON)
PRIMARY RESPONSE AREA—WEST AND NEAR NORTHWEST SIDES
WEATHER—TEMPERATURES IN THE LOW 70S

"STILL ALARM"

At about 2:00 p.m. companies were stilled out to a fire on North Waller Avenue. The first units on the scene reported, "Nothing showing on a 2-story brick occupied building." At the front door firefighters were met by a woman who told them she smelled smoke in her apartment. She added that she called 911 yesterday at the same time for the same smell, and that the fire department couldn't find anything. When I arrived, I entered the apartment and caught a very slight smell of burnt food. Using thermal imaging cameras, companies checked both apartments and the basement but could not find anything unusual. I advised the woman of our findings and told her to call us back if she smelled it again.

"PIN-IN ACCIDENT"

At around 1:30 a.m. I was dispatched to a "Pin-In Accident" at Central and Irving. Engine 94 was the first to arrive and corrected the location to Irving and Linder. Upon arrival Engine 94, Tower Ladder 23 and Ambulance 47 reported a three-vehicle accident.

Vehicle #1—wrapped around a tree with one occupant pinned in

Vehicle #2—a minivan with no occupants on the sidewalk next to Vehicle #1

Vehicle #3—a parked car on the street with no occupants

Per protocol, Engine 94 led out and charged a 2 ½" line and had their dry chemical extinguisher ready while extrication was in progress. As the crew from Tower Ladder 23 was getting their extrication tools ready, the paramedics from Ambulance 47 approached Vehicle #1 on the driver's side to assess the victim's condition. They quickly pronounced the sole occupant of the vehicle dead on arrival.

Throughout my career I've been to a lot of these types of accidents. I can't recall ever seeing a vehicle completely wrapped around a tree like this one. The driver's side rear fender was actually inches from touching the front fender and the tree was embedded in the driver's door.

The crew from Tower 23 worked diligently but the victim was so deeply entangled in the car that I had to turn the extrication over to Squad 2. It wasn't that the crew from Tower 23 couldn't handle the job, it was that their tools had reached their limits. The Squad carries more sophisticated equipment, and their members receive extensive training on things like this. With a blanket covering the victim, Squad 2, assisted by Tower Ladder 23, went to work. In situations like these our practice is not to remove the victim from the car but to remove the car from around the victim. After about twenty minutes of cutting, bending and prying, the extrication was complete. With the driver now out of the vehicle, I had Squad 2 triple-check to be absolutely certain there was no one else in, around or under the car. You never know. If someone happened to be walking down the street at the wrong time the crashing vehicles could have struck them. The final search of the scene was negative. Chicago Fire Department ambulances do not normally transport DOA's. In this case however, there were no police wagons available, and a crowd of onlookers and television cameras were gathering. At the request of the police supervisor on the scene, and with permission from an EMS supervisor, Ambulance 47 transported the victim to the closest hospital.

Below is an article I read online the next morning:

A man died in a hit-and-run car crash early Saturday morning in the Portage Park neighborhood on the Northwest Side, police said. The crash happened around 1:40 a.m. in the 5400 block of West Irving Park Road, said Chicago Police Department spokeswoman Officer Amina Greer. A 2002 Honda Civic and a dark-colored van were traveling east on Irving Park Road at a high rate of speed when the van struck the Honda. The Honda then struck a tree, Greer said. A male adult, who was driving the Honda, was pronounced dead at the scene of the crash, Greer said. The man's exact age was not immediately available. No one else was in the Honda except for the driver. The occupants of the van ran away from the scene of the accident, Greer said. As of early Saturday morning, no one was in custody. The police Major Accident Investigation Unit is investigating the case, and no other information was available.—Chicago Tribune

08/31/15
ASSIGNMENT—BATTALION 6 (ENGINE 123's QUARTERS, 51ST & LEAVITT)...THE OLD 19TH BATTALION
PRIMARY RESPONSE AREA—SOUTH SIDE
WEATHER—TEMPERATURES IN THE MID 80S

Nothing out of the ordinary today.

SEPTEMBER 2015

09/06/15
Assignment—5-1-5 (Special Operations—Engine 5's Quarters, DesPlaines & Jackson)
Primary Response Area—City Wide
Weather—Temperatures in the low 90s

Today was an EXCEPTIONALLY busy day.

"PERSON IN THE WATER"

At 7:15 a.m. I was dispatched from quarters to a "Person in the Water" at DuSable Harbor. A male in his 40's was reportedly working on his boat when he fell into the Harbor. Prior to my arrival the CFD Fast Boat, that just happens to be moored in the same harbor, arrived quickly, and pulled the man out of the water. He declined medical attention.

"PERSON ON THE TRACKS"

Around 9:30 a.m. I caught a run over the radio for a "Person on the Tracks." A distraught woman wandered off the Cumberland CTA train station platform and on to the track bed. CTA security cameras picked it up quickly and power to the location was shut down immediately. Prior to our arrival, a CTA worker was able to coax the person off of the tracks and escort her back to the station safely. The woman was transported to the hospital by CFD ambulance for evaluation.

"CAR INTO THE BUILDING"

I was dispatched to a "Car into the Building" at 2:00 p.m. but was Held En Route a few minutes later.

Being that I was in a citywide response buggy, around 3:00 p.m., I took a ride to survey the site of Taste of Polonia, a large annual Polish festival on Chicago's northside. While there, I happened to notice that one of the members of a performing polka band was a relative of mine. I gave him a wave from the side of the stage and was acknowledged with a short trumpet toot. I was at the festival site for about 30 minutes noting street closures, fire lanes, entrances and exits.

About 7:30 p.m. I headed over to the fuel depot at North Ave. and Throop St. After topping off my tank, I drove up the street to visit with some old friends at Engine 106's quarters. Around 9:00 p.m., while chatting with the officers, we heard an announcement over the radio, "A Still & Box and a Level I Hazmat at the scene of the freight train fire at 93RD and St. Lawrence on the orders of Battalion 23." The next radio transmission came seconds later, "5-1-5 take in the Still & Box and Level I." I acknowledged the run and jumped on the Kennedy expressway at Sacramento and headed south. According to the GPS on my *iPad*, the distance from Engine 106's quarters to the fire was about 17 miles.

"STILL AND BOX–FREIGHT TRAIN FIRE"

Upon arrival, Battalion 23 immediately requested a Still and Box alarm when he found a large volume of fire on two flat train cars heavily loaded with long wooden telephone poles.

He requested a Level I Hazmat seconds later when he saw that a couple of train cars downwind of the fire were tankers. The train was located on an embankment above street level in a residential area.

As I exited the Dan Ryan expressway at 95TH and headed east I could already see flames and dark smoke powerfully billowing fifty feet into the night sky. When I got close to the scene, I snaked around the winding streets and found a place to park my buggy about a half block upwind. From there I donned my turnout gear and breathing apparatus and headed up the embankment towards the fire.

When I got up on the tracks, 2-2-6, Deputy District Chief Greg Matthews gave me an assignment, "Kev, there are supposed to be representatives from the railroad somewhere on the scene. Go find them and get the train's consist." (The consist is a list carried on every train that describes what each car is carrying. Basically, it's another name for shipping papers.) "Got it boss," I replied.

Looking down the tracks about 200 feet, I could see the headlights of a pickup truck that I assumed was the railroad people. As I began walking in that direction, two guys standing next to the truck spotted me and began waving papers. My assumption was correct. These were the railroad reps, and they had the consist. Using our flashlights 2-2-6 and I pored over all the documentation until we found what we needed. The first car downwind of the fire was an empty flat car. Good. The next car was a boxcar filled with sugar. Good. The third car down was the tanker but was listed as empty. The last known substance it transported was sulfuric acid. Good, we should be okay.

A few minutes later the Hazmat Team (5-1-1) arrived, and I briefed them on the information we had. Because the utility poles were more than likely treated with creosote or some other chemical preservative, our decision was to first check the air quality near the fire. Next, even though we felt pretty good about the tank car being safe, 5-1-1 took temperature readings of it just to make sure it wasn't hot. It wasn't. We were good all the way around. After about forty-five minutes of companies pouring water on the fire, it was now mostly out. The wooden poles, however, were so tightly stacked on the train that even with exceptional effort, it was almost impossible to get water on every smoldering ember. About 11:00 p.m. 2-2-6 struck out the Still and Box, secured the Level I and released me from the scene. Several engine companies were kept there for another couple of hours soaking the poles with thousands of gallons of water.

On my way back to quarters I heard over the radio that Battalion 1 was still on the scene, downtown, of another Level I Hazmat that originally came in as I was on my way to the train fire. This one was for elevated carbon monoxide readings in a high-rise building located in the south loop. A friend of mine, newly promoted Battalion Chief Rich Nelson, was in Battalion 1 for his first time. Rich is a very sharp guy but as I know from firsthand experience, some things can be pretty overwhelming when you're the new guy. Also, from listening to the radio earlier in the shift, I knew Rich was having an exceptionally busy day in the first battalion. So as a courtesy I decided to slide by to see if I could be of any assistance. When I was about a mile away, I heard Rich's radio update to the fire alarm office, "Battalion 1 to Main. Secure the Level I on my orders. The source of the CO was a vehicle left running in the parking garage below the building. We used fans to ventilate the CO that made its way up the elevator shaft to the residential area above. Readings throughout the building are now zero." I was only a few blocks away, so I continued in.

I arrived just as companies were picking up their equipment and pulled my buggy up to where Rich was standing in the street. With that "what a day!" look on his face, he walked over to my buggy and we both had a good laugh about how hectic Battalion 1 can be. I told him that even though it was a Sunday just before midnight, it was Labor Day weekend, and with the large number of tourists and partiers still on the streets, the night was still young. I took the long way back to quarters and drove through downtown to check out the late-night vibrancy of the Labor Day weekend.

"PERSON THREATENING TO JUMP"

About three minutes after backing into quarters, around 11:45 p.m., I was dispatched to a "Person Threatening to Jump" at Lawrence Ave. and the Kennedy Expressway. The first thing that came to mind was that this location was only a block or so from where the Taste of Polonia fest was going on earlier. Even though the event ended hours ago, some bars in the area host after-parties. A lot of "jumper" runs turn out to be drunken drama, but just as every other run, they have to be treated as the real thing.

While responding, I decided I would stay on the expressway and take the underside position of the incident. This way, if this were a bona fide incident, I could block traffic. Also, this is where our inflatable jump bag would be set up if needed. I was about five minutes away when I heard the first company on the scene report, "Engine 108 is on the scene at the Kennedy. Do you have any more information on this? We don't see anyone." Just as I pulled up under the Lawrence Ave.

bridge, the alarm office replied, “Engine 108 and all companies responding to the Person Threatening to Jump, we got another call saying that the person is now on the Ainsle bridge over the Kennedy.” This was just up ahead of me, so I continued past Lawrence up to Ainsle and reported to Battalion 10, “5-1-5- to Battalion 10, I’m on the scene down below at Ainsle. I don’t see anything down here and I didn't see anything back at Lawrence.” He radioed back, “Battalion 10 to 5-1-5. I’m up here with both the Chicago and State Police. They couldn’t find anything either. You can go home. I’m gonna return all companies.”

With that, I turned off my emergency lights and drove ahead to the next exit at Central Ave. As I approached the Milwaukee Ave. Bridge over the Kennedy, I noticed a woman approximately in her 30’s, standing alone looking over the guardrail down onto the expressway. Not wanting to startle her I slowly pulled up near the curb to where she was standing and rolled down my window. “Everything okay?” I asked. When she turned in my direction it immediately appeared to me that this young woman had been drinking. Laughingly she replied, “I’m fine, I’m fine.” I stayed parked at the curb and watched as she walked away. When she reached the bottom of the bridge a male about the same age appeared from out of the bushes and took her hand. I watched as the two walked away laughing hysterically. My guess is that this was either a prank or someone mistook this couple as contemplating a jump off of the bridge. In order to bring closure to the original jump incident I called the fire alarm office on the radio and told them what I found.

"STILL ALARM–FREIGHT TRAIN FIRE"

I was lying in bed half asleep about 4:00 a.m. when another run came over the house speakers, "5-1-5, Freight Train Fire, 2700 E. 100TH St." As soon as I heard the address, I figured this was most likely a rekindle of the same train fire we had earlier. While en route, my thoughts were that once the fire was extinguished and all companies left the scene, the train would be moved south to a large rail yard at 106TH street. I figured that the oxygen introduced into the pile of logs by the movement of the train, helped reignite hidden areas of smoldering embers that we couldn't reach with hose streams earlier.

About ten miles into my sixteen-mile trip, I heard Battalion 24 report, "Battalion 24 to Englewood, I'm in the train yard at 106TH. We've got a rekindle of that train they moved here from the earlier fire. There's not much fire but we're gonna have to work on getting water back here."

It didn't sound like anything Special Operations would be needed for, so I slowed down my response, but continued in while I waited for Battalion 24 to hold me up. I made it all the way to 106TH street when I thought maybe Battalion 24 didn't realize that the helicopter and I were responding. (For reconnaissance purposes, the CFD helicopter responds automatically to all train fires.) When I arrived, I parked just outside the train yard and called Battalion 24 on the Fireground radio channel, "5-1-5 to Battalion 24. Just for your information you're getting a Special Operations response on this. You have me and the helicopter." "I'm sorry, Kev. I didn't realize you were dispatched. Thanks for comin' out but you can go home." she replied. Her next radio transmission was, "Battalion 24 to Englewood, hold the helicopter and I'm releasing 5-1-5."

I got back to my firehouse from the above run at 4:45 a.m. My shift would be over around 5:30 so I didn't even try to get in a nap before going home. I packed up my stuff, made a pot of coffee and read the paper until my relief came in at 5:45. Just out of curiosity, before sitting down at the kitchen table, I checked the mileage on my buggy. Since filling up earlier in the shift, I put on 108 miles in sixteen hours...and never left the city limits.

09/09/15

For some reason I don't have a record of where I worked on this day. Nothing much must have happened, or it would have been noted.

I did have one entry in my personal journal on this date that read: "The critically injured firefighter from a month ago is awake and smiling. He will be moving from the hospital to a physical care facility very soon. He's expected to make a full recovery."

09/18/15

ASSIGNMENT—BATTALION 19 (ENGINE 54's QUARTERS, 71ST & PARNELL)...THE OLD 18TH BATTALION

PRIMARY RESPONSE AREA—ENGLEWOOD

WEATHER—TEMPERATURES IN THE MID 80S

The day was pretty quiet. The four fire runs I had all turned out to be false. I did, however, have one bona fide fire in the evening.

Just before lunch, an off-duty paramedic from my battalion called. Due to a family issue, he needed an emergency trade so he could be off the following day. While I was out doing my morning rounds, he stopped by my firehouse, filled out the trade forms and left them on my desk. His phone call was to confirm that I found his paperwork and that everything was okay for him to be off tomorrow. We're always very accommodating when it comes to emergency trades. I told him I would make sure everything was fine and I would personally hand deliver his paperwork to District Headquarters today.

After dinner I rolled out of quarters about 6:30 p.m. My first order of business was to visit each firehouse in my battalion to drop off paperwork. After my last firehouse stop, I headed to District with the emergency trade forms. The ride to District took me pretty far out of my battalion and, sure enough, just as I was a half block from headquarters, the fire alarm office called me on the radio, "Englewood to Battalion 19, take a still at 73RD and Ackley." From my present location at District Headquarters, the address given was about six miles back the other way. I acknowledged the run, "Battalion 19, Fire, 73RD and Ackley. Office, be advised that I'm responding from District." By announcing over the air that my response would be delayed, first arriving companies would be alerted that one of them, the ranking member, would have to take charge until I got there. Before turning around, I drove the remaining half block to District Headquarters and pulled up on the apron. Through the buggy window, I quickly handed the trade forms to a firefighter sitting out front, "Give these to the Deputy," I said, "I'll call him later. I just caught a run."

"STILL ALARM"

No sooner than I pulled away, the fire alarm office began giving me my "lineup" of companies.

Doing this usually means they are getting a lot of calls on the reported address or they see something on the street cameras. Basically, it's a strong indication that you have a bona fide fire. Still miles away, my reply to the alarm office was, "Message received. Again office, I'm responding from District. I'm still pretty far away. Also make sure the 23RD Battalion is aware." Battalion 23 was responding to this fire as the RIT Chief. She needed to know that she'd probably beat me to the scene and would have to take charge until I arrived.

Unbeknownst to me, Battalion 23, Chief Carol Jackson, was at the fuel depot at 103RD and Stony Island, only a few blocks from my location when SHE got the RIT assignment. As I came over the bridge on 103RD street I could see her lights only about a half-mile ahead of me. She must have seen me in her rear-view mirror when she responded to the alarm office, "Battalion 23 message received. I'm responding from the fuel depot. I think Battalion 19's not too far behind me. Let companies know that BOTH chiefs are responding from a distance." The alarm office confirmed her communication and announced, "Companies to 73RD and Ackley be advised that both chiefs are responding from a distance." Chief Jackson was still about a half mile ahead of me. When she got on the inbound Dan Ryan, I lost sight of her lights.

A few seconds later the first company reported, "Engine 47 is on the scene at 73RD and Ackley. It looks like we have back porches going on a six-flat." This preliminary report now gave me an idea of what we would be dealing with. Often a report of "back porches going" means there could be quite a bit of fire.

About a minute later Battalion 23 reported, "Battalion 23 is on the scene at 73RD and Ackley. I'll take command until Battalion 19 arrives." Another minute passed when I pulled up behind her parked buggy and followed her radio transmission with, "Battalion 19's on the scene, office. I have command. I'll get back to you in a minute with more."

I jumped out of my buggy without donning my fire gear and went to the front of the building where I caught up with Chief Jackson. "I got it Carol," I said, "you can go put on your gear." Making a quick assessment of the scene, I didn't see any fire but there was a definite smell of wet smoke in the air. I saw that one line was led out from Engine 47 to the rear through a vacant lot next door. The truck had their main ladder to the roof and Engine 122 had a line into the front door. I then followed 47's line to the rear where I got a look at how things were going back there. Most of the 3-story back porches were lightly charred indicating there was probably quite a bit of fire but that it was extinguished quickly. I looked up and saw Engine 47's crew working their line on the third-floor porch.

"Battalion 19 to Engine 47...what do you have?"

"The fire's out. We're washing down and overhauling."

"Battalion 19 to Engine 122...what do you have?"

"No fire on the first or second floors. We're on the third washing down some hot spots where it got into the kitchen."

"Battalion 19 to Truck 30...how 'bout you?"

"Roofs open...Primary and Secondary searches complete and negative. We're overhauling with the engines now."

"Battalion 19 Message Received."

With the above information I switched my radio from Fireground to Englewood and gave the following report,

"Battalion 19 to Englewood, the fire is out. Primary and secondary searches are complete and negative, and companies are in the process of overhauling and washing down."

I still wanted to get a look at things inside, so I followed Engine 122's line into the building up to the third floor. It was still a bit smoky, but we were in good shape. On my way downstairs I looked out of the second-floor hallway window and saw that my immediate boss, 2-2-5, Deputy District Chief Debra Keys, was standing out front. She wasn't due to respond here unless the alarm was escalated. My guess was she showed up because she was on the street when the alarm came in and took it in when she heard both battalion chiefs were responding from a distance.

As I exited the front door, I noticed Chief Keys giving me a look that clearly said, "Why are you in the building without your fire gear on?" I walked over to where she was standing to give her a briefing and to get reprimanded about not having my gear on, but before I could say a word, she cut me off and said, "Looks like you got this." While giving her my briefing I found that my assumption was correct. She did take in the fire because she was in the area and heard that both battalion chiefs were responding from a distance. My report to her on the fire was that Engine 47 did a great job getting water on the porches fast, while Engine 122 led out a line to the interior to keep the fire out of the apartments. I also explained that both trucks did a nice job of making sure there were no tenants inside. I added that everything happened rather quickly. It was literally only three or four minutes between their arrival and 47's message that the fire was out.

Before leaving, Chief Keys made a couple of suggestions including requesting Human Services for the displaced tenants. I graciously thanked her for her critique and for her advice. However, just before she walked away, she added, "and Kev, one more thing...if you're gonna go into a fire building put your gear on." Yep...she got me, and I conceded, "Thanks Chief. Message received."

When everyone was picked-up and in service, before leaving the scene, I had all the companies gather in front of the building for a quick meeting. First, I commended everyone on a job well done. I then pointed out that from what I could see of the remains, it looked like there had been quite a bit of fire when they arrived, and their quick and efficient actions kept this thing from becoming something big. I then dismissed the firefighters and did a quick critique with only the officers. The only thing I recommended was that, when there is no chief officer on the scene, they be more proactive on the radio with progress reports like, "we have water on the fire," "primary searches are underway," etc. I then dismissed all companies and returned to quarters.

> 09/21/15
> Assignment—5-1-5 (Special Operations—Engine 5's Quarters, DesPlaines & Jackson)
> Primary Response Area—City Wide
> Weather—Temperatures in the low 70s

Before construction work began on the Chicago Riverwalk project, the construction contractor and ranking members of the Chicago Fire Department, worked together to create a plan on how best to handle emergency incidents that might occur on site. With a solid pre-plan in place, construction supervisors and fire department bosses conducted on-site drills with fire companies and ambulance personnel in the area near the project. At these drills, firefighters and paramedics were shown all the designated access points as well as specific and general on-site hazards.

"CONSTRUCTION SITE ACCIDENT"

Around 8:30 a.m. I was dispatched to a "Construction Site Accident" at LaSalle and Wacker Drive, the site of the Chicago Riverwalk project. Further information on the computer in my buggy read, "Construction Site Accident on a Barge with Possible Crush Injury." Most construction companies are very good with sticking to the emergency plan. I was pretty confident they'd have things ready for us when we arrived.

(There is a particular dynamic presented at construction site accidents: the construction worker "brotherhood." When one of their own is injured, they go to work quickly trying to help. We in the fire service are very understanding of this mindset and, although we have overall control of emergency scenes, we will often utilize on site construction equipment and its operators to assist in rescue operations.)

En route, I heard over the radio that Truck 3 was on the scene and was directing incoming companies to Lower Wacker Drive. Because of our pre-plan, I knew exactly how to access this point and arrived within minutes. Getting out of my buggy I was met by Chief Leo Bascom of Air Sea Rescue. Leo explained, "We have one injured worker on the barge. Squad 1 already has him in a Stokes basket and they're securing him now. There's a crane overhead. We think the best way to do this is to use the crane to bring the basket right over to this ambulance here. C'mon, I'll show you."

I grabbed my life jacket and Leo led me down the riverbank. Together, we went up a ladder, across a narrow I-beam and down another ladder onto the barge where the injured construction worker was being tended to. The patient had been hit across the shins with a steel plate that was being lifted by a crane. Everyone including the patient was calm and everything looked good for a smooth removal. Members of Squad 1 and Truck 3 were almost finished securing the patient into the basket and had already begun rigging it for the crane lift.

Leo then tugged my shirt and pulled me off to the side. He quietly told me the police boat was moored against the river side of the barge, and that their crew was pressing him to take the patient on their boat to a drop off point along the river at another location. To me this didn't make sense. "Why put him on the police boat when there's an ambulance right here?" I asked. Leo shrugged, "I don't know. That's what they want to do." On rescue incidents like these the Fire Department is in control. I'm not one to pull rank, but in this instance I did, "No. The ambulance is right here. We're not taking this guy for a boat ride first. Besides, we have a firefighter/paramedic with the patient now who can only hand him off to someone of equal or higher medical qualifications. I'll talk with the police." By this time a high-ranking police officer was on scene. I explained to him that we had previously drilled with the construction company on a Stokes basket/crane rescue and, with the ambulance already in a good position, this was the best way to do this. The police supervisor understood, said he'd talk to his officers on the boat, and if we needed anything, to let him know.

With the decision made, Leo and I went back to where the patient was and spoke to a construction supervisor. We told him once we had the patient secured to the basket, we wanted his crew to rig it to the crane. (These guys know their stuff. They hoist tons of steel overhead in the downtown area everyday. We totally trusted they would rig their co-worker with just as much care and caution.) The supervisor agreed to our plan. I was then introduced to the crane operator and another guy who was going to provide hand signals. When everything was ready to go, the crane slowly began lifting the patient. Affixed to the basket was a tag line manned by a third construction worker. As the basket carefully moved along, I guided the man on the tag line across an I-beam then on to a wooden plank leading from the barge to the shore. Piece of cake! When the basket was over land, the crane operator lowered it on a dime to the waiting ambulance crew. The patient was transferred to a stretcher and transported to a local hospital in good condition.

This was a great example of how those pre-planning drills, conducted early on in the project, helped firefighters and construction crews work together to make this incident go smoothly and safely.

After lunch, around 1:30 p.m., I drove to the 31ST street harbor to meet the CFD SCUBA team who would be removing their two rescue jet skis from Lake Michigan. With the summer boating and beach season coming to an end, these handy little machines were being removed from the water to be stored at our department warehouse until spring. Standing at the water's edge, I observed as the divers and one firefighter from Support Services took the jet skis out of the water and loaded them onto a trailer. Watching this operation, I had that nostalgic feeling you get when you realize that summer's over. As they drove off, I thought to myself, "I won't be around in the spring when those skis are put back in the water. Only two more months and I'll be retired and no longer an active member of the Chicago Fire Department."

"BOAT IN DISTRESS"

I got my second and last run of the day at 7:00 p.m. when I was sent to a "Boat in Distress" at 63RD and Lake Shore Drive. The first arriving companies quickly held all responding units when they found that the boat in distress had only run out of gas and was tied to the shore waiting for a tow. No distress.

> 09/24/15
> ASSIGNMENT—BATTALION 19 (ENGINE 54's QUARTERS, 71ST & PARNELL)...THE OLD 18TH BATTALION
> PRIMARY RESPONSE AREA—ENGLEWOOD
> WEATHER—TEMPERATURES IN THE HIGH 70S

"STILL AND BOX–BUILDING COLLAPSE"

About 11:40 a.m., while in quarters, I was dispatched as Safety Chief to a Still and Box for a Building Collapse on the near southside. The job of the Safety Chief is pretty basic: arrive at the scene, report to the Command Post, do a 360-degree walk around the site, then take up position near where members are working and monitor conditions to keep everyone safe.

The first company to arrive on the scene reported a confirmed incident with at least one person buried under rubble. They also immediately requested a full Building Collapse Response that would bring to the scene numerous specialized rigs, equipment and members who are specifically trained for this type of incident. A subsequent report seconds later, by the first arriving engine, added that the building appeared to be undergoing some sort of rehab construction or partial demolition and there were workers on site.

(Side Note: I truly believe that most people possess a noble quality that compels them to help others in times of need, especially in life-or-death situations. Although lives have been saved and people rescued because of selfless acts of others, many times these would-be rescuers have become victims themselves. Collapse situations are one of the most dangerous incidents that an untrained "rescuer" can involve themselves in. The removal of one critical piece of debris can potentially cause a collapse even larger and more devastating than the first. This could result in trapping not only the original victim, but also would-be rescuers and complicating extrication efforts. Everyone including police officers, construction workers, passers-by, and even first arriving fire units must fight the urge to jump on the pile and start digging randomly. If a victim is not on the surface and safely accessible, the job of the first in fire companies is to gather information and start creating a safe work area for incoming technical rescue teams. Creating a safe work area begins by shutting down any heavy equipment that may still be running near the site. Vibrations from a running dump truck or bulldozer can possibly trigger another collapse. Also critical to safe and efficient rescue operations is the cordoning off of a "collapse zone" and the gathering of information that will hopefully include what was happening at the time of collapse, the number and location of victims, and the type of building construction.)

At this particular incident the information gathered by the first arriving engine and truck was, that prior to the collapse, only one man was under the roof. Two others were on the roof and rode it down as it collapsed. They were accounted for and safe as were the remainder of the crew that was not near the building at the time. The workers also pointed out the exact location where the victim was standing when the roof came down.

The structure involved was a 1-story brick rectangular building about 20'x 50'. The construction crew was working on Side B when one end of a 2'x 20' concrete Flex-Core roof panel dropped down and pinned one of the workers. The collapse also blew out a large portion of the B Side wall exposing the interior where the victim was buried. The other end of the concrete panel, on Side D, remained atop the opposite wall in a precarious position.

Upon arrival I put on my gear and reported to 2-2-1, the Incident Commander, Deputy District Chief Andy Bajorek. "Chief," I said, "I'm Safety. I'll do my 360 and get back to you ASAP." I then did my walk-around and reported the following:

- No electric or gas service was currently connected to the structure.
- The opposite end of the panel that fell was still precariously resting atop the D Side wall.
- The two remaining walls on either side of the gaping hole created by the collapse had loose brick above where the extrication operation was taking place.
- Several cracks in the walls of the remaining structure had to be constantly monitored for movement.

Only a few blocks from the incident was the Chicago Fire Department Headquarters. Many of the big bosses, who were listening to the radio, responded to the scene when they heard the first company's report confirming a collapse with someone trapped. One of the ranking members who came from Headquarters was Assistant Deputy Fire Commissioner, Ed Nagle. ADFC Nagle heads up the Special Operations Division and is arguably one of the most knowledgeable technical rescue people on the job.

Ed, who is a hands-on guy, was in the rubble at the "last seen point" along with the Special Operations Battalion Chief and the captain of Squad 1. Led by ADFC Nagle, a search and extrication plan was quickly implemented.

As members of Squad 1 cut through concrete and steel attempting to locate the victim, a team of firefighters carefully removed loose debris and placed it in 5-gallon plastic buckets. The buckets were then passed to the outside using a chain of other firefighters. So as not to cause further collapse, this work had to be done with the utmost care. About thirty minutes after the arrival of the first fire companies, the victim was visible but still buried under a large amount of heavy debris. As soon as he was semi-accessible, a firefighter/paramedic climbed in to evaluate his condition. After a quick examination the man was pronounced DOA.

Now, in order to remove the victim, several obstacles had to be overcome. First, the heavy end of one of the collapsed concrete panels had to be lifted slightly to unpin the victim's legs. This was done using heavy rescue air bags that, when inflated, have the ability to lift thousands of pounds. As the section of concrete was inched higher, heavy-duty cribbing was inserted to assure it would not come crashing back down. Once the roof panel was lifted about two inches, the victim's legs were freed. The second obstacle was now to remove another smaller piece of the concrete roof section that was pinning the victim's chest and head area. Once again, air bags and cribbing were used. When the roof section was completely off of the victim, rescuers slowly began removing him from under the remaining loose rubble.

The operation was halted only once when it was found that a steel tension cable inside the Flex-core concrete was caught up under the victim's arms. Peering under the rubble on his hands and knees, ADFC Nagle assessed the entanglement and called for the air-powered grinder. Using this tool, members were able to cut the cable and remove the victim who was then placed into a waiting Stokes basket and transported by ambulance to the hospital.

When the job was completed and all companies were picked up and in service, ADFC Nagle called everyone together and commended them on a job well done. He commented on how well the first arriving companies performed their duties of reconnaissance and scene securement, and also complimented everyone else on sticking to their assignments and supporting the operations of Squad 1.

> 09/27/15
> ASSIGNMENT—BATTALION 14 (ENGINE 109'S QUARTERS, 22ND & KEDZIE)
> PRIMARY RESPONSE AREA—WESTSIDE, LITTLE VILLAGE
> WEATHER—TEMPERATURES IN THE MID 70S

"STILL ALARM"

I just pulled out of quarters about 7:15 p.m. and was heading south on Kedzie to Engine 99's house for my first night visit, when I was sent to a Still Alarm at an approximate address of 23RD and Rockwell. Fire runs given as approximate addresses usually mean that people are seeing smoke from a distance or calling in from across a street, down an alley or even a few blocks away.

I turned on my lights and siren, made a U-turn on Kedzie

and began heading back north. About four blocks ahead of me I could see Engine 109 responding. Then, over the radio came, "Battalion 15 to Main, start a Working Fire Response into Battalion 14's still. I'm about a mile away and see a lot of smoke coming from that area. I'm taking it in too."

Now, driving east on Cermak with Engine 109 still about four blocks ahead of me, I kept glancing up to my right trying to see the smoke Battalion 15 was reporting. Between buildings and at intersections I caught glimpses of an eerie, dark blue, dusk sky with black smoke billowing past the large full moon.

(Side Note: Tonight there would be a Supermoon Lunar Eclipse. At this time the moon was large and bright but not in full eclipse for another two hours.)

When I got to Western Ave. I turned south and heard Engine 109 report on the scene. His report was that he had a fire in a factory followed by, "Hold all responding companies. We can handle it."

"WHAT?!" I thought, "a fire in a factory, all that smoke and he's holding all companies?!" I kept my lights and siren on and continued in.

Arriving at 23RD and Rockwell I got a better look at what we had. There were two very large rubbish piles burning in a block long vacant lot that was once the site of a factory building. What happened was, my radio cut in and out just as Engine 109 was reporting on the scene. Through the garbled radio transmission, what I didn't hear was his full report saying, "We have a rubbish fire where the extra alarm factory fire was a few months ago." Whew! Because the burning piles of rubbish were in the middle of a very large open area with no exposure problems, I radioed to the fire alarm office,

"Battalion 14's on the scene. Hold the Working Fire

Response. We have two large rubbish piles in a vacant lot. I'm gonna keep my two engines and one truck here for now."

In order to get water to the middle of the large lot, I had Engine 23 drop a supply line to Engine 109 and then drive to the first hydrant on the street. Engine 23 would then have a positive source and could supply Engine 109 all the water they needed. After about ten minutes the fire alarm office called me and asked for a better description. My assumption was that one of the big bosses was listening to the radio and heard the same broken report I heard earlier about a "fire in a factory," and wanted to know what was going on. My response was, "I have two very large rubbish piles in the middle of a very, very, very, large vacant lot. No exposure problems. I have Engine 23 feeding 109 with an in-line operation. We'll be here for about a half hour." Once we got a positive flow of hydrant water it only took about twenty minutes to fully extinguish the two fires.

After completing my night rounds, I returned to my quarters. As I pulled up to the rear overhead door, I saw one firefighter in the parking lot looking up at the sky. The lunar eclipse was now in full swing and the Supermoon looked awesome! I pulled my buggy inside then called my wife to remind her about the lunar eclipse. She thanked me for the call and said the park across the street from our home was filled with people staring up at the sky, and that she and our daughter were heading out to join them.

> 09/30/15
> Assignment—Battalion 6 (Engine 123's Quarters, 51st & Leavitt)...the old 19th Battalion
> Primary Response Area—Southside
> Weather—Temperatures in the high 60s

No fires or anything out of the ordinary this day.

OCTOBER 2015

10/06/15
Assignment—Battalion 7 (Engine 91's Quarters, Diversey & Pulaski)
Primary Response Area—West Logan Square, Near Northwest Side
Weather—Temperatures in the mid 60s

"RIT"

Some time in the mid afternoon I was dispatched to a fire as the RIT Chief with Truck 29. The fire, on the second floor of a 2½-story frame, was quickly extinguished by the first arriving companies. By the time Truck 29 and I set up our RIT operation, the fire was pretty much out, and companies were performing overhaul and wash down.

While standing by, near the front of the fire building, I was approached by a police sergeant who seemed pretty angry about something. He explained to me that two of his officers at the scene had complained to him about an off-duty firefighter who was in the alley earlier "helping" pull hose. He told me that at the rear of the fire building, his officers observed a heavy-set man in an orange shirt pulling on fire hose and yelling at the firemen. When the police officers told him to back off and let the firefighters do their job, the man replied loudly and aggressively that he was an off-duty firefighter. And, according to the police, the man continued his tirade with several sarcastic and degrading comments about police officers in general. So as not to escalate an already hectic scene, the police officers said they kept their cool and ordered the man to walk away from the scene immediately. They also added that if he didn't leave NOW this would turn into a situation no one REALLY wanted. With this, the man backed off but remained on the scene watching the fire from a yard across the alley. The police officers then told their sergeant they were okay with him watching from a distance and let it go at that. I thanked the police sergeant for reporting this and told him I'd notify our commanding officer on the scene.

I waited until the fire was out before informing the deputy district chief on scene of the story I just got from the police. "Okay Kev, thanks. You can pick up. I'll speak with the police," he replied. Upon leaving I purposely drove through the alley just to see if this "off-duty firefighter" was still around. I wanted to see if I recognized him, but I didn't see anyone in the alley fitting the description.

Later that evening, at dinner, I asked a few of the guys from Squad 2 if they saw or heard anything about this incident while they were in the rear of the fire building. One of the guys replied that he did see our fire investigators talking with someone who fit the description. I never found out why the investigators were interviewing this guy but there are a couple of possibilities:

- The guy was an off-duty firefighter and may have witnessed something that would provide some investigative information.
- He was not really an off-duty firefighter but possibly a person of interest.

Unfortunately, I often don't get the rest of the story. This was one of those cases. I don't know how this ended, but something I'm pretty sure of is that IF this guy was really a firefighter, the story would have made its way to every firehouse in the city in a day or two. I never heard any more on this.

> 10/09/15
> ASSIGNMENT—BATTALION 7 (ENGINE 91'S QUARTERS, DIVERSEY & PULASKI)
> PRIMARY RESPONSE AREA—WEST LOGAN SQUARE, NEAR NORTHWEST SIDE
> WEATHER—TEMPERATURES IN THE MID 70S

As usual, I reported for work at about 5:30 a.m. While putting my gear in the buggy I was approached by a man who said he was a photographer. He claimed he was working on a project for the Fire Department and presented me with paperwork saying he had permission to ride-along with either Squad 2 or Battalion 7 today for a few hours. A quick phone call to District Headquarters confirmed that the photographer, Nate, did have official permission to ride along. Over coffee in the kitchen, he explained that the objective of his work was not so much to get dramatic fire photos, but to document "a day in the life of a firefighter." During our discussion one of the firefighters in the room asked me about my upcoming retirement, "Getting close, huh Kev?" he asked. "Yep, a few more weeks," I replied. Hearing that I would be leaving the job soon, Nate thought that photographing me going about my daily routine would be a great fit for his project. I told him that was fine, so he put his photography gear in the buggy, and we left quarters to start the morning rounds.

Our first stop was Engine 76 where Nate photographed the 0800, morning roll call. Then it was on to the remaining two firehouses in the battalion where we picked up the daily paperwork and delivered it to District. While there, I introduced Nate to Acting Deputy District Chief Tom Burke who told me, "If anything happens close to your still district you have my permission to take it in for the photographer." About five minutes later, while still at District, a fire was reported over the radio on the 4900 block of Potomac. With the Chief's permission, we took it in. By the time we arrived things were under control. Nate took lots of photos of companies picking up hose and putting tools away. We only had one other run before Nate had to leave. It was for a Level I Hazmat, a gas leak, which turned out to be false.

> 10/12/15
> Assignment—Battalion 7 (Engine 91's Quarters, Diversey & Pulaski)
> Primary Response Area—West Logan Square, Near Northwest Side
> Weather—Temperatures in the high 70s

Nothing.

> 10/15/15
> Assignment—Battalion 7 (Engine 91's Quarters, Diversey & Pulaski)
> Primary Response Area—West Logan Square, Near Northwest Side
> Weather—Temperatures in the low 60s

"STILL ALARM–ALLEY GARAGE"

Not much happened this day, just one garage fire. A professional exterminator was hired by an apartment building owner to rid his garage of rats. The owner met the exterminator at the site but forgot to bring the keys to the garage. The exterminator told the owner that access to the inside of the garage wasn't necessary. He said he could work from the outside by placing a rat smoke bomb under the concrete slab through an exposed hole. He put the smoke bomb under the slab, lit it and covered the opening with stone and gravel. While standing out front, the owner and exterminator noticed what they thought was a lot more smoke than should be coming from the smoke bomb. Apparently, there was a crack in the concrete floor that allowed the heat from the canister to touch off some combustibles inside the garage. Upon arrival the first engine forced entry, found a small fire inside and used a hand pump to extinguish it.

10/18/15

Throughout the last year or so, I worked several of my off days because of trades made with other battalion chiefs. Today I was off on a payback for one of those trades.

10/21/15
Assignment—5-1-5 (Special Operations—Engine 5's Quarters, DesPlaines & Jackson)
Primary Response Area—City Wide
Weather—Temperatures in the mid 70s

Nothing.

10/27/15
Assignment—Battalion 3 (Engine 14's Quarters, Milwaukee and Chicago)
Primary Response Area—Near Westside, West Loop
Weather—Temperatures in the high 50s

Nothing out of the ordinary. About one month to retirement.

10/30/15
Assignment—Battalion 3 (Engine 14's Quarters, Milwaukee and Chicago)
Primary Response Area—Near Westside, West Loop
Weather—Temperatures in the low 50s

Once again, photographer Nate joined me for the day. He got some nice shots of Engine 14's roll call and of our morning rounds, but no fires.

Later that evening was a large annual Halloween bike ride through the streets of Chicago. Using an on-line map of the bike route the captain of Engine 14, my old friend Bill Haddon, figured out that the riders would be coming through 14's still district a few blocks east of the firehouse around 7:00 p.m.

So, after dinner, Bill took photographer Nate with him on the engine and headed over to Chicago and Halsted. I met them there and, leaving ourselves a clear exit path in case we got a run, we parked and watched as thousands of bikes went by with people dressed in crazy Halloween costumes. Nate shot a lot of photos and after about fifteen minutes the last bike passed. Engine 14, along with Nate, went back to quarters and I went on my evening rounds.

NOVEMBER 2015

11/05/15
Assignment—Battalion 15 (Engine 39's Quarters, 33rd & Ashland)
Primary Response Area—Back of The Yards, Brighton Park
Weather—Temperatures in the high 60s

Nothing.

11/11/15
Assignment—Battalion 3 (Engine 14's Quarters, Milwaukee and Chicago)
Primary Response Area—Near Westside, West Loop
Weather—Temperatures in the high 60s

Nothing.

11/14/15
ASSIGNMENT—BATTALION 7 (ENGINE 91'S QUARTERS, DIVERSEY & PULASKI)
PRIMARY RESPONSE AREA—WEST LOGAN SQUARE, NEAR NORTHWEST SIDE
WEATHER—TEMPERATURES IN THE MID 50S

"INVESTIGATION"

About 7:15 a.m., while I was doing paperwork in my office, Engine 91 was dispatched from our quarters to a "Transformer on Fire" on North Kimball. When they arrived, the officer reported via radio that there was no sign of a transformer on fire and asked the fire alarm office for more information. They replied, "That's all we have 91. One cell phone call reporting a transformer on fire at that location." The officer of Engine 91 reported back, "Okay. We checked both alleys. There's no one here to speak with us. We don't find anything. We're returning to quarters." When they got back around 7:30, the officer told me the address they came from was a senior citizen home.

(Many times, when a transformer "blows" it will make a loud explosive sound and sometimes a flash. After the initial "boom" everything usually looks pretty normal. A fire company will respond and check for wires down or residual fires on the pole, in nearby trees and on the outside of buildings.)

At 8:00 a.m. I was dispatched along with Engine 43 to an "Investigation" at the same address that Engine 91 had just returned from. "Investigation" runs are kind of ambiguous. They don't give you a lot of information. You may get something in the comments section of the run sheet, but not often. I left the firehouse and responded with lights and siren. While still en route I heard Engine 43 report, "43's on the scene of the Investigation. We have a 4-story nursing home here." Still ambiguous.

When I arrived at the address I reported on scene and entered the lobby. Inside, I was met by a building engineer who told me he heard a loud "boom" in the alley about 45 minutes earlier. He went on to add that immediately after the boom, his building lost electrical power. He said he checked the alley and didn't see anything burning but did call 911 to report the sound and the subsequent power outage. He also said the second time he called he told the 911 call-taker that a senior citizen facility was affected by the outage. (When a senior building is involved in a power outage the fire department responds to check for people stuck in elevators and in need of electrically powered oxygen equipment.)

Using a standard set of questions, I confirmed with the building engineer that:

- The building was on backup generator power.
- The elevators were working.
- All special needs patients were taken care of.

With these three things in order, I informed the building engineer there was nothing more we could do. That's when the engineer told me that he called 911 the second time because he thought the fire department might be able to get the power company to respond faster. I told him all I could do was put in a second request, which I did while he was standing in front of me. In my radio request I included, "Please let ComEd know that this is a senior home." With that I released Engine 43 and put myself in service.

Today was Doug Maki's last day. Doug is a lieutenant on Truck 35 and would be officially retired the next morning at

8:00. Before I was promoted to battalion chief, I worked periodically as a captain and lieutenant on Engine 76, the engine quartered with Truck 35. It was always a fun day working with Doug. We'd sit at the front desk for hours chatting about all kinds of things, including 1970's drag racing, and when there were only 12 teams in the National Hockey League. I was happy to be working in the 7TH battalion with Doug on his last workday.

After completing my morning administrative duties and having lunch, I returned to Engine 76's quarters where Doug's co-workers were hosting a reception in honor of his last tour of duty. The kitchen was crowded with off-duty members who stopped by to wish Doug well. His family was also present, and the room was abuzz with laughs and conversation over cake and coffee. Making my way through the kitchen I found a spot at a table next to an old friend who had left the job years ago. Unfortunately, as we were catching up on things, our conversation was cut short when I got a run for a fire on Diversey Avenue.

"STILL ALARM"

Arriving at the Diversey address we found a crowd of people standing outside of a large corner building with a store on the first floor and apartments above. The owner of the store met us outside and told us someone set off an M-80 firework in the doorway of the building leading up to the apartments. Companies investigated and found there was no fire, and no one was injured. I notified the alarm office of what we had and that I was turning the scene over to the police. All fire companies were released, and I reported "in service on the air."

"STILL ALARM"

At 4:30 p.m. I was dispatched to another Still Alarm on North Whipple. Prior to my arrival, Engine 106 reported on the scene with smoke showing from a 1½-story brick building. With that, the fire alarm office notified me that I was now getting a Working Fire Response.

I just arrived on scene, and was still in my buggy, when I heard companies inside report via radio that they had a small furnace fire that was quickly extinguished using their hand pumps. With that report, I held the Working Fire Response and entered the basement to take a look. The smoke had dissipated but there was a familiar pungent odor. I could tell immediately there was plastic burning. This was confirmed by Engine 106 and Truck 13 who were just finishing up as I walked in. "PVC?" I asked. A few of the firemen nodded and answered, "Yep." As I stepped further into the basement one of them turned, and in a scolding manner, said, "Hey...get outta here! You only got a few days left on the job. You don't need to be breathing any more of this stuff." Smiling at the concern for my health, I turned and left the basement thinking about how much of "this stuff" I've inhaled over the last 30 years.

As I spoke with the building owner out front, Truck 13 used their electric fan to remove the odor from the basement and first floor apartment. When everything was clear, companies picked up and returned to quarters.

Earlier in the day I accepted a dinner offer from the crew at Engine 106. I spent a lot of time at that house when I was a floating lieutenant and captain. I got to know those guys pretty well. With only a few days left until my retirement, they wanted to give me a nice send off with one of my favorite firehouse meals, Ben Pakula's homemade pizza!

I got to Engine 106's house about a half hour before dinner. The crew and I shared a few stories, had some laughs and for old times sake I even pitched in and helped with the Saturday crossword puzzle. When dinner was served, I was told to sit in the "Jesse Diaz seat" at the head of the table. (It's an inside joke. Jesse is one of the senior guys in the house. When he's working, he's very territorial about his place at the table.) He was off today but did receive a texted picture of me sitting in his seat, to which he replied, "Only when I'm off Kev, Happy Retirement!"

After a great pizza dinner, the crew surprised me with a large, frosted cake that read, "Good Luck Kevin." This was always one of my favorite houses to work in. They always had a very hard working and fun group.

(Side Note: During dinner about four of the guys in the house were complaining of pounding headaches..."PVC?"..."Yep.")

I left Engine 106 around 7:30 p.m. and headed for the fuel depot. While filling my tank, I noticed the woman who runs the facility staring at the roof of my buggy. When I turned to see what had her attention, I saw something red and green fluttering around on top of my car. Taking a closer look, I found a 3-foot by 3-foot ladybug kite affixed to the luggage rack of my buggy with wire ties. Looking back at the woman I smiled and told her I was retiring in a few days, and that I had just left a firehouse full of jokers. I finished pumping my gas and laughed about how silly this must have looked as I drove down the streets. I called the lieutenant of Engine 106, my old pal, Adam Volkmann,

"What's with the ladybug kite?" I asked.

"What ladybug kite?"

"You know what kite!"

This went on a few more times before Adam replied, "Ladybugs are good luck. Good luck in your retirement, Kev."

"You guys are nuts. Tell everyone I said thanks again for dinner."

I didn't have wire cutters with me, so the ladybug flapped behind me all the way to Engine 76's quarters where I was heading for my last night visit with Doug Maki.

When I got to 76's quarters, the earlier retirement gathering had been all cleaned up, the house lights were down, and things were quiet. Standing on the apparatus floor looking out the glass overhead doors, Doug and I reminisced about the good times we had on the job. He would be done in a few hours, and I had only a few more days. We wrapped up our chat and I told him I'd see him in the morning. (The crews of Engine 76 and Truck 35 planned a "morning after the last day" thing for Doug at a small northside establishment. The bar opens at 7:00 a.m. on Sunday mornings. Companies often do this for a retiring member, so that those who were working the day before can stop by and wish the new retiree "good luck.") I left 76 around 9:00 p.m. and headed back to my quarters...the ladybug flapping behind me all the way.

"RIT"

With my scanner on low I went to bed about 10:30. At about 4:00 a.m. I was awoken by the voice of Sean Keating, "Battalion 18 to Main, I'm on the scene on Cicero. I've got a fire in a 3-story brick building 200' by 150'. Office, it looks like it's going through the roof. Gimme a Box."

Knowing that I'd be responding to this fire in some capacity, I started getting dressed and planning my route. Sure enough, a few seconds later I was dispatched as the RIT Chief with Truck 35, Doug Maki's truck.

Everyone who heard that initial report by the 18TH Battalion just KNEW that because of the size of the building and the amount of fire reported, this was going to escalate to an extra alarm. Everyone responding also KNEW that we'd probably be there until we got relieved by the on-coming shift in a few hours.

Upon arrival at the scene, I met Doug in front of the building. As described in Battalion 18's initial report, this was a large brick structure with fire visible at roof level. Surveying the building from the street, Doug and I noted a good push of bottled-up smoke emitting from boarded up windows on the top floor, and we could hear companies inside reporting, "heavy fire in the cockloft." My initial thought was that companies inside were going to be pulled out very soon, and this would become another "surround and drown" event.

As RIT protocol requires, Doug and I did a complete walk around the building to determine areas of entry and exit in case of a Mayday. Realizing this would soon most likely go from an interior attack to an outside defensive one, we also noted the height of the building with collapse zones in mind. We then returned to our staging area in front of the building to standby.

Just as we got there, the officer of Engine 117, the engine company working on the third floor, radioed down, "117 to Battalion 18, we got water on the fire in the cockloft. We think we might have it knocked! I need another truck up here to open this thing up!"

Deputy District Chief Bob Hagen had just arrived on the scene and was now in command. Hearing Engine 117's request, he immediately sent another truck to the third floor. Then suddenly, as if someone closed a valve, the fire disappeared and the smoke dissipated. With a surprised look Doug said, "I think they got it." I replied, "Holy shit, I think you're right!" Subsequent radio reports confirmed the main body of fire was out, and the third floor and cockloft were going to need extensive overhaul work.

The first responding companies, Engine 117, Engine 96, Tower Ladder 14 and Truck 26 all did a GREAT JOB stopping this fire. Everyone helped 117 get their line up to the third floor so they could get water on the fire quickly. Because of their aggressive interior attack, what all of us thought was going to be an "all-nighter," was over in an hour and a half!

While standing by, around 5:30, I called my quarters and spoke with Steve Florek, the chief who was going to relieve me,

"Hang tight Steve. It looks like we're almost done. I should be back by 6:00 or 6:15."

"Okay Kev, just call if you wanna get outta there. I'll come relieve you," he replied.

"Thanks, but I'm good. I'll call if I think it's gonna go past 6:30."

Truck 35 and I were released from the scene around 6:00 a.m. While walking back to our rigs I hollered over to Doug, "I'll see ya at the bar in a couple of hours but I'm gonna run home first." "Yeah, me too," Doug replied.

As I approached my buggy, which was parked about a half block away, I noticed there was an interior light on. "Oh no," I thought. I put the key in the ignition and...nothing...my battery was dead. I knew if I called for our city mechanic to come out, I'd be waiting there for another two hours. Anxious to get relieved and go home, I began asking every ambulance and police car still on the scene if they had jumper cables. No luck. Finally, a firefighter from Engine 117 came up to me and said he had cables in his personal car back at the firehouse a few blocks away. So, with Battalion 18's permission, I took his buggy with the firefighter to get the cables. We returned and with a jump from the running buggy mine started right up. A little embarrassing? Yes, but no big deal.

I got back to my own quarters about 6:30. Steve and I chatted over coffee for about an hour before I headed home to shower, then off to the bar.

I got to the morning after gathering around 8:30 a.m. The place was filled with off-duty firefighters, many of whom were at the fire a few hours ago. In addition to Doug's retirement, everyone was talking about what a great job those companies did putting that fire out so quickly. I stayed for a couple of hours and had a whole lot of laughs.

On my way home it hit me kinda hard, the countdown was on. Only THREE more workdays and I'M done.

11/20/15
ASSIGNMENT—BATTALION 8 (ENGINE 125'S QUARTERS, NARRAGANSETT & FULLERTON)
PRIMARY RESPONSE AREA—WEST AND NEAR NORTHWEST SIDES
WEATHER—TEMPERATURES IN THE MID 40S

Quiet Day. A couple of runs, no fires.

Sometime in the early afternoon I got a call from Luis Acevedo, the lieutenant of Engine 57.

"Hey Chief, we heard you're gonna be working at our house next day. I'm calling to see what you want for dinner in honor of your retirement."

"Wow, that's really nice of you, and as long as you're offering, I think you KNOW what I want."

"Message received Chief, we thought so but wanted to check to be sure. See you next day!"

TWO more workdays to go...

11/23/15
BATTALION 17 (ENGINE 57'S QUARTERS, DIVISION AND WESTERN)...THE OLD 12TH BATTALION
PRIMARY RESPONSE AREA—HUMBOLDT PARK, LOGAN SQUARE
WEATHER—TEMPERATURES IN THE LOW 30S

Engine 57's quarters is located in the Humboldt Park area of the city, an area heavily populated by people of Puerto Rican descent. Since I've been on the job, Engine 57 has always had many Hispanic firefighters assigned there, many who grew up in the area. I always felt at home and liked working in this firehouse because I, too, grew up in a neighborhood nearby that was heavily Hispanic, mostly Puerto Rican. Many of my younger year's baseball, football and floor hockey games were played at Humboldt Park and the nearby Clemente High School. Over the years I've met several firefighters from this house who I've actually competed against back then. I once put in for an assignment at 57 early in my career but got beat out by someone with more seniority. This was always one of my favorite firehouses.

This day's shift was pretty quiet. I only had a few runs, nothing serious. Throughout the day I went about my administrative business and chatted with crews at the three other firehouses in the battalion. The conversation at each house was mostly me answering questions about what I was going to do in my retirement.

(Side Note: Andy Thorpe, the battalion chief regularly assigned to these quarters was off today. He and I came on the job the same day in July of 1986, and at the end of the next workday we would be leaving the job on the same day as well.)

At 6:00 p.m. I returned to my quarters and parked my buggy in its place on the apparatus floor. As soon as I got out, I could smell the aroma of home cooked Puerto Rican food. They KNEW!

The cook, Alicia Silva, who used to own a Puerto Rican restaurant in the Humboldt Park area, and the rest of the mostly Latino crew, prepared one of the best home cooked Puerto Rican/Cuban meals I've ever had. There was chicken, pork, arroz con gandules, tostones, pasteles and empanadillas. The dinner was great, and they even topped if off with a "Happy Retirement" cake. What a nice send-off. Great house. Great crew. Great cooks!

After dinner I went out to do my evening rounds and to top off the fuel in the buggy.

About 10:30 p.m., I closed the door to my room and got in bed. As I laid in my bunk, that bittersweet thing kicked in hard again. After my next workday this thirty-year ride would be over. Through my mind ran a ton of thoughts about "the job" including how much I wanted to be a fireman when I was a kid and how hard I worked to not only get hired but to make my way up through the ranks. I eventually dozed off. No runs all night.

ONE Day to go...

11/26/15
Assignment—Battalion 3 (Engine 14's Quarters, Milwaukee and Chicago)
Primary Response Area—Near Northside, West Loop
Weather—Temperatures in the low 30s

Well, it's finally here...Thanksgiving Day 2015...my last workday as a Chicago firefighter.

I always enjoyed attending "last day" receptions but really didn't want one or any big "send-off" in my honor. So, with that in mind, I purposely chose Thanksgiving as my last workday. I figured off-duty members, who might come on any regular day, would be with their families for the holiday.

A few weeks prior to my last shift, knowing that the regular assigned chief in the 3rd Battalion would be off, I called the department's Manpower Section to ask if I could have that assignment for my last day. I was told, as long as the regularly assigned chief wasn't called to work overtime that day, it's a done deal. Hearing that I requested his spot for my last day, the chief assigned to Battalion 3 called me. As a courtesy, he said even if he were called to work overtime on that day, he would take the out-of-house assignment so I could work my last shift in the 3RD Battalion at Engine 14's house.

Being able to finish out my career at this house meant a lot to me. As a young kid, Engine 14 and Truck 19 were two of the companies I watched working at many fires in my neighborhood. It was the first firehouse I ever walked into on a grammar school field trip. My toy fire trucks were numbered after Engine 14 and Truck 19 and, in 1969, my first interaction with real firemen was from this house.

Back in the late 1960's, in an attempt to stop people from opening fire hydrants during the hot summer months, the city ran a program called "Splashdown." This program required all engines and trucks throughout the city to go "on the air" for a couple of hours each day to safely block off a street, temporarily install a sprinkler cap on a hydrant, and get kids wet. Engine 14 and Truck 19 did most of their "Splashdown" duty using a fire hydrant by Eckhart Park, across the street from my house. Because they were the new guys, Charlie from Engine 14 and Ken from Truck 19 were the two firemen assigned the task of entertaining the kids. Every child and parent in the area knew Charlie and Ken.

In 1996, as a young relief lieutenant, I was working at a firehouse on the southside. Before the shift began, an older firefighter from another house who was detailed in for the day, sat across the kitchen table from me, "I'm on the engine with you today kid," he said. Something about this guy struck me. It took a bit of thinking, but after a minute I asked,

"Hey, were you on Truck 19 a long time ago?"

"Yeah, I was a candidate there in '69."

"Do you remember doing Splashdowns at Eckhart Park?"

"Yeah."

"Do you remember the one kid who would never get wet but would ask you tons of questions about the fire department?"

"Oh my God...WAS THAT YOU?"

"Yep. That was me."

"Well, I must have gave you all the right answers BOSS!"

"You certainly did, Ken."

Another reason I wanted to work my last day at Engine 14 was because Bill Haddon, the captain of the house, was a good friend of mine. Bill and I met when I transferred into Engine 30 in 1988. We worked together as firemen until 1994, when I was promoted to lieutenant. We also grew up in the same neighborhood and knew a lot of the same people, but we didn't know each other back then.

I reported for duty at the usual time of 5:30 a.m. and relieved Liam O'Boyle. Liam and I came on the job the same day back in 1986. He came on as a paramedic and then crossed over from the EMS side to the fire side years later. Probably because it was my last day, Liam and I chatted a little longer than usual this morning. We shared a few stories about the job, and talked about how we both REALLY wanted to be firemen when we were kids. Finally, our conversation led to both of us agreeing on how lucky we were, not only to fulfill our dreams of being firemen, but also to ultimately reach the rank of battalion chief. We shook hands, wished each other the best, and Liam left.

"WATER FLOW ALARM"–MY LAST RUN

Around 6:45 a.m. Engine 5 and Truck 2 were dispatched to a Water Flow Alarm on West Adams. (Water Flow Alarms are pretty common and usually false. Most of the time they are caused by a broken sprinkler pipe or a pressure surge in the city water supply.) When 5 and the truck arrived, they found an old 6-story factory building that had been converted into business offices. Because of the Thanksgiving holiday, the building was completely locked up and appeared to be unoccupied. As the crews walked around the building looking for any sign of fire, one of them put his hand on the outside sprinkler connection and found that it was vibrating. (A vibrating sprinkler connection pipe is an indication that the building's fire pump in the basement is running, and that water is flowing somewhere inside. It doesn't necessarily mean there's a fire, but it does mean that entry to the property must be made to find the flow.)

Causing only a couple of scratches to the front doors, Truck 2 forced entry. Once inside companies began a systematic investigation. When they reached the 4TH floor, they found a heavy flow of water coming from under one of the unit doors into the hallway. Entry was made and companies discovered one sprinkler head off and still discharging water but no sign of fire. The officers immediately had their crews work simultaneously to find the fire pump room, shut off the water and bring up several heavy tarps carried on Truck 2. Using these tarps firefighters would create dams to help contain the water to the 4TH floor and to stop it from flowing into the elevator shaft. (It doesn't take much water to put elevators out of service.) The captain of Engine 5 then notified the fire alarm office,

"Engine 5 to Main, we have no fire here. We forced entry and found a sprinkler head off on the 4TH floor. We're working to shut the water down now. See if you can notify a building manager through the alarm company and send me a battalion chief. We have a lot of water here."

This would be the last run of my career. At 0715 hours (7:15 a.m.) the computer voice came across the house speakers, "Battalion 3, Water Flow Alarm at 620 W. Adams."

I arrived on the scene at the same time as the building manager and a maintenance man. It was my guess that their quick response was because both lived close by. They had probably been notified by their private alarm monitoring company as soon as the Water Flow was detected, and fire companies were dispatched. All three of us walked into the lobby where the captain of Engine 5 explained,

"There's a sprinkler head off on the 4TH floor. There's no

fire. It looks accidental. We shut off the supply valve in the hallway and I got a couple of my guys shutting off the main valve in the basement now. Chief, we only called for you because of the amount of water damage."

All of us then walked the stairs to the 4TH floor where we saw about two inches of water in the hall and in the room where the sprinkler head activated. There was also a small amount of residual water slowly flowing out of the sprinkler head. I turned to the lieutenant on Truck 2,

"Tell your guys in the basement to find and open the drain valve. That'll stop the residual water."

"They're on it right now Chief."

I then began gathering the information I needed for my paperwork and advised the building manager on what needed to be done,

"You can keep a couple of our tarps here, but you'll have to fill out a form with the lieutenant of the truck. He'll stop by in a day or two to pick them up. Call your sprinkler company now and have them come out to replace the head that went off and get the system back in service. I'm sure you'll wanna call your insurance company and get a cleaning service out here too."

As we were leaving, the building manager thanked and complimented us for not damaging his front doors, and for everything we did to minimalize the water damage. I grabbed my radio and transmitted what would anti-climatically be my final official run report to the fire alarm office,

"Battalion 3 to Main, Engine 5, Truck 2 and myself are in service and returning to quarters."

At 11:00 a.m., after completing my morning rounds, and delivering the daily paperwork to District Headquarters for the last time, I returned home to Engine 14's house. After lunch there would be a small open house in honor of my last tour of duty. This was just how I wanted it. Nothing big.

On their way to Thanksgiving dinner at my in-law's home, my wife and daughter stopped by the firehouse. I introduced them to everyone in the kitchen and gave them a quick tour of Engine 14's quarters and my office. As they were getting ready to leave, Captain Bill called out, "Hang on. You gotta see this!" He went to the refrigerator and pulled out a large cake that read "Good Luck in the Future, Kevin." Also drawn in icing, was a depiction of my 2000 Ford Ranger riding off into the sunset. I owned that truck for the past thirteen years. It had become my firehouse trademark. Over the last few years, I must have heard a million times, "Are you still driving that thing?!"

Throughout the day more people than I expected stopped by to wish me well. The steady flow of working and retired members who came was actually pretty heartwarming. In addition to those who stopped by in person, I also received quite a few phone calls and well wishes via text messages.

As mentioned earlier, today was also Andy Thorpe's last day. He and I came on the job the same day in 1986 and were leaving on the same day in 2015. For the last few years Andy had been the chief of the 17TH battalion. At his quarters, he too, was enjoying a social gathering in his honor. A few weeks earlier, the members of Andy's battalion and some of my friends decided to merge our traditional "morning after the firehouse" last day gatherings. It was agreed that our morning meeting would be held at a bar in Bucktown called Mickey's. Mickey's was chosen because of its 6:30 a.m. opening time.

Around 7:00 p.m. I went out for my final night rounds. At Engine 22's quarters, the on-duty captain rang the house bells summoning all members to the front of the house for a photo. While posing for the camera someone mentioned our meeting at Mickey's the next morning. Hearing this, one of the paramedics said, "You know...Mickey's doesn't sell alcohol that early. They're open, but they only do coffee and rolls. We found THAT out when we organized a paramedic party there one time."

UH-OH! The word was already out in three battalions that we were meeting at Mickey's right after work the next morning. It was now around 7:45 p.m. I immediately called Andy to tell him we would have to try and find a new location...and fast. He and I and the crew at his house did some frantic web searching and made a bunch of phone calls trying to find any bars in the area that would be open and serve alcohol at 6:30 a.m. on the day after Thanksgiving. We had no luck, and the clock was running out. At around 9:00, as one last effort before cancelling, Andy and I decided to cruise our respective battalions in hopes of finding an alternate place. My first stop turned out to be a winner, Zebrzydowska, an old Polish bar on Division Street. After confirming with the bartender that they'd be open at 6:30 the next morning, and that they serve alcohol at that time, I called Andy and told him about my find. The two of us and several firefighters from different houses quickly spread the word about the new location. Whew! Zebrzydowska saves the day! Taking a deep breath, I drove back to quarters.

Pulling up onto the firehouse apron, I did a quick flash of my buggy lights. With this, the firefighter on watch opened the overhead door to let me in. I backed into my spot on the apparatus floor, turned off the ignition and pressed the Available in Quarters button on my computer screen. As I stepped out of the buggy, I got a weird feeling. Except for a couple of lamps on the officers' desks, a glow and hum from the pop machine, and the flickering of the television screen in the kitchen, the house seemed exceptionally quiet and dark. All the lights on the apparatus floor and kitchen were out for the night. The engine, truck and ambulance were all parked in their usual positions facing the front doors. Before heading into the kitchen to catch the end of the Bear's game with the captain and a few of his crewmembers, I took a slow walk around the apparatus floor and began thinking...thinking that this was my last night in the firehouse. Being a Chicago fireman was what I always wanted since I was a young boy. Now, in a few hours, it would be over. I wasn't sad, and I wasn't second-guessing my decision to retire. I was grateful, but feeling just a bit nervous, "Am I gonna miss all of this?" After once or twice around the apparatus floor I had one more thought, "I couldn't have made a better choice for my last day, Thanksgiving."

In the dimly lit kitchen were about five, half-asleep firefighters on sofas and lounge chairs watching the end of the Bears vs. Packers game. I pulled up an old office chair and sat down at the table next to Captain Haddon. He and I small talked until the game ended. The Bears won 17-13. "Okay." The Captain announced in a humorous way, "Kitchen's closed, see ya in the mornin'." With that, everyone got up, stretched a bit then filed out and headed to their bunks.

Once in my room, I finished up the day's paperwork, then relaxed with a crossword puzzle before turning out the lights. My last night on the job was eerily quiet. Not one of the rigs in the house went out the entire night. Not even the ambulance.

At 5:00 a.m. I was awoken by the alarm on my phone. I got out of bed, washed up, packed my overnight bag and bedding, and went down to the kitchen for coffee. At around 5:30 Battalion Chief Eddie Gannon relieved me of duty for the last time. Eddie and I knew each other for years. At the back of the buggy, we spoke for a while talking about my retirement plans and his, "When are you leaving?" I asked. Laughing he replied, "Oh, I've got at least a few more years before I can even START thinking about retiring." He then helped me load my gear and personal belongings into my truck out front. "Congratulations Kev," Eddie said as he shook my hand firmly. "Thanks man, you be safe," I replied. Eddie then turned and went back into the firehouse.

Warming up my truck on this cold morning in front of Engine 14's house, and just before I pulled off the apron for the last time, the inevitable thought came over me, "Wow, this is really happening. I'm no longer a Chicago firefighter." I then slowly made a U-turn on Chicago Avenue in the direction of home, a short, but on this morning, a long, four blocks away. Dealing with this strange feeling, I found myself driving only about fifteen miles an hour. At 6:00 a.m., on this chilly November morning, the day after Thanksgiving, the streets were extra quiet. I don't think I saw one car or one pedestrian. This, and the pre-winter darkness, added to making this morning even more surreal than I ever imagined it would be.

It was only a few minutes after leaving 14's quarters that I got home. I parked in my garage, removed my gear from the back of my truck, and placed it in the corner where it had been kept for years in a makeshift locker. Before going into the house, I stood in the garage for a few seconds looking at my helmet hanging on the wall and my firecoat that read, Battalion Chief Stawiarski. With that, I remember snapping out of the surrealness, cracking a smile, and thinking, "What a great ride!"

Grabbing my overnight bag, I went inside the house. My wife and daughter, who both knew of my morning plans, were still asleep. So, quietly, trying not to wake them, I took a quick shower, had a bite to eat, and headed over to the morning after gathering.

I got to the bar around 7:15. I kinda figured that because the gathering was in honor of two of us, there would be a pretty decent turnout. Approaching the front door of this old neighborhood tavern, I could already hear what sounded like a large crowd inside. When I opened it, the volume increased twenty times! The place was packed shoulder to shoulder! Only two steps inside, I was greeted with laughter, well-wishes and a cold bottle of beer. Shaking hands and clanking bottles all the way, I headed over to the back of the bar where Andy was talking to a few people. Before I even reached him, my voice was hoarse from thanking my now, "former" co-workers for coming to celebrate. When I finally made it over to Andy, we threw a pile of money on the bar, and the party continued for the next few hours with remarkable stories, laughs and sincere well wishes from great friends...I couldn't think of a better way to leave the best job in the world!

ALL JOURNAL ENTRIES REVIEWED AND APPROVED: RETIRED BATTALION CHIEF STAWIARSKI.
JOURNAL CLOSED.

ACKNOWLEDGMENTS

IT WOULD BE nearly impossible to note every person who supported, encouraged, or inspired my choice to pursue and attain my dream of becoming a Chicago firefighter. A sincere thank you goes out to all my family, friends, workout partners and firefighters I met prior to getting on the job. You have no idea how much your support meant to me.

Also in order is a special extension of gratitude to those co-workers and bosses who broke me in on the job and mentored me throughout my career. There are way too many to name and I wouldn't want to leave anyone out. I sincerely thank all of you and every member of the Chicago Fire Department that I've had the privilege to work with.

To my friends Al, Mike, Ray and Ryan. You have no idea how much your unselfish time and instrumental constructive feedback contributed to me finally getting this book thing over the finish line. To each of you I offer a wholehearted thank you.

Thanks also to another CFD friend, Mike, for his help with the book's cover.

A deep, heartfelt thank you also goes out to my daughter, Samantha, whose sheer presence in our home inspired me to train hard, work hard and to be as safe as possible. In addition, I thank her for some of the early editing work she did on this writing.

Most importantly, I thank my wife, Kim. Her support and

encouragement began way back when we were dating and the idea of becoming a firefighter was still only a dream. I can undoubtedly say that without her I would not have attained all three of my promotions and enjoyed my career as much as I have. Thank you for everything, especially all those days you helped me study (and almost drove me nuts) by hammering me with test questions over and over and over and over and over and over and over!

UPDATE 2023

OVER SEVEN YEARS have passed between the day I retired and the time I decided to make this writing public. Since then, I've been asked some of the same questions very often. I guess now would be a good time to respond.

IF YOU LOVED THE JOB SO MUCH, WHY DID YOU RETIRE AT AGE FIFTY-FIVE INSTEAD OF STAYING A FEW MORE YEARS OR UNTIL MANDATORY RETIREMENT AT AGE SIXTY-THREE?"

Well, there were a few reasons. 1) The city presented a monetarily enticing offer for those who would retire between the age of fifty-five and sixty. When I did the math, for me, it was a no-brainer. 2) During my stretch on the fire department I was lucky enough to not sustain any major injuries or illnesses. I figured that an early retirement, while still healthy and in good shape, was right for me. 3) With such an enticing offer in front of me, it was easier to reason out that by leaving I would be creating an opening for someone new to come on the job. I had fun, raised a family, saw so many interesting things and made a good living. Why not make room for some young kid to do the same?

DO YOU STILL VISIT FIREHOUSES?

For most of my career I was a relief officer. Other than being assigned as a firefighter to Engine 30 for six years and Truck 58 for about three, I was never really a part of any specific firehouse family. All the houses, where I worked as a reliever, always accepted me as one of their own, but in my mind, it was always their house, and I was a guest. In my first year of retirement, I did take up a few offers from several houses to stop by for homemade pizza night, Saturday corned beef and cabbage and a home cooked Puerto Rican feast. Stories were told, and laughs were many, but I also started to realize I was no longer part of the active team. It's hard to explain. I will always be accepted as one of the family, but time moves on, and things have to be left behind. Pretty much the only time I'll visit a firehouse now is for those "last day" gatherings that happen mostly in November. These gatherings are a good way for me to get my fill of seeing old co-workers, telling stories and remembering the distinct smell of a firehouse apparatus floor.

DO YOU MISS BEING A FIREFIGHTER?

This is the question I get asked most frequently. The answer is "yes" and "no." I could go on and on, but I won't. Here are a few things I miss and a few things I don't. I do miss the excitement and unpredictability of what type of run would come in next and when it would be. I don't miss long days followed by long nights without sleep. I do miss the camaraderie and great company. I don't miss the pressure and heavy responsibility that inevitably came with my supervisory positions. I do miss helping people in need. I don't miss living by a rigid work schedule.

DO YOU KEEP IN TOUCH WITH OTHER RETIRED FIREFIGHTERS?

Yes. I've had breakfast and lunch meetings with retired friends many times since leaving the job. This is probably my favorite way to keep the memories of being a Chicago firefighter alive.

Made in the USA
Columbia, SC
04 February 2025